RENEWALS 691-4574
DATE DUE

JUL 2 8

AF

Origins of Church Wealth in Mexico

Origins of Church Wealth in Mexico

Ecclesiastical Revenues and Church Finances, 1523–1600

John Frederick Schwaller

University of New Mexico Press
Albuquerque

Library of Congress Cataloging in Publication Data
Schwaller, John Frederick.
Origins of church wealth in Mexico.

Bibliography: p.
Includes index.
1. Catholic Church—Mexico—Finance—History—
16th century.   2. Catholic Church—Mexico—Clergy—
History—16th century.   3. Mexico—Church history—
16th century.   1. Title.
BX1428.2.S38   1985   282'.72   85-1122
ISBN 0-8263-0813-9

Design by Milenda Nan Ok Lee

© 1985 by the University of New Mexico Press.
All rights reserved.
First edition

Contents

Introduction   1
Chapter 1   Tithe Collection   19
Chapter 2   Tithe Distribution   55
Chapter 3   Parish Revenues   83
Chapter 4   Pious Works and Alms   111
Chapter 5   The Critical Decade   149
Chapter 6   Conclusions   173
Notes   187
Bibliography   205
Map Appendix   213
Statistical Appendix   219
Tithe Collection Conditions   225
Index   233

Figures

1. Tithe Division   57
2. Cabildo Salaries   61
3. Division of the Tithe, 1564–66   65
4. Division of Revenues   71
5. Salary Cuts—Musical Staff   75
6. Codex Sierra   100
7. Chantries in the Cathedral of Mexico   119
8. Chantries in the Cathedral of Michoacán   120
9. Gross Tithe Revenues: Mexico, Michoacán, Guadalajara   151
10. Gross Tithe Revenues: Puebla, Oaxaca   151

To Anne

Acknowledgments

This book began as a series of conversations around *tapas* and drinks in Seville, with Jacques Barbier, and several others. While working in the Archivo de Indias, Barbier and I had mused on the possibility of constructing economic indicators for use in colonial Latin America. In my research on the church I had come to the conclusion that while not perfect, the records of the tithe could, if used judiciously, serve in that function. Over several weeks the group of us tossed around the advantages and shortcomings of several potential indices. Although my research went on into questions more social than economic, this debate stayed in the back of my mind. This book results from those musings. No longer do I contend that the tithe is a perfect indicator, but this work does serve to describe and analyze the wide range of income sources available to the church, and the means whereby those sources of income were allocated and utilized. The end result is to cast some light on the overall contours of the economy of New Spain at the end of the sixteenth century.

The germ of this book came from one chapter in my dissertation, which I have expanded. Consequently the research presented here began in approximately 1974. During 1974–76, I studied in Mexico initially under the auspices of a Benito Juárez–Abraham Lincoln Fellowship of the Mexican Secretaría de Relaciones Exteriores. The second year of my stay in Mexico was funded by a Training Fellowship of the Organization of American States. From Mexico I traveled to Spain, where the U.S. Office of Education underwrote my research through a Fulbright-Hays Graduate Student Research Abroad Fellowship. To all of these institutions I acknowledge my debt. In more recent times, at least parts of this book have been financed by seed grants from Florida Atlantic University, a grant from the American Philosophical Society, and a U.S. Department of Education Fulbright-Hays Award for faculty research abroad.

I wish to extend my thanks to many individuals and institutions here and abroad for their help in my work. In Mexico I held an affiliation with the Instituto Nacional de Antropología e Historia, and worked under the direction of Dr. Antonio Pompa y Pompa. My deepest thanks go to him and to the then subdirector of the Instituto, Dr. Fernando Cámara Barbachano. As a result of this affiliation I also came to know and appreciate Dr. Enrique Florescano, current director of INAH, and Dr. Alejandra Moreno Toscano, past director of the Archivo General de la Nación. To my many friends at INAH, I feel a deep gratitude. In the Archivo General de la Nación, Dr. José Ignacio Rubio Mañé proved to be a wonderful help, and I enjoyed and profited greatly from our conversations. Likewise the then director of the Biblioteca Nacional, Dr. Ernesto de la Torre Villar offered me every courtesy and assistance. At the Archivo de Notarias del Departamento del Distrito Federal I wish to thank the director, Lic. Carlos Barrios H., and to the *encargada* of the Centro de Documentación of the Instituto de Estudios y Documentos Históricos, Claustro de Sor Juana, Dr. Lupita Flores. More specifically the staffs and assistants in all of these archives proved to make the research itself challenging and diverting. To my friends, *porteros*, and others, I send many thanks.

A large part of this research was conducted in the Archivo del Cabildo Eclesiástico Mexicano, located in the cathedral of Mexico. I owe a special debt of gratitude to His Eminence Miguel Darío Cardinal Mirando, now retired, archbishop primate of Mexico. Without his kind permission to consult the ecclesiastical archives of Mexico, much of this would have been impossible. I also wish to recognize the memory of the Very Reverend The Dean of the cathedral chapter of Mexico, Msgr. Rafael Dávila Vilchis, who died shortly after I concluded my initial research in Mexico. I also wish to thank the Venerable The Archdeacon of Mexico, Dr. Octaviano Valdés, whose own research in history has given us much. Lastly, my appreciation goes to the Rev. Martín Rivera, master of ceremonies of the cathedral, and now secretary-archivist of the chapter, Msgr. Luis Reynoso, then secretary-chancellor of the archdiocese of Mexico, and certainly to Sr. Carlos Cruz, private secretary to the cathedral chapter, who helped me daily.

In Spain, I wish to thank Doña Rosario Parra, director of the Archivo General de Indias, in Seville. To all my friends on the staff, too numerous to mention, I send my deepest thanks, especially to Doña María Antonia Colomar. As a special expression of gratitude, I recognize the staff of *subalternos* of the archive. These men occupy a special place in our hearts and minds, and are a major topic of conversation among those who investigate in the archive. I likewise express my thanks to the director, staff, and investigators of the Escuela de Estudios Hispano-Americanos for their help and friendship. Again, the list is too long to include them all, but a special thanks to Dr. Javier Ortiz de la Tabla. The directors and staffs of the Archivo General de Simancas and of the Archivo Histórico Nacional also extended great assistance and courtesy to me, and I thank them for that.

The number of people I need to thank among academic colleagues could easily occupy more space than already devoted. I will thus limit my expressions of gratitude in print, in the hopes of extending them more personally. Among the individuals who have aided me in a very primary fashion are Prof. Charles Boxer, under whose guidance this study began, Prof. John H. Parry, who was party to the later developments, Profs. Charles Gibson and Woodrow Borah, who in their kind manners aided a neophyte, and

Prof. Robert E. Quirk, who directed my dissertation. Among my friends, colleagues, and mentors, I wish to thank John Lombardi, Mark Burkholder, Jacques Barbier, Alan Keuthe, Doug Inglis, John Kicza, Richard Salvucci, Sylvia Arrom, Stanley Hordes, Paul Ganster, Elinor Melville, Richard Greenleaf, John TePaske, Engel Sluiter, Jim Lockhart, Bill Taylor, and countless others. Needless to say, these scholars have given me inspiration, advise, and suggestions. Any errors or shortcomings of my work are purely my own. I also wish to thank Thelma Spangler and Betty Lofgren for their tireless efforts.

Lastly I want to express my deep gratitude to my parents, Henry and Juliette Schwaller, my brother Henry Schwaller, and to our family firm, for providing me with moral and monetary support on and off for too many years. I also want to thank my son, Robert Clemens Schwaller, for inspiring me to finish. This work is not all my own. Without my wife, Anne Cardot Taylor Schwaller, pen would have not been put to paper, nor notes taken. She has helped me in every possible way, from sharing dusty bundles of manuscripts, bumpy rides in the Mexican hinterland, trans-Atlantic adventures, conversations, debates, arguments, and all of the other joys and sorrows of the itinerant academic. Her labors in the archive on my behalf form the core of the research of this book. If this book achieves success it is due in large measure to her aid and support, ideas and suggestions. I remain indebted.

Origins of Church Wealth in Mexico

Introduction

By the middle of the eighteenth century the Catholic church was by far the single most powerful institution in New Spain, rivaling even the royal government. The power of the church, political, spiritual, and economic, was to pose a major threat to the central government of Mexico well into the twentieth century. Yet this institution did not appear fully developed but underwent a long process of growth, beginning in the decades following Cortés's conquest of the Aztec empire. In order better to understand the process through which the church attained such power, this study will look at the origins of the economic power of the church in colonial Mexico.

Historians writing of the late eighteenth- and early nineteenth-century church have viewed it at the end of a long process of development.[1] The power and wealth of the church did not blossom immediately upon the creation of the institution following the conquest. Rather, it resulted from a long period of development which encompassed most of the sixteenth century. Church officials made several attempts in this period to secure the financial success of the church. This study will analyze the major sources of income, how they were distributed and utilized, and the success or failure of each one, in order to determine the foundations from which the church grew in Mexico.

When studying the church, one is often impressed by its monolithic appearance. In fact there are major divisions within the institution, dating back centuries. In the New World, the major administrative division was between the religious orders and the normal episcopal hierarchy. Members of the religious orders, such as Franciscans, Agustinians, and Dominicans, are called the regular clergy, signifying that they follow a special rule of life and conduct (*regula*) beyond the simple priestly vows. Furthermore, many of these orders, especially the Franciscans, are mendicant orders, meaning that they are supported exclusively from alms and begging. Thus, while members of an order such as the Society of Jesus (Jesuits) are clearly members of the regular clergy, they are not mendicants since they may receive money from more sources. The other major group within the church is the secular or diocesan clergy. These priests are part of the normal ecclesiastical hierarchy, which includes the parish curate, bishop, archbishop, reaching all the way to the pope. The word *secular* recognizes the fact that they live out in the world (*saeculum*), rather than in monasteries like the regular clergy. *Diocesan* signifies that the priest must accept the authority of a bishop or archbishop. The regular clergy has its own hierarchy of abbots, provincials, and generals which parallels the hierarchy of bishops and archbishops. This study will focus on the secular clergy.

In colonial Mexico the secular clergy fell administratively under royal authority. As a result of papal concessions and royal decrees, the power to appoint most members of the normal ecclesiastical hierarchy was given to the monarchs of Spain.[2] These appointments ultimately needed papal approval, which was always forthcoming. Furthermore, the popes had donated the right to collect the ecclesiastical tax, the tithe—a 10 percent tax on agricultural production—to the Spanish kings.[3] The monarchs were then obliged to pay for the cost of missionary activity and for the maintenance of the church. In 1512 the tithes were redonated to the church, partially relieving the monarch of his financial responsibility. The kings, nevertheless, maintained their authority to intervene in most ecclesiastical matters, and effectively mediated between the pope and the church in the New World. In practice, the kings of Spain had unlimited administrative control over the church in their American colonies.

The secular clergy was divided territorially into bishoprics. Initially all of Mexico was a single diocese, created shortly after the first explorers had sighted the coast of Yucatán. This diocese, called the *Carolense*, provided a framework for further ecclesiastical activity in the newly discovered region. It was later transferred to Tlaxcala in recognition of that "republic's" assistance to Cortés in the conquest. In fact the first bishops of Mexico and Tlaxcala arrived in the colony at about the same time, 1527–28, so it is difficult to ascribe a clear primacy to one or the other. Thereafter, as the conquest continued and new territories received Spanish settlers, episcopal authority followed them. Oaxaca, specfically the city of Antequera, received a bishop in 1535, followed shortly by Michoacán, the city of Pátzcuaro, in 1538. The last diocese of central Mexico, Guadalajara, created in 1546, eventually lay in a different administrative territory, New Galicia, with the rest pertaining to the *gobierno* of Mexico. (See Map Appendices.)

The territories encompassed by these dioceses ran roughly north and south. Oaxaca straddled the Isthmus of Tehuantepec, reaching as far north as the mouth of the Papaloapan River. In the southwest it bounded neighboring Tlaxcala at the mouth of the Ometepec or Rio Grande. The diocese consisted of four regions of Spanish settlements: Coatzacoalcos, Villa Alta, the Oaxaca Valley, and Nexapa near Tehuantepec.

The diocese of Tlaxcala had its capital moved to Puebla shortly after that city was founded. The territory of the diocese ran from the boundary with Oaxaca on the east to a line beginning in the north in the Tamiagua Lagoon to a point some twenty miles south of Acapulco on the Pacific. Some of the richest agricultural land lay in the diocese, especially the very fertile Atlixco Valley, which soon became one of the breadbaskets of the entire colony.

The most important ecclesiastical jurisdiction of the colony, Mexico, became an archdiocese in 1547, with the other bishoprics suffragan to it, including Guatemala, Chiapas, Yucatán, and eventually the Philippines, in addition to those already mentioned. It contained the largest Spanish population and some of the most fertile soils, in the Valley of Mexico and in a corridor stretching to Querétaro in the north and westward to the Toluca Valley. The Pánuco River formed its northern boundary, running to the west to a point fifteen leagues northwest of Valles, where it passed south to the Pacific coast. The border with Michoacán lay about ten leagues (thirty miles) north of Acapulco.

Michoacán passed far into the northern districts beyond San Luis Potosí. To the east and to the north of Mexico lay New Viscaya, whose ecclesiastical history relates to a period beyond that encompassed by this study. The boundary of Michoacán with Guadalajara began north and west of San Luis about ten leagues, passing five leagues west of León and on to the Pacific just north of Manzanillo. Thus Michoacán encompassed several very distinct regions: the mines and dry land to the north, the agriculturally rich Bajío and lake district in the center, and the Pacific coastal mountains and plain to the south. Like Puebla, the capital of the diocese was moved from Pátzcuaro to Guayangareo, later known as Valladolid, and still later as Morelia.

The far west and north fell to the diocese of Guadalajara. The first capital was Campostela, later moving to Guadalajara. Its size and sparse settlement made it administratively a difficult territory. Only the mining districts of Zacatecas, Fresnillo, and Sombrerete attracted Spaniards to the far north. The central area of the diocese offered good agriculture and saw the beginnings of cattle raising.

Before studying the financial condition of the church, a few words on the currency would be appropriate. In general, the financial records of the time contain at least four different units of currency. The most common name was the peso. In fact, three different types of pesos appeared:

the *peso de oro de minas*, the *peso de oro común*, and the *peso de tipuzque*. The first two were silver coins while the last was an alloy. The other main type of currency was the *ducado* or *ducado de Castilla*, also a gold coin; it was used for measuring salaries paid to royal officers. For all intents and purposes, these currencies merely served as bookkeeping conventions, for the only coin in actual circulation was the *peso de tipuzque*. The value of these coins was assessed in terms of a medieval Moorish gold coin, the *marevedí*. The *peso de oro de minas* was worth 485 *marevedises*, the *peso de oro común*, 300, the *peso de tipuzque*, 272, and the *ducado*, 375. Because of their closeness in value the *peso de oro común* and the *peso de tipuzque* were regularly confused in common parlance.[4] In this study I have resolved all currencies to the *peso de oro común*, unless otherwise noted.

The peso was in turn further subdivided. Each peso was composed of eight equal parts (thus the origin of pieces of eight) called either *reales* or *tomines*. The silver coin ultimately was literally divided like a pie into the eight pieces. For accounting purposes only each of the eight pieces was further divided into twelve *granos*. Thus the peso was equal to ninety-six *granos* or eight *reales*.

The secular and the regular clergy depended on two different sources of income, an important financial distinction. The regular clergy focused its attentions primarily on alms, in keeping with the mendicant tradition. The Jesuits and other orders soon turned to owning rural estates, the profits from which could support their on-going activities.[5] Yet the capital basis for these ventures remained gifts from the faithful. The secular clergy, however, received direct payments from the crown for some of its parochial activity, and the tithe supported its overall administration. One group of parish priests received annual salaries from local Spanish encomenderos who were required to provide for the spiritual well-being of the Indians under their charge.[6] While the secular clergy accepted alms, they surely ranked as a much smaller source of income than either salaries from the crown and encomenderos or the tithe.

The wealth of the church should be considered on both an individual and an institutional basis. In the case of the regular clergy, one can ignore the private wealth of the individuals, since most of the orders required a vow of poverty from their members. Thus there was little concept of individual wealth or income. The order provided for the regular priest. The secular priest was free, within certain limits, to be an economically active person. He retained primary responsibility for his own sustenance. If he failed to find a job he had little institutional support to fall back on. There were many sources of individual income, from parochial salaries and dues to chantries and other ecclesiastical endowments. Thus, while the individual priest had to concern himself over his own livelihood, the church as a whole also needed financial support. Within the realm of church finances there emerged a distinction between monies used for ecclesiastical salaries and monies used for capital outlay and administrative costs.

As an institution with financial needs the church should be considered in the context of the times. Other than the royal government, no institution had as broad a scope of activities or as large a staff. While there are no hard figures on the total number of secular priests in New Spain at any given time in the sixteenth century, there are several estimates. In 1575 the archbishop of Mexico reported on all the priests working in his diocese. This list included 155 men.[7] That figure can be taken as a minimum, because numerous other priests resided in the archdiocese but were not employed in an ecclesiastical function. Some received a livelihood from the university, others from private endowments; others managed their own estates or served their families. In 1582, the bishop of Puebla-Tlaxcala prepared a similar report.[8] That list of priests included 118 men. But again, other priests lived in the diocese at the time who did not appear. Nevertheless, using these figures as bare minimums, one can estimate that the population of secular priests around 1580 in the dioceses of Mexico, Puebla, Oaxaca, Michoacán, and Guadalajara would be about 550 priests employed in clerical function.[9] This was certainly greater than the total number of royal bureaucrats, including corregidores and their assistants. Thus just to support this work force the financial needs of the church were tremendous.

One must also consider the financial needs of the individual priest. As noted, the secular clergy took no vow of poverty. They could be economically active, as long as they avoided out-and-out commercial dealings, such as wholesale or retail trade, direct nonecclesiastical employment by a member of the laity, and the base occupations, such as artisanry. As a professional, too, the secular priest probably expected a higher salary than a common clerical worker, such as a notary's assistant. While the number of secular priests with university degrees hovered around 25 percent in the sixteenth century, these men certainly had higher salary expectations. Those priests employed in the major cities, such as Mexico, Puebla, or Oaxaca, had greater salary demands because of the higher cost of living.

A feeling for the cost of living and the expectations of priests living in the city can be found in a letter from a member of the cathedral hierarchy in Mexico, the *maestrescuela* D. Sancho Sánchez de Muñón, to the king written in 1568.[10] In the letter Sánchez de Muñón posited that a priest living in Mexico City needed a minimum of 300 *pesos de minas* (480 *de oro común*) annually to provide food and support for himself and his servants. He argued that this figure constituted a bare minimum, and 800 to 1000 *pesos de minas* was more reasonable. As examples, he cited the cost of housing, about 120 *pesos de minas* a year; clothing, likewise about 120; transportation—a mule, feed, and trappings—about 80 per year; household expenses not including food, about 60; and the care of servants and the occasional purchase of a slave, on average, 100 pesos (all *de minas*).

The cost of living in Mexico City can be evaluated against the salaries of other similar officials. Perhaps most comparable to the priests would have been university professors. In 1594 the salaries of university professors ranged from a low of 165 pesos for the instructor of rhetoric to a high of 413 for the teacher of grammar. Most of the other professors earned between 248 and 330 pesos annually. This falls far behind what Sánchez de Muñón indicated as necessary for living in Mexico City.[11] The other end of the salary scale was occupied by the viceroy. After some initial fluctuations, the salary of the viceroy of New Spain was fixed at 20,000 ducats a year, about 25,000 pesos. The president of the audiencia enjoyed a salary of about 4,375 to 7,500 pesos.[12] The range of salaries for the *oidor* was much lower, from 2,000 to 3,000 pesos annually.[13] At the lowest end of the royal bureaucracy the alcaldes mayores, corregidores, and their assistants received from 100 to 300 pesos annually. One should note that the king barred high royal government officials from conducting any business activity in the region in which they served. The degree to which lower officers were forbidden is open to question. Thus, the wide disparity between their salaries can be in part ascribed to this. University professors and local magistrates could have outside income. Overall, these figures give one a basis against which to judge ecclesiastical incomes of the same period.

The church was quite specific on the question of the minimum ecclesiastical income. In order to prevent persons from being ordained without sufficient support, every candidate for the holy orders had to present testimony concerning his potential income, or *congrua*. The minimum acceptable annual income for the purposes of ordination was set at 300 pesos. Nevertheless, many priests were ordained with just under 250 pesos of annual income.[14] Five different types of sustenance, called *títulos*, were recognized for ordination. For the members of the regular clergy, the *título de mesa común* was the only possibility, since their order would support them financially. For secular clerics, four other categories were used: patrimony (*patrimonio*), chantry (*capellanía*), benefice (*beneficio*), and language (*lengua*). *Patrimonio* and *capellanía* were quite similar in practice and often combined. These titles required that the candidate receive his minimum annual stipend from funds invested in his behalf, either as his legal due from the estate of his parents, his patrimony, or from the income of a pious work, a chantry. The *título de beneficio* could be fulfilled by receiving an appointment to any canonically endowed position. In the early sixteenth century there were very few benefices, but the number grew through the period, especially after 1574 when the king took over the patronage of rural parishes. Lastly, the *título de lengua* was fulfilled if the individual spoke one of the native Indian languages of Mexico because the knowledge of an Indian language guaranteed the candidate of a job upon ordination.

While the rest of this work will focus on the hard questions of money—revenues and disbursements—one should keep in mind even in one's most callous moments, that the church was an institution to be revered. The society in which the church operated recognized its labors as being valuable, and as such was willing to support those efforts. One becomes keenly aware of this when studying almost any realm of church finances. Even though the tithe was a mandatory 10 percent tax on production, there were very few cases of noncompliance. The only major suits concerning tithe collection occurred between the large taxpayers and the church. The group of encomenderos carried on a lengthy suit over the extent of their tax burden. Likewise the heirs of Cortés, the Marqueses del Valle, had several legal disputes with the church over the level and extent of their tax liability. Most other producers either willingly paid or did not end up in the courts.

One can further appreciate the respect with which the populace viewed the church in their pious works and alms. While some minor alms were required by law of all testaments, in nearly every case studied the testator gave far beyond the legal minimum. While in this analysis pious works are viewed more as financial institutions for the propagation of wealth, in fact they represented the deepest religious and spiritual concerns of the patrons who created them. They served to perpetuate the feelings of piety of the benefactor. The universal and infinite nature of the pious work also must have impressed the common people, in an age of tremendous flux and change. Thus while individuals received important financial benefits from the pious works, they perceived it as offering important spiritual ones as well.

The clerics themselves invested much of their time in financial dealings. Parish priests were concerned about the collection of their salaries, while the upper clergy had to oversee the collection and distribution of major sources of income, such as the tithe. It often seems that the clergy were petty and acquisitive in their financial dealings, but again one must remember that they had every faith that their efforts were of transcendent importance. While the regular clergy conducted much of the early missionary activity, seculars still could look upon their parochial service as missionary. They were the very representatives of the church militant and triumphant. The most exciting ecclesiastical field in which to work was the New World, with its offer of conversion and salvation for countless millions of Indians. Thus the concern the clergy expressed over financial questions must be seen as a reflection of concern over the tremendous task that lay before them. The level of ecclesiastical income could very well determine the success or failure of Christianity in any given area. Indeed, the ultimate secure financial basis for the church resulted from the connection between the church's need for income and popular expressions of piety as developed in the Counter-Reformation.

The social structure of colonial New Spain, toward the end of the sixteenth century, was closely linked to the economic structure. In general, Spanish law recognized two fictional "republics," in essence two separate societies occupying the same geography with individual enclaves. These two groups, Spaniards and Indians, were legally independent of each other, self-governing, and equal. Nevertheless, the practical effect of the Spanish colonial policy was the creation of a subservient Indian group under the domination of Spanish overlords. The inevitable mixing of these two groups, dating from the earliest Spanish contacts with the native, produced the mestizo. The presence of blacks in Spain, both as slaves and freemen, resulted in the appearance of mulattoes in the New World. Some of the conquerors belonged to those groups. Zambos, the offspring of a black and an Indian also appeared. Thus, even by the end of the sixteenth century, Spanish colonial society was a multihued assortment of people. In general, the practical social structure placed the Spaniards at the pinnacle, followed by many of the mixed groups and free blacks, with Indians occupying a place just above the slaves. Insofar as Spanish law regulated the activities of all these groups, this social structure can be rightly called a caste system.[15]

The economic structure can be resolved into three major sectors: agriculture, mining, and commerce. Leading these in importance was agriculture. It was the basis for all other sectors and the lifeblood of the colony. Without local food production the colony could not survive. Fears of just this problem had arisen during the early Spanish occupation of the Caribbean Islands, especially since Spaniards were loathe to eat local foodstuffs. Thus, only with the creation of agricultural estates producing cattle, wheat, and other Spanish food products could the New Spanish economy grow. Furthermore, agriculture provided the raw materials used by the other two sectors of the economy. Closely linked, then, to agriculture were the mining industry and commerce. Protoindustrial complexes such as weaving mills and other *obrajes* can be seen as linked to the commercial sector.

If agriculture was the most important sector by virtue of its supporting the others, then the mining industry held preeminence in its role as a producer of capital. In an essentially precapitalist, preindustrial, bullion-based economy, the production of gold and silver directly affected the available capital in the system. Taxation, royal regulations, and other factors tended to limit the impact of this capital on the colonial economy, since so much of it was destined to the overseas markets of Europe. Nevertheless, a great deal of mining wealth did enter the local economy, thus providing for overall growth.

Commerce was the sector that served the other two. The protoindustrial component improved, refined, and prepared the raw materials for sale either to local or foreign markets. The commercial sector also handled the raw goods produced by the agricultural sector, moving them in the various market systems. Lastly, the commercial sector tended to acquire capital from the mining sector and used it to expand the local economy and to bring the necessary foreign goods into the economy.

Once one realizes how the three sectors were interconnected, it is necessary to trace this development backwards in time to analyze the flow of capital in the system and the means whereby limited resources were distributed to provide for stability. In colonial Latin America the allocation of vital resources and the process of capital distribution for start-up were intimately linked. The most important institution for the accomplishment of this was the encomienda.[16] Initially this was a grant of Indians to a Spanish conqueror or colonist to provide him with labor. Owing to various political and ethical concerns, by the 1550s the encomienda was changed to a simple grant of tribute, confirmed by the crown, from an Indian population to a colonist or conqueror. In the outlying or fringe areas of the Spanish-American empire, however, the encomienda retained its earlier identity as a labor-allocation institution. Once the encomienda lost this identity in central Mexico, a new institution was created to replace it, the *repartimiento*. Under this system Indians were still required to provide labor for Spaniards, but now they were organized by the royal government, were limited in the time they had to serve, and received wages for their efforts. The goal of this and other later labor systems founded by the crown was to encourage the Indian population to enter into the wage economy.

Because the lifetime of the encomienda was limited by legislation at mid-century, the encomendero had several decisions to make concerning the institution's long-term benefits to him. One option was simply to use the encomienda-generated income to pay daily living expenses. Under this option, when the encomienda was lost to the family, nothing was left. So the wise encomendero took the income from the grant and invested it in diverse ventures. Some might be used to buy and develop an agricultural estate, some might be used as start-up capital for mining or commerce. Other capital might be loaned to family or friends, or invested with others to form a company. In these cases, the encomendero could at least attempt to forestall ruin and perhaps create long-term wealth for himself and his family. He had to diversify to ensure long-term gain to the family. For the overall economy, these investments were tremendously important in providing the capital necessary for its early development.[17]

The inheritance of wealth in this system was very difficult, since so many factors mitigated against it. The underlying principle of the Spanish inheritance law, embodied in the Laws of Toro, was that all children should receive a fair portion of their parents' wealth. While the law did stipulate exact limits whereby one heir might be favored over the others, equitable distribution was the rule. Thus, Spanish parents in the New World had to plan carefully the careers of their children and the inheritance each might receive, in order to guarantee that a substantial amount of capital might be held by at least one. That would be the amount necessary to continue the family line and socioeconomic position, with both income and capital for the heir. The priesthood and convents provided parents with some means of limiting second-generation offspring. The child's inheritance might be used for education, in the case of a priest, or for a conventual dowry for the girls entering the orders. In these cases, if the child's total inheritance were not used during his or her lifetime, it could be passed on to a nephew, son of the major inheriting sibling. In this manner, wealth was concentrated into one or two reproductive lines. Although the children of a couple might inherit equitably, the grandchildren, by being limited, might receive a greater concentration.[18]

Certain investments were also used to circumvent the inheritance laws. One was the *mayorazgo,* or entailed estate. The *mayorazgo* required a royal license for its foundation, but once granted the recipient could stipulate that a given percentage (47 percent) of his estate be bound together as a unit. This inheritable unit might include real property, personal possessions, and income-generating investments, including encomiendas. Once bound together, however, the estate could not be alienated but was inherited wholly by the eldest son. Thus, although the *mayorazgo* did avoid the problem of breaking up an estate, it was extremely illiquid. Should economic conditions decline or the success of a family dim, there was little or no way to free the capital bound up in the estate, short of another royal license, which was tremendously expensive. The other type of investment used to circumvent the law was the pious work. This institution will be discussed at length in Chapter 3. It had many of the same characteristics of the *mayorazgo,* but usually involved less capital.

The social structure of the colony was intimately related to the economy outlined above. While the Indians and mixed groups played a critically important role in the actual production of goods and services, their role in investment and capital formation was limited, mostly by the caste laws which prevented them from pursuing occupations at that level. Therefore, most of the entrepreneurs came from the ranks of the Spaniards. This did not, however, totally exclude the castes from occasionally attaining some economic power. On close examination, one realizes that even among the Spaniards there were subtle differences between the entrepreneurs of the one economic sector and another. The generalizations that follow are just that and do not constitute hard-and-fast rules about the social composition of the sectors.

The agricultural sector consisted of two rather distinct groups at the end of the sixteenth century. In general the agricultural sector supported all of the major social groups, from Indians to Spaniards. Among Spaniards, the very wealthy and the small farmer both participated. A kind of segregation seems to have occurred. Those regions that supported wheat and other grains were divided into smaller plots, supporting many smallholders. Cattle and other livestock required much larger estates, and in turn the owners tended to be wealthier. The ecological requirements of these two different types of agricultural production also dictated a geographical segregation. Some regions, such as the southern Toluca Valley, Atlixco, and most of the Valley of Mexico, supported small vegetable and grain agriculture. On the other hand, the northernmost regions of the Valley of Mexico, the Tula-Xilotepec region, and the northern Valley of Toluca all saw great concentrations of livestock. The southern areas were well watered while the northern ones were drier.[19]

Still tentative are conclusions about the creation of the agricultural estates. It seems that many of the larger haciendas had their origins as adjuncts to encomiendas. In the early days of the encomienda, the encomendero could not require his Indians to travel great distances to provide their labor services. Moreover, he was required to be a landowner and have his residence in the same province as the Indians. Thus, before the 1560s encomenderos acquired lands near the villages of their encomiendas. In the later period, when labor services were outlawed, the encomenderos maintained their estates and acquired labor through other means, such as contract wage labor or debt peonage. Thus, between the encomienda and the hacienda there is a continuum in the person of the agricultural entrepreneur, a continuum not present in the institutions themselves.

At the other end of the social scale, many relatively poor Spaniards held and exploited small plots of land. These smallholds specialized in grain and vegetable production, as noted. Usually they required little capital investment, other than the seed and draft animals. These were yeomen farmers who lived a simple rustic life. If they did amass excess capital it would be invested in more land or improved equipment and housing. But, in general, they lived on the margins of the elite society of the cities. Alongside these farmers were mestizos and other mixed groups, who in many ways were indistinguishable from the poor Spanish. Of course, the Indian population also engaged in agricultural production to meet their own needs, and to a degree to serve the general agricultural market.

Within the mining sector, a similar pattern seems to have occurred. Most of the mining entrepreneurs, owners of mines and refining mills, were Spaniards. It is likely that very few mestizos were mine owners. Unlike the agricultural sector, these men tended to live in the mining districts, unless tremendous wealth allowed them to maintain an additional residence in the city. In general, the composition of the mining elite varied between the older mining regions of central Mexico, such as Taxco or Pachuca, and the mines of the north, such as Guanajuato or Zacatecas. There is more evidence of encomenderos actively participating in the early development of the central mines. By the end of the century, locally born mine entrepreneurs had taken over in the central mining district, as part of a second generation. The northern mines opened later, suffered some stagnation in the latter part of the century, and then enjoyed a rapid increase in wealth before yet another downturn in the 1630s. Thus, there was not as much possibility for a second generation. Spanish inheritance laws, already seen in the agricultural sector, played an equally destructive role in the passing on of wealth among miners. For obvious reasons, it was far more difficult to divide a mine than an agricultural estate. Labor in the mines came from three major groups. Initially Indians in the encomienda played a central role. Later, as personal service was outlawed, the miners relied increasingly on black and mulatto slaves. Finally, especially in the north, there was a mixed system of local Indians, imported Indians (Tlaxcalans brought up to the mining districts), and slaves.

The commercial sector was divided between wholesale and retail merchants. This distinction was socially important, since nobles were prohibited from engaging in retail commerce or industry. In the 1580s, an aspirant to a seat on the town council of Puebla was barred from taking possession of his office because he owned an *obraje* and thus lacked the nobility necessary for so high a public office. Furthermore, there was an almost strict geographical division between the two groups. The great merchants, engaged primarily in the overseas trade, lived and operated out of Mexico City. The smaller retail merchants, who might engage in some internal wholesale activities, were scattered throughout the colony. A similar distinction might have been true with regard to their places of origin. In general, it seems that the internal market merchants by century's end were locally born, while overseas merchants tended to be peninsular born.

Under the large-scale merchants ranged a whole host of itinerant peddlers and small shopkeepers. This group was probably the most heterogeneous of all, including Spaniards, mixed groups, and Indians. Nevertheless, one imagines that each tended to have a more specific market among his own ethnic group. Indeed, the small shop was a means of upward socioeconomic mobility for the middle and lower castes. Yet at all times, merchants, from the small shopkeeper to the great magnate, were dependent on other factors in the economy for their success. Without production in the agricultural and mining sectors, the merchants could not hope to prosper. Likewise, with the occasional loss of a fleet, market conditions could become extremely difficult.

The economy of sixteenth-century Mexico underwent a slow growth. As more land went under European cultivation, as further mining districts were discovered, and as trade with Spain and the New World developed, the overall activity of the economy grew. Along with this growth was an equally steady inflation, as noted in price trends for some basic commodities. The exact contour of the economy in the last quarter of the century has been a topic of great debate. The role the economy played in the life of the church will be considered in Chapter 5 with some indication as to the precise movement it took. Suffice it to say that the economy expanded rapidly prior to 1580, probably leveled off or fell slightly in that decade, and rebounded in the last decade of the century. This growing economy provided significant opportunities for investment and gain.

1. Tithe Collection

For the sixteenth-century Mexican church, the tithe was by far the most important source of revenue. This 10 percent tax on agricultural production paid for the cost of running the cathedral, the salaries of its officers, and the salaries of its staff. Some parish priests received part of their salary from the tithe as well. Concern over the tithe, its collection, and distribution occupied much of the time of many ecclesiastical and lay figures. The system of collection and distribution was complex and closely defined by royal and canon law. Often practice conflicted directly with the legal requirements, creating seemingly endless disputes. Furthermore, the collection and distribution of the tithe helped to foster a precapitalist entrepreneurial class and to make the church an important feature in capitalist development.

General Considerations

The history of the tithe, as it refers to Mexico, has Caribbean and Spanish precedents.[1] While tithing itself originated in the early days of Christianity, the practice in Spain at the turn of the sixteenth century set the precedent for New Spain. Papal bulls of Alexander VI and Julius II gave the Spanish crown the right to collect and use all of the tithes of the Indies, in return for royal support of the church and missionary efforts in the new lands.[2] These privileges became part of the bulwark of the Patronato Real. A royal cédula, dated October 5, 1501, legally defined the tithe for the Indies.[3] This decree listed all of the commodities upon which the tithe had to be paid and how it would be applied. While the word *tithe, diezmo,* implied a 10 percent levy, this did not apply to all items.[4] In general the royal legislation dictated the tithe pattern already in effect in the archdiocese of Seville or Granada.[5] In medieval Spain there were two types of tithe, personal tithe and praedial tithe. The former functioned like an income tax, a tax on personal gain and production. The latter was a tax on the products of the earth, from mining, agriculture, or other exploitation. Only the latter was applied in the New World, and then only partially.

The second major contribution to the foundation of the tithe system came from a document called the Concordat of Burgos.[6] While not a true concordat, the meeting in 1512 between Ferdinand and the bishops of Santo Domingo, Concepción, and San Juan de Puerto Rico did clarify the financial status of the newly created churches. In the document Ferdinand specifically allowed the bishops to enjoy the tithe and to use the funds in the work of the church. While redonating the tithes to the church, the king withheld one-ninth of the total for himself along with the right to all the tithe on gold, silver, precious stones, and metals that was paid in Spain. Thus, in the years before the conquest of Mexico, the pope first granted, or donated, the tithes to Ferdinand and Isabela, who in turn renounced them, redonating these revenues to the church.

In the first few months after the fall of Tenochtitlán, Charles I began to take a more active interest in his rights over the tithe. In a cédula of October 1523, he ordered all treasury officials to oversee the tithe collection or collect it themselves.[7] Since the king had received the rights to the tithe, he had a moral obligation to have it collected. In a moment of magnanimity Charles also declared that all his own lands and profits from the New World fell under the tithe, just like any other person's.[8] Eventually this ruling came to mean a sizeable income for the church. With these major rulings and agreements established, the tithe question arrived in Mexico just months after the fall of the Aztec empire.

In October 1524, Cortés wrote to Charles describing the aftermath of the conquest. Perhaps in response to the 1523 cédula, Cortés presented his opinions concerning the ecclesiastical development of the territory and noted that he had ordered the collection of the tithe. He wrote that the collections included 1523 remittances but not previous years. Cortés justified this position by noting that any crop yield before 1523 would have hardly covered the expense of collecting the tithe because of the war continuing in many places. The tithe for the two years 1523–24 for the Valley of Mexico and surrounding areas was 5,500 *pesos de ley perfecta*.[9] While Cortés later mentioned that the tithes for Veracruz and Medellín reached 1,000 *pesos de ley perfecta*, no other figures had yet arrived in Mexico for the outlying districts.[10] By 1524 the first *cura* of Mexico, Benito Martínez, had died, and the king named Francisco Garzón in his place.[11] In the same year the value of the tithe for Mexico rose to 4,100 *pesos de minas*, up from 5,500 for the previous two years combined.[12]

With the erection of the first dioceses in New Spain, those of Tlaxcala and Mexico, the tithes legally belonged to the church administration, following the precedent of the Concordat of Burgos in 1512. Thus the bishop, or archbishop, and cathedral chapter held joint responsibility for collecting and distributing these funds. The theory behind the tithe dictated that it would pay the costs of the church. In the sixteenth century this never occurred. Even by the end of the century, the tithe alone could not provide an income for all the local *curas*, plus the money necessary to support the bishops and cathedral chapters. The formulation of a royal tithe policy concerned three groups: Spanish commoners, who always had to pay the tithe; Indians; and the king, nobility, and encomenderos.

As noted, in 1522 Charles I declared that the crown would pay the tithe on all products not otherwise exempted, but only in the Indies. In Spain, the king guarded all of his prerogatives including the right not to pay tithe. The crown's decision to pay the tithe in the New World constituted an important precedent. Since originally the Indians had paid their tribute in commodities and labor, the king further declared that encomenderos had to pay the tithe on all tribute income paid to them in titheable goods.[13] This meant a sizeable addition to the archdiocesan coffers, but the matter did not stop there. If the encomenderos had to pay the tithe on commodity tribute, then the king himself also had to pay, according to his own ruling. The crown and encomenderos thus guaranteed at least part of the church's revenue. In several other cédulas, the king further ordered that the viceroy and all other royal officials had to pay the tithe, although in Spain they did not.[14] Breaking another long tradition, the king ruled that the members of the military-religious orders were liable to pay the tithe. This differed sharply from the situation in Spain, where the orders' position as defenders of the faith gave them an exemption from the tithe.[15] Likewise nobles tithed in Mexico, but not in Spain.

The Spanish tithe system, which applied to all non-Indians, quickly fell into place. The Indians paid little tithe during the sixteenth century, in comparison to the tithe of the Spanish. What they did pay was limited to three things, the *tres cosas*, established by Bishop Zumárraga.[16] Zumárraga considered three European commodities—wheat, cattle, and silk—important enough to tithe. The cultivation of silk initially played a role in the tithe. Cultivation declined, however, in the face of royal opposition and the introduction of goods from the Orient. Silk faded out altogether later in the century.[17] The other two commodities always played an important role, in spite of the Indians' reluctance to adopt them.

The king's resolution to limit the Indian's tithe to the *tres cosas*, following the initial decision of Zumárraga, should in no way be construed as humanitarian. After having received the rights to the tithe for his missionary effort, Charles I had no intention of paying for all of the church's activity from his own treasury. A series of cédulas defined royal responsibility in the area of ecclesiastical finances. In 1533 the king ruled that as long as the question of the Indian tithe remained unsettled, he and the encomenderos would pay local *curas'* salaries. That same cédula directed the royal treasury to increase Indian tribute levels to the degree required to guarantee proper payment for the priests.[18] The famous *tres cosas* became a royal decree in 1544, following considerable debate and investigation.[19] In spite of this limited authorization for tithing the Indians, revenues did not reach a level at which all clerics could receive their pay from the tithe levies. Royal subsidies continued. Finally in 1566, Philip II ordered that no curate be paid from the royal treasury. Treasury officials had to see that the tithe was used to pay the priests, and only when the tithe did not reach the level sufficient to pay them would the king intervene. As strict as the ruling sounds, in the vast majority of cases no one knew how much the tithe was really worth for any given *partido*. After 1576, only the districts of Atlixco and Veracruz in the diocese of Puebla-Tlaxcala, Coatzacoalcos in Oaxaca, and Pánuco in Mexico, and four parishes in New Galicia had *curas* whose salaries came partly from the tithe. In fact fewer *curas* received their pay from the tithe after 1566 than before. Only the cathedral parish of each see continued to rely totally on the tithe for salaries.

Church authorities collected the *tres cosas* separately from the rest of the tithe, by royal mandate. They could not rent the collection to a third party, rather they had to collect it directly. Church officials often sold the right to collect the rest of the tithe to outsiders. Provisions existed for the royal collection of all tithe, should the revenue amount to less than the quantity necessary to cover minimum salaries. The cédula that enacted this provision appeared in 1541, and it set the minimum at 4,444 *pesos de minas*.[20] Nevertheless, this did not affect Mexico greatly, since by 1538 the tithe reached nearly 10,000 *pesos de minas*. The degree to which the royal treasury entered into the tithe collection in less prosperous dioceses is unclear.

The royal treasury oversaw the earliest tithe collection. The Cortesian tithe, cited earlier, fell to the *real hacienda*, as did the collections for 1530 and 1535, and one assumes the entire period from 1523 to 1535.[21] But by 1536 the Mexican church had taken charge of administering the tithe collection, renting part of it out to others.[22]

The royal treasury rented out the earliest tithes according to territorial jurisdiction. Although the church took over the administration, this pattern continued throughout the sixteenth century in Oaxaca, Michoacán, and New Galicia. Nevertheless, as soon as the tithe collection fell to the church in the diocese of Mexico, the chapter rented and collected it according to commodity. In any given year the cathedral chapter had to decide whether or not to rent the tithe or administer it directly. In many years the decision roused deep animosities in the chapter. Direct administration cost less, since ecclesiastical officials took charge of the process as part of their other duties.

The rental of the tithe, however, provided the church with immediate cash and no far-flung collection responsibilities. Normally the parties renting the tithe paid the church a certain percentage of the bid price upon signing the contract, and provided a sufficient number of *fiadores*, individuals pledged to pay the entire sum to the church, should the collection fail. The rest of the contract value came due at the end of the time period stipulated in the contract according to a payment schedule.[23] While the collectors, either the renter or the ecclesiastical administrators, actually received goods, produce, and livestock from those paying the tithe, except for a few common grains, they would sell the produce and give only the money to the church. The whole process could take quite a while. In at least one case, the renter of the tithe on cattle had a secondary partner. They agreed to store the calves collected in the tithe for a period of three years. One partner provided the ranch, the other provided the feed. At the end of three years they resolved to split the profits, that is a second generation of calves they produced. Whether or not they paid the church three years late, or paid the church immediately, made no difference as long as the church was paid. In the meantime the tithe renter could use the commodity collected for his own investment.[24]

Tithe rental provided the means whereby a precapitalist entrepreneurial group might come into existence. The renters speculated on the collection of the tithe. They provided the church with ready cash in the initial rental and then assumed the liability of collecting the tithe, hoping to make a profit on the difference between the cash given to the church and the actual value of the goods collected. Furthermore, the renters could speculate with the goods collected, as seen in the case above, thus attempting to increase their profit.

In any given year, the chapter might rent part of the tithe and collect another part directly. For example, the tithe for Querétaro and San Juan del Río constituted a territorial unit, one of the few used in tithe collection in the Mexican archdiocese, administered directly by a chapter member (see Document Appendix). Nevertheless, most tithe farms went according to commodity and not territory. The categories came directly from the 1501 cédula defining titheable goods.[25] The church recognized ten categories: (1) pigs and goats; (2) cheese, wool, and milk; (3) Spanish grains, such as wheat, barley, and oats, and garbanzos, and other beans from Europe; (4) Indian crops, such as corn, pinto beans, chiles, and melon seeds; (5) fruits and vegetables; (6) sugar, honey, wax, cacao, cotton, chickens, turkeys, and pigeons; (7) silk, indigo, and cochineal; (8) cattle; (9) mules and horses; and (10) sheep. The year's crop formed the basis for the annual tithe levy. For ten bushels of a given commodity produced in a year, one went to the church. For livestock, the tithe covered animals born during the year, not the entire flock. Since the animals collected were usually one year old, when recording, say, sheep, documents often refer to lambs.

The *fondo excusado* constituted a special, separate part of the tithe and its collection.[26] This fund represented the tithe paid by the average household in each *partido*, or collection area. In the archdiocese, at the end of the century, this was one single household. Oaxaca, however, had four. The household was to be neither the largest nor the smallest in the district. In actual practice it was the second largest.[27] The chapter collected the fund separately from the rest of the tithe and allocated it to the account of the fabric of the cathedral, for both maintenance and construction. For ease of collection the tithe administrators must have tried to lump it in with the rest of the tithe. In July 1540, a royal cédula ordered that if the ecclesiastical officials included the *excusado* in the collection of the rest of the tithe, it had to be removed before the disbursal of the funds.[28] This distinction could have affected the reported gross tithe revenues, since by the 1560s the *excusado* represented some 7 percent of the whole tithe.[29]

Beyond these general guidelines for the imposition and collection of the tithe, variations existed from diocese to diocese and from year to year. In confronting the collection of the tithe, the basic decision to be made was whether to administer the collection directly or rent the collection to outside bidders. Strong arguments could be rallied to support either position. In favor of rental, the church could have all its money very quickly, usually in less than one year, while direct administration often required several years to finish a single collection. On the other hand, direct administration netted the church far higher revenues, since all the tithe ended in its hands, with only small amounts expended for the salaries of various collection functionaries. Tithe rental returned less money to the church because the renter was essentially betting that he could make a profit between the money he paid to the church and the money collected.

In the case of the diocese of Oaxaca the cathedral chapter usually rented the tithe, seeking the quick funds.[30] In the archdiocese of Mexico, however, both methods of collection were used equally often. In fact direct administration might even have been more common than rental. In Michoacán it seems that rental was more common. In general, in the smaller dioceses, in terms of Spanish population, the cost of administration, the delay, and the constant need for money led to frequent tithe rental. In the archdiocese, and probably in the diocese of Puebla, the denser Spanish population made direct administration easier, and higher revenues served as a temptation to reject tithe rental in favor of direct methods. The dichotomy is, however, in itself an oversimplification. Even when the bulk of the tithe was rented, some was often collected directly, and vice versa.

Several functionaries took part in the tithe collection procedure whatever mode was finally decided upon. The cathedral chapter had the primary obligation to collect the tithe, a task it usually approached with great interest because its members' salaries came from it. The chapter annually elected two of its number to serve as the *hacedores de diezmos*, rotating in the office. The primary obligation of the *hacedores* was to oversee the collection and distribution of the tithe for the whole chapter. They entered into contracts with the tithe renters, checked over the accounts of both administrators and renters, and witnessed the division of the tithe among the various recipients. To keep the office separate from the day-to-day affairs of tithe collection, the officers were normally ineligible to serve as collectors themselves.

The other officials involved in tithe collection and distribution were the *contador* and two mayordomos. The *contador* was the cathedral accountant. He recorded all the income and expenses of the cathedral chapter and kept all of the records of the tithe. He worked in close cooperation with the *hacedores* and the tithe collectors. When funds were disbursed the chapter ordered the *contador* to issue a *libranza*, pay order, which was presented in turn to the mayordomo. The mayordomo actually had physical control of the church funds, kept in a locked chest which required three keys to be opened. The *contador*, mayordomo, and *hacedores* each held one of the keys, thus any one or two could not open the chest without the others. The mayordomo also was responsible for purchasing the items necessary for the cathedral and church in general.[31] In fact there were usually two mayordomos, one for the physical plant of the cathedral (the *mayordomo de fábrica* or *ecónomo*), the other served the chapter directly and had charge of overall financial activities (mayordomo). The fabric of the church included not just the structure but the ornaments, vestments, and ritual supplies (wax, wine, and wafers). Thus, each mayordomo had control over a part of the liquid cash. In Mexico one man served both offices until about 1580. In the very early years, the mayordomo also acted as the tithe administrator. The *sacristán*, while not a tithe officer, was responsible for the security and maintenance of the physical property of the cathedral, and as such worked closely with the mayordomo, and later the *mayordomo de fábrica*. When the cathedral needed to have financial documents drawn up it was the mayordomo's responsibility. Consequently, in suits involving the cathedral, or in the collection of the tithe, the mayordomo acted as an agent of the chapter. He authorized loans of church funds, mortgages and rental of church property, and in short oversaw the whole range of financial operations of the church.

Mexican Tithe Collection, 1576–78

Some of the nuances of tithe collection can be better understood by following the process over a period of time. Daily decisions by the cathedral chapter and other collection officials often had an important impact on the tithe collection. Consider, for example, the period 1576–78. As will be seen later, this period was a decisive one for the Mexican church. A great epidemic struck New Spain in these years, resulting in tremendous loss of life among the Indian population. By the mid-1580s this affected the tithe collection. Nevertheless, there is no reason to believe that at the time the church officials collecting the tithe were aware of the ultimate impact of the pestilence. Thus, as far as the tithe collection was concerned, the period under study did not differ greatly from previous times. If in fact there was concern over a possible lowering of tithe revenues, the period might demonstrate a bit more resourcefulness of purpose on the part of the collection officials, thereby manifesting a wider range of techniques used in tithe collection. From records available, it seems that the full impact of the Indian mortality was not felt for at least four, and possibly six, years. Furthermore, a detailed study of the epidemic period (Chapter 5) will demonstrate the measures taken to protect revenues when church officials finally became aware of the long-term financial ramifications.

The Mexican cathedral chapter decided to rent the tithe for 1576 but to administer it directly for the next two years. References in the discussion of this question lead one to conclude that before 1576 the tithe had been collected directly for some time.[32] What follows is a discussion of the various actions regarding tithe collection taken in 1576–78 by the cathedral chapter of Mexico and its agents, along with an analysis of the background and implications of these actions.

The year 1576 began with an attempt by the chapter to prosecute Francisco González, a previous renter of the tithe on sheep, who had not fulfilled his contract. Suits like this were common. Usually the first indication of trouble on the part of a renter was a request for a delay in repayment (*espera*). When one fell seriously in arrears on an obligation, the entire sum would be refinanced. Only in the very last instance would the church actually prosecute. Clearly the tithe officers felt that they stood a better chance of collecting at least part of the money through negotiation. Lawsuits had a tendency to drag on, costing more and more, and thus seriously diminishing the church's net return. In the case of González, a new payment schedule was negotiated.[33]

The cathedral chapter then turned to several items relating to the crown and the royal treasury's participation in the tithing procedure. First the chapter considered the rental of the tithe for the province of Pánuco. As noted, Pánuco was one of the few regions in which tithe revenues actually paid the salary of the local parish priest. The region was rather distant from Mexico, thus complicating tithe collection. Whatever the reason, this was the only portion of the archbishopric of Mexico where royal treasury officers took control of the tithe collection. In spite of papal grants and royal orders, in the archdiocese of Mexico, it was not common practice, with this one exception. Royal treasury records indicate that the crown had overseen the Pánuco tithe from the earliest times through the 1580s.[34]

In January 1576 the *maestrescuela* of the cathedral was empowered to negotiate with the royal treasury officials about the Pánuco tithe. The result of their talks allowed the royal treasury to continue to take an active role in the tithe collection for Pánuco. In October it auctioned the tithe rental for Pánuco to Bartolomé Mexía for the year 1577, with a contract bid of 1,040 pesos. He later ceded this obligation to Antonio Núñez Caldera. Subsequently, Núñez Caldera either won the auction or received it from another for the years 1577–83 (excepting 1578 and 1581). In fact the only important tithe worth collecting was on cattle. In the rental documents for Pánuco the goods to be collected were variously listed as "cattle," "cattle and grain and other things," or simply "the tithe pertaining to His Majesty."[35]

Later in January the cathedral chapter instructed its agent at court in Spain to begin pressing for a ruling on the obligation of religious orders to pay the tithe.[36] This issue was destined to become a major conflict between the secular and regular clergy. The regulars argued that as part of the church they were not subject to the tithe. The seculars countered by pointing out that as long as the regulars opposed direct episcopal control, they were not truly a part of the local hierarchy and thus could not claim immunity from the tithe. Furthermore, the seculars bitterly complained that much prime agricultural land was falling outside their taxing authority, to the overall detriment of the church, owing to acquisitions of the regular orders. By the end of the century, the chapter began to take more active measures to restrict the growth of the regulars' estates. In 1596 it offered to lessen the tithe obligation to 5 percent for the regidor Alonso de Valdes, if he agreed to purchase an estate from the friars of San Jerónimo in Chapultepec.[37]

In February the cathedral chapter began to award the tithe rental contracts. The contracts were granted after a public auction, *remate*. These auctions took one of two forms. Either they were well publicized in advance and held at a single sitting, like our modern auction, or they were placed in *pregón*. This entailed announcing a bidding period well in advance. Then a period of time, from a week to a month, would be set aside for the collection of bids. The auctioneer or crier, *pregonero*, would announce the auction daily and call for bids. After the period had ended, the contract went to the highest bidder.

Nevertheless, several things could stand between a successful bidder and the actual contract. The most important of these, for the church, was the posting of bonds, *fianzas*. Each tithe collector had to present other individuals willing to act as bondsmen or cosignatories. These people obligated themselves to fulfill the contract, if for some reason the renter was unable. If the highest bidder could not post sufficient bond, he would not win the contract. In these instances the second highest bidder would begin petitioning the church officials to award him the tithe contract instead.

In February 1576, eight tithe contracts were issued. They included the tithe on sheep, cheese and wool, horses and mules, wheat, corn, sugar, cattle, and garden crops. While other goods were rented out for collection, they did not appear in the chapter minutes. One of the more interesting of these other tithe rental contracts was the one for "anise, ginger, cane [bamboo?], reeds, woad [a dye-stuff], rhubarb, bricks, lime, pottery, glass, honey and syrups."[38] In 1576, the tithe was generally rented according to commodity and not region, with the exception of Pánuco.

Although omitted from the minutes of the cathedral chapter, the tithe on sugar was also a question at this time. For all intents and purposes it was collected regionally, since the only area in the archdiocese where sugar was produced in any quantity was the Cuernavaca Valley. Within that territory the largest producer, by far, was the Cortés estate. But between 1565 and 1591 the estate and the church officials were embroiled in a suit over the nature of the tithe payment. The church argued that, based on royal orders, the tithe on sugarcane was to be paid in sugar, at 5 percent.[39] The sugar producers countered by demanding that the tithe be paid on the agricultural product, the sugarcane. This would have severely limited church revenues because the cane had little intrinsic worth if it was not processed and refined into sugar. Since the large producers all had their own sugar mills, if they paid the tithe in cane they could look forward to collecting a fee for refining it.[40] In 1593 the church court ruled against Cortés and the other large producers. They immediately appealed to the pope, but were unsuccessful in overturning the judgment.

In the early 1570s, the church conducted another suit against the Cortés Marquesado on what were called the commutations. In the last half of the sixteenth century the tribute paid by the Indians was increasingly paid in cash, rather than in goods or services. The process whereby the tribute was fixed in cash was called commutation.[41] The church adhered to the principle that even if tributes were commuted to cash the encomendero still had the obligation to tithe on the original commodity. The encomenderos argued that since there was no tithe on cash income, the commuted tribute could never be taxed. By 1590 the crown ruled against the encomenderos, itself included, and made the commutations liable to the tithe, based upon the goods which they represented.[42] As with other rulings applied to encomenderos, the crown also tithed on the commuted tribute. In the case of the tribute and the commutation, the tithe applied only to the titheable goods. Thus if the tribute consisted of woolen blankets, the tithe was assessed on the raw wool, not the value of the blanket.[43] In the case of the Marquesado, court papers indicate that the value of the commutations for the twenty-one months from September 1569 through April 1571 came to 935 pesos.[44] This was levied only on clothing from Yautepec, Tepoztlan, Oaxtepec, and Acapistla, and fowl from those four villages and from Coyoacan, Tacubaya, and Cuernavaca.

Because of the difficulties inherent in ascertaining the proper level of tithe on both tribute and commutations, the church entered into negotiations with both the encomenderos and the royal treasury. These decisions, arrived at collectively, were then formalized. In late 1576, Alonso Pérez, the encomendero of Tezontepec, agreed to pay 250 pesos to the church for the commutations on his tribute for the period 1571–78, at the rate of 31¼ pesos per year.[45]

By the end of 1576, the cathedral chapter found itself discussing the benefits and liabilities of renting or collecting the tithe. It tentatively decided to go ahead and rent the tithe if someone offered more than the past year. Nevertheless, by March 1577, the chapter members changed their minds and voted to administer the tithe directly. After making that basic choice, a whole new set of issues had to be resolved. The implementation of the administration system took well over a year. It was not until July 1577 that an administrator was named for the collection, Canon Diego Caballero Bazán. Caballero was a titular member of the

Michoacán cathedral chapter but never actively served his prebend. The viceroy of Mexico, the Marqués de Villamanrique, several times accused him of being the most mercenary priest in the territory, concerned more with financial affairs than spiritual ones.[46] His father had been a middle-level bureaucrat, secretary of the audiencias of Santo Domingo and Peru. He was probably related to one of the wealthy sugar estate owners in the Cuernavaca region, Diego Caballero. While his particular skills might have placed him in bad graces with the viceroy, he seemed particularly well suited to tithe collection.

The rest of 1577 was spent in dealing with the failure of earlier years' tithe rentals. In September the chapter resolved to renegotiate the obligation incurred by Alonso Rodríguez de Bonilla in the rental of the tithe on grain for 1574–75. An agreement was reached on the 8,750-peso debt only after Rodríguez was imprisoned.[47] On two other occasions the chapter dealt with the inability of Juan de Badillo to pay his various tithe obligations for the current and past years, including his responsibility as successor to Rodríguez de Bonilla's debt.[48]

Moving into 1578 the chapter continued to deal with additional problems created by their decision to collect the tithe directly. In March it addressed the question of the salary to be enjoyed by the *hacedores* for their added work load. In general, the *hacedores* received a fixed salary for overseeing the tithe collection. Under direct administration their tithe duties increased tremendously, since now every detail of collection had to be decided not by a tithe renter but by the church. Therefore, the chapter resolved to pay 1 percent of all money collected, up to a maximum of 30,000 pesos gross revenue, or 300 pesos to the *hacedores*. While so far no records give the total value of the 1578 tithe, it was probably higher than 30,000. The *hacedores* would continue to receive their usual salary if the chapter decided to rent the tithe.[49]

As noted earlier, the tithe was usually collected by commodity. Under church administration it seems that the collection was carried out by province. In May 1578 the cathedral chapter resolved to divide the archdiocese into collection districts for ease of administration. At this time it is not clear exactly where these districts were. Nevertheless, the archdiocese is divided naturally into several rather clearly defined geographical areas. The Valley of Mexico is the most prominent, followed in importance by the two neighboring valleys of Toluca and Cuernavaca. To the south are the coastal plains and highlands of the modern state of Guerrero, often referred to as the province of Acapulco and its mountains. Then to the north of that is the mining district of Taxco. North of Mexico City is the fertile province of Tula and the mines of Pachuca. The northern frontier of the archdiocese was the region of Querétaro, being successfully exploited by this time, and Pánuco, one of the earliest Spanish settlements.

The chapter may have divided the central basin even further, since it accounted for the largest portion of agricultural production in the archdiocese, and thus the largest tithe revenues. The Valley of Mexico contained four general regions. To the southeast lay the province of Chalco, including land as far south as Amecameca. To the east-northeast was Texcoco, passing to the north as far as the Acolman-Teotihuacan area. Moving west one found the large Huehuetoca-Tepotzotlán region, which dominated the northwest corner of the valley. It also included Tlalnepantla, Zumpango de la Laguna, and Cuautitlan. Then to the west-southwest was the large fertile Tacubaya, Tacuba, Coyoacan zone, much of which had been in the Cortés estate.

By the middle of 1578, the church officials decided to replace Caballero Bazán as tithe administrator with one of their own chapter members. The first prebendaries appointed were the Racioneros Rodrigo Muñoz and Antonio de Salazar; later in the year Salazar was replaced by Juan Hernández, also a *racionero*.[50] This decision no doubt reflected the opinion that it was cheaper still to hire members of the cathedral chapter to oversee the tithe collection than to employ outside personnel.

In June 1578, the chapter drew up the conditions under which the tithe administrators would operate[51] (see Document Appendix). In earlier years the chapter had written guidelines for the verification of the tithe on tribute, but it had never before written guidelines for the general tithe collection. The document contained twelve points. The agreement outlined both the manner in which the tithe was to be collected and how it was to be distributed. The administrator had to notify the chapter of the arrival of any tithe in kind and to inform everyone of any distribution of the goods. The obligation of arranging the distribution of the tithe revenues among the authorized recipients fell to the administrator. He established the time for the division, but he charged the mayordomo with the actual allocation.

The administrator faced complex paperwork. He kept all contracts for collection and sale of the tithe. In an account book he recorded the day, month, and year of all receipts of money and goods. He also saved contracts with the lower-level collectors stipulating the quantity of money and goods each had to collect. In turn each of the collectors maintained a record book of all collections, using witnesses to verify the entries.

The administrator was responsible for hiring the local collectors and establishing their salaries and obligations. The collectors had to post bonds to guarantee the faithful completion of their duties. The administrator hired teamsters to bring tithe goods to Mexico City. The mayordomo, in turn, paid them their fees, based upon the contracts issued by the administrator. In storage and shipping, good grain had to be separated from damaged grain, so that the bad would not spoil the good. Likewise, in order to avoid the complaint that one individual received good grain in the distribution and another bad, no goods could be allocated individually but rather to everyone at the same time. Lastly, the chapter reserved the right to change or modify the conditions of the tithe administration at any future date. The administrator received 200 pesos annually for his efforts.

Later in 1578 two interesting things occurred. In September, Bartolomé de Espinosa was appointed as the tithe collector for grains in the province of Chalco.[52] This appointment indicates that the Valley of Mexico was divided into separate collection districts at this time. Also significant, his authority was limited to the collection of grains and not other goods, implying that even under direct administration collectors specialized in single commodities, or related groups, rather than all tithes for a given region. In practice, though, as in the case of sugar in the Cuernavaca Valley, the major crop of the Chalco province was grain, with limited production of other goods.

In November, the royal audiencia ordered the chapter to pay certain monies to Cristóbal de Estrada, the tithe renter of wheat for 1573. The chapter had collected the tithe directly from two wheat farmers for that year and kept the money. Estrada protested to the audiencia, since by having won the rental contract, all the wheat tithe revenues legally belonged to him. The court ruled in his favor, and the church had to pay him the money. The actual judgment demanded that the money be given back to the farmers, who in turn handed it over to Estrada.[53]

At some time in 1578, the *racionero* Servan Rivero had been placed in charge of collecting the Indian tithe, the *tres cosas*.[54] As seen earlier, this tithe was to be collected separately from the rest. Although the general guidelines for the *tres cosas* called for direct collection, it was often rented out.

The collection of the tithes for the period 1576–78 stretched out over several years. In 1579 the chapter had to renegotiate two of the outstanding contracts. One was with Antonio Rosales, the renter of the wool tithe for 1576–77, the other with Pasqual Crespo and Juan Pinillos, renters of the corn tithe for 1576.[55] In July of 1580 the renter of the anise, spice, and dye tithe, mentioned above, also defaulted on his contract, thus requiring renegotiation.[56] Finally, in 1582, the chapter took positive action against those who had failed to pay or collect the 1577 tithe by drawing up excommunication papers against them.[57] This delay between the actual harvest and the final tithe collection was quite common. Francisco de Paz, the tithe administrator for 1579–83, testified in an investigation of tithe collection that "until the tithe for a year has been collected, three, four, or five years pass, which means that year of 1577 remains to be collected until 1585."[58] Nevertheless, by 1597 the chapter still had not collected the money for the rental of the tithe on wool for 1576, twenty years earlier![59] At least part of this delay, however, must be attributed to the 1576 epidemic. As mentioned, though, it could take several years for the financial implications of a disaster of this scope to be felt or even recognized by the cathedral chapter.

Additional Considerations

From studying the tithe collection records in other dioceses, one can gain additional insights into the collection system. One of the basic principles of the tithe collection was that clerics could not rent the tithe because of their vested interest. This restriction was embodied in royal law, which specifically forbade any interested party from receiving a rental contract.[60] As with other such prohibitions, there were ways of complying with the letter of the law while violating the spirit.

Cathedral chapters usually chose one of their members as the administrator of the tithe. Clearly this was acceptable within the law. Although the chapter members received their wages from the tithe, serving as an administrator was quite different from renting the tithe. The one merely oversaw the collection process; the other attempted to profit while conducting the collection. Nevertheless, in the diocese of Oaxaca the prebendaries sometimes did rent the tithe. One case was that of the archdeacon, later dean, of the chapter, D. Sancho de Alzórriz. D. Sancho, in addition to his seat on the chapter, also served as the local commissar for the Inquisition.

In 1586 Alzórriz was accused of illegal dealings in mules and other commodities. He defended himself saying that for most of his fifteen years in Oaxaca he had either rented the tithe or purchased tithe goods from the church. In two specific cases Alzórriz took over the rental of the tithe from another. In the first, in 1574, he purchased the tithe rental contract from the original collector. He did this in partnership with Antonio Gómez Páez, a resident of Oaxaca. In the second case, Alzórriz split a tithe contract. Lucas Jáuregui rented the whole tithe for 1584–85 for 16,000 pesos, 8,000 pesos per year. In January 1585, Jáuregui transferred the collection of the second year to Alzórriz, except for the tithe on fowl, which Jáuregui had already rented to a third party. In both of these cases Alzórriz became the de facto renter of the tithe, even though he did not originally win the rental contract. In the final ruling the bishop of Oaxaca, D. Fr. Bartolomé de Ledesma, decided that Alzórriz had broken the law by participating so actively in the tithe rental, fined him 100 pesos, and enjoined him, and all other prebendaries, from ever renting the tithe, directly or indirectly, or participating in commercial activities.[61]

In the archdiocese of Mexico this royal proscription was evaded by appointing clerics as collectors of the tithe while giving them a percentage of the collection rather than a specified salary. The end result of this action created an effective situation similar to a tithe rental, except that the church still received its money later rather than sooner. It did, however, provide an adequate incentive to ensure the faithful and vigorous collection of the tithe, while protecting the collector from the enticement of profit inherent in the rental.

The tithe for the northern province of Querétaro and San

Juan del Río was usually administered in this fashion. In 1591, the cathedral chapter established a set of conditions for the precentor, Dr. D. Alonso Larios de Bonilla, to regulate the collection in Querétaro[62] (see Document Appendix). His first order of business was to make a general accounting of previous years' collection from the four individuals who had rented and administered the tithe in the province. That done, Larios de Bonilla set out for the province, being certain to carry with him copies of the royal audiencia judgment, which ceded the province to the archdiocese, rather than to the diocese of Michoacán. This ruling also listed the names of the estates, haciendas, and ranches in the territory and served as the master list for the collection.

As administrator, Larios de Bonilla had an account book wherein he would list each estate along with its total production and the tithe payment. He paid particular attention to sheep, goats, and other herded animals because the tithe on them had to be split between Mexico and Michoacán, since they grazed part of the year in both dioceses. For his work Larios de Bonilla received 10 percent of the total collection. The cattle tithe had been rented in the past. If Larios could improve past years' revenues, he could enjoy 10 percent of the new income. He received 5 percent of the tithe collected on grains, wool, cheese, sheep, fruit, grapes, nuts, and cattle. Only on the increase from previous years could he keep the full 10 percent of the tithe. He also held legal power to sell all of the goods collected, either for cash or on credit. This was a measure of simple expediency, since shipping costs from Querétaro to Mexico would be greater than the value of the goods. Larios de Bonilla must have done a good job, because as long as he lived he continued to make an annual tithe collection trip to Querétaro during the summer. The percentage he was allowed to keep, however, declined to 6 percent by 1594.[63]

Collection Costs and Speculation in Tithe Goods

The question of shipping costs was very important. For many years Indians were required to pay their tithe in the cabecera of their region. This meant that the Indians bore much of the cost of transportation. It did, however, facilitate collection by centralizing the goods in the chief towns.[64] In an attempt to lessen the burden on the Indians the crown ultimately ruled that the responsibility for shipping lay with the church and collectors, not the Indians.[65]

Shipping accounts for 1583 show the high cost of transporting tithe goods. In general, the cost was so high that only commodities gathered in the Valley of Mexico were worth bringing into the city. Only very occasionally did the church bring goods in from Toluca. In 1583 the shipping costs for the tithes on corn, wheat, and barley from Chalco amounted to just over 1,063 pesos.[66] This covered the transportation of 2,296 bushels of wheat, 1,367 of corn, and 249 of barley. The shipping cost was 2 *tomines* per bushel for wheat and barley, and 2.5 for corn. That year wheat sold at auction for 13 *tomines*, corn between 4 and 6.[67] Shipping amounted to half the value of the corn and one-seventh the value of wheat. The cost of collection and shipment of the tithe from Tacubaya and Atzcapotzalco amounted to 1,160 pesos in 1582.[68]

Another cost of directly administering the tithe was the storage of the collected grains. Because of the size of the church's income from grains, it was worthwhile to store some of it to be sold when the prices were highest, thus maximizing income. Secondly, many members of the cathedral chapter preferred to receive their share of the tithe income in kind, rather than receive money and then have to later purchase foodstuffs.[69] These considerations required the church to store at least part of its tithe revenues, mostly grain.

For example, the desire to keep some grain for later sale

or distribution appeared in 1579 when the cathedral chapter resolved to place all wheat in storage until there was sufficient quantity to distribute among the tithe recipients.[70] The storage facility was always referred to as a casa or *casa de diezmos* but in fact must have been something like a storehouse or shop converted for storage. In 1583 the chapter ruled that renting an additional storage facility had proven too costly and resolved to use the mayordomo's house instead.[71] No indication was given as to his response to that action. The decision was obviously a bad one since the following June the chapter ordered the tithe administrator to look for a new storage house, given the poor condition of the grain.[72]

Based on some actions taken in 1585, it seems clear that the church speculated with its tithe grain. First in August the chapter ruled not to sell any corn from the tithe until the end of September. Then in late September, the members decided to continue to withhold some of the produce from the market. Ultimately, in November the chapter members voted to hold the grain until the price reached 8 or 9 *tomines* per *fanega*.[73] While this price was clearly higher than the 4–6 *tomines* of grain sold at royal tribute auction, it was below the record 12–18 reached during the agricultural crises of the 1590s.[74] Even the moderately high price of 1585 was reached and exceeded by the church in 1586, when corn from Teotalpa was resold to Indian farmers at 12 *tomines* in March, while Toluca corn went for 10 *tomines*.[75] Speculation did help offset the cost of storage. In 1590 the rent for the storage house was 350 pesos.[76] That expenditure was rather small, given the large quantities of grain the church had at its disposal with which to speculate. As noted above, chapter members wanted their tithe share partially in kind. Divided among all the chapter members, the rental of the storage house was rather inexpensive, leaving one with the conclusion that their speculation served to augment church revenues.

The Indian tithe question preoccupied sixteenth-century

clerics and administrators alike. Some variation existed on the established rule of the "three things." As late as 1577, the cathedral chapter sought a resolution from the viceroy on the issue.[77] By 1586, the chapter was still petitioning the crown to extend the Indian tithe to include all European products, not just the three things.[78] Complying with royal orders the church usually administered the Indian tithe directly. Yet in 1597, the chapter ordered that the Indian tithe be rented to an individual "who will collect it with mildness and without severity even though it be for less than it is worth."[79] That year the whole Indian tithe was rented for 2,076 *pesos de minas.* In the same year the tithe on lambs rented for 4,800 pesos, for comparison.[80]

Meanwhile, it seems that Indians in areas like Querétaro paid tithe on more than just the three things outlined in the early royal and episcopal decrees. In the instructions to the general administrator in 1591, seen above, the chapter ordered him to collect from the Indians [*naturales*] all the items from Castile that were raised or harvested: fruit, nuts, grapes, and small livestock [*ganado menor*].[81] It is likely, too, that the chapter was implementing, on its own, the proposal made to the crown some five years earlier, hoping ultimately to receive royal approval. In the last years of the sixteenth century the chapter even rented the collection of tithe corn from Indian communities in the Cuernavaca Valley.[82] Thus, although the principle of the three things seems to have been well established, there was certainly variation in the rule.

As noted above, the king received one-ninth of the total tithe revenues in recognition of his role as patron of the church, based on papal bulls and royal legislation. Although in the sixteenth century the king regularly returned this money to the church, it first had to be removed and handed over to the royal officials. The royal treasury participated actively in this part of the tithe collection system. The treasury became involved in several ways in the collection of the king's portion. Royal decrees had merely ordered that the "royal ninth" be removed before any other allocation of the gross tithe.⁸³ The royal treasury officers often became very picayune when it came to collecting the ninth. In 1576 the diocese of Oaxaca approached the treasury officials about collecting the tithe on the commutation of tribute to the crown paid by Indians in the diocese. The treasury officers replied that since that cathedral owed several years' payments of the royal ninth, the treasury would keep the commutation tithe as payment. The Oaxaca cathedral chapter replied that the crown had traditionally given the money back to the cathedral, and thus it would be merely a sham to deposit it only to have it given back again. While recognizing this, the treasury officers stood their ground. Finally Andrés Ruiz de Rozas, encomendero of Ocelotepec, offered to post bond for the cathedral so that the treasury would disburse the commutation tithe. His bond covered the possibility that the royal decree redonating the ninth might not be forthcoming.⁸⁴

In the diocese of Puebla-Tlaxcala a very odd pattern of collecting the royal portion emerged in the last decade of the sixteenth century. It was treated as a distinct fund, like the *excusado* or Indian tithe, and rented separately. In 1593 the ninth was rented to Diego Mexía de la Cerda for 5,600 pesos. Clearly Mexía did not go to each agricultural producer and collect one-ninth of the tithe due that year. He must have been purchasing a right to enjoy the ninth, after the end of collection. To do that he first had to pay the purchase price to the royal treasury according to a payment schedule. In this case he won the rental auction on January 19, 1593, and paid off the obligation on August 20, 1594, nineteen months later. Clearly he based his action on the assumption that the final figure for the royal ninth would exceed the 5,600 he bid.⁸⁵

This rather odd practice continued into the seventeenth century. In 1609 the *visitador* Lic. Diego de Landeras y Velasco formally denounced the practice. In his report he wrote that the royal ninth for the three years 1603–05 had been rented for a total of 20,850 pesos. When the tithe collection was finished the royal ninth actually reached about 50,000 pesos, a loss of over 9,000 pesos per year.[86] From the tithe records for Puebla-Tlaxcala we know that the 1603–05 tithe reached 381,985 pesos, yielding 42,443 pesos for the royal ninth. While less than Landeras's estimate, this sum is far closer to the *visitador's* figure than to the rental contract for the ninth.[87] In all likelihood the cathedral chapter had to allow the renter to enjoy some profit between the rental and actual value. It seems unlikely, however, that the renter enjoyed the full ninth. Clearly the church pursued the logic that the royal treasury desired its money sooner rather than later, and this practice allowed it. Initially the treasury might have preferred to receive less money quickly, but in time the treasury saw less and less of the actual value of the royal ninth, ultimately less than half, and it was forced to take some decisive action. In 1620 the crown ordered that the ninth be taken from the gross tithe revenues, and in no other fashion. This clearly addressed the practice in Puebla-Tlaxcala.[88]

Turn of the Century

Tithe collection in the archdiocese of Mexico in the last decade of the sixteenth century and the beginning of the seventeenth century was dominated by one man, Canon Antonio de Salazar. He was first appointed to the cathedral chapter of Mexico in 1572 as a *racionero* and promoted to canon in 1585. He came from an old Mexican family. His maternal great-grandfather and maternal grandfather were both conquerors: his maternal grandmother's father was Miguel de la Palma, and her husband was Alonso de Avila. Avila, a member of the Cortés expedition, received several Indian villages in encomienda. He passed part of his holdings on to his son-in-law, Gonzalo de Salazar, as a dowry around 1534. This included one-half of each of the towns of Matlactonatico and Jujupango. Salazar and his wife, Antonia de Avila, had at least five sons: Pedro, Hernando, Gonzalo, Agustín, and Antonio. Antonio and Agustín joined the secular clergy, both attaining prebends, Agustín as canon in Puebla. Gonzalo entered the Agustinian order, while Pedro and Hernando remained in secular life. Hernando inherited the family encomienda.[89]

Canon Antonio de Salazar was first hired as tithe administrator in 1590 with a salary of 400 pesos, plus 100 more for a servant. This rapidly grew until by 1597 he received 1,200 pesos a year. As tithe administrator, he gained almost total control over the collection. Although technically he administered the tithe directly, in fact he oversaw the rental of most of the components of the tax. In 1592, for example, he either rented or assigned the collection in twenty-three contracts. Of these, seven were agreements with local clergy, to oversee the collection in the parishes they served. The rest were tithe rentals. As in past years Salazar divided the tithe basically according to commodity and then by province. He rented the major commodities such as grains and cattle by province. Secondary commodities such as sheep, mules, pigs, and goats were rented for the whole archdiocese. This was a pattern that would continue throughout Salazar's tenure as administrator. Another important feature of his administration was the listing of haciendas included in the collection authority given to the renters.

Once the rental by auction was completed a notary drew up two documents. One of these was an obligation from the renter to the church for the amount of the rental, often including a schedule of payments. The second document empowered the renter to collect the tithe in the name of the church. In this document, during the administration of Antonio de Salazar, individual estate owners were listed. In the absence of more complete tithe collection data these lists are excellent pictures of the land tenure pattern at the time.

The most detailed rental documents cover the regions immediately surrounding Mexico City.[90] One area began in the south with the Chalco province, and covered land from Amecameca in the south to Chimalhuacan Atengo in the north. By century's end this district included the most estate owners, according to the tithe rental documents. The next area was the Texcoco region, including the territory immediately north of the Chalco province, eastward to the border with Tlaxcala, and north to Acolman and Teotihuacan. To the west from there, one passed into the Tepotzotlan district. According to the tithe rental papers this region covered the territory immediately to the north of Mexico from Tepotzotlán in the west to Ecatepec in the east. Beyond Tepotzotlán to the north was the huge district that centered on Huehuetoca going as far north as Izmiquilpa, as far east as Pachuca and Epazoyucan, and westward to the mountains near Toluca. This district included the rich Tula Valley and plateau to the north. The tithe documents also outlined the land ownership in areas to the west and southwest of Mexico. The two major districts in this area were Tacuba, and the larger region of Coyoacan, which included Tacubaya and San Mateo Huitzilopochco (modern Churubusco).

By the end of the century most of the dioceses of Mexico had adopted the practice of renting or administering the tithe by provinces. In Oaxaca there traditionally had been four regions for tithe collection: Antequera (Oaxaca City), Coatzacoalcos, San Ildefonso–Villa Alta, and Nexapa-Tehuantepec. Each of the districts functioned as a separate component of the whole. In each, one estate was identified for the payment of the *excusado*.[91] In the diocese of Michoacán, by the end of the sixteenth century, the number of tithe collection districts had grown rapidly, with the development of the agricultural region of the Bajío and the mining districts to the north. Traditionally Michoacán had three districts: the core area of Michoacán, Zacatula, and Colima. By the last decade of the century three more districts had been added: Irapuato, Silao, and San Miguel el Grande (modern de Allende).[92] In the diocese of Guadalajara, up until the 1560s there were four collection districts: the core area around Guadalajara, Campostela—the first capital of the region—, Purificación, and Culiacan. Again with the growth of the mining districts, especially Zacatecas, undoubtedly the number of districts increased.[93] In one document dated 1572, the tithe figures were broken down into eighteen zones, for Guadalajara.

In the case of the archbishopric of Mexico, the *fondo excusado* reflected the tithe revenues from just one single estate, rather than one estate from each collection district, as was allowed. In 1589 this estate was that of Hernán Gutiérrez, although no indication is given of where the estate was or how large it was.[94] In 1600 the *fondo excusado* was rented out for collection. According to the rental contract the estate chosen for that year, and several subsequent ones, was that of D. Juan Altamirano, a member of the prestigious order of Santiago. The *fondo* was rented for the sum of 1,240 *pesos de minas*.[95] This means that Altamirano's estate had an annual production in excess of 20,000 *pesos de oro común*, which compares with the total tithe revenues from Tenancingo of that year, which were sold for 1,900 pesos.[96]

The churches of New Spain became closely involved in the agricultural life of the colony as a result of their reliance on the tithe as their major source of income. Only estates owned by ecclesiastical corporations were exempt from paying the tax. The allowance of this exemption became a major ecclesiastical issue in the seventeenth century. At the same time, reliance upon the tithe made the finances of the church somewhat insecure, since pestilence, drought, or other tragedy could destroy much of the agricultural production of one diocese, if not the whole colony. Nevertheless, although there were other sources of income for the church, none received as much attention or provided as much for the administrative costs of the institution.

The tithe collection established some other practices which continued throughout the colonial period. Among these were speculation in collected grains, rental of the tithe to wealthy entrepreneurs, and the on-going conflict between the secular and regular clergy over tithe payment. The importance of the tithe made the church a major factor in the commodity market of the colony and one of the major forces in the development of capital formation and of capitalist agriculture.

If direct administration of the tithe collection brought the church in close contact with the individuals of the agricultural sector, the rental of the tithe brought them into contact with the entrepreneurial group. As noted earlier, the records of tithe collection are very fragmentary for the sixteenth century. In those cases where contracts are available, often the document merely includes the names of the participants with little indication of their occupation or even the nuances of the agreement. From the limited information available, three types of individuals seem to have been active in the rental of the tithe: persons with a use for the tithe products, merchants, and others with regional interests. For instance, in tithe rental a person owning a ranch would often rent the tithe on cattle, or a miller rent the tithe on grain, or a weaver rent the tithe on wool. Numerous examples of this type of tithe contract exist. Earlier in this discussion, Antonio Núñez Caldera appeared as the renter of the cattle tithe from Pánuco. Núñez Caldera owned a large estate in the Pánuco region. In fact his estate was either so large, or so well located, as to lie in part of two dioceses, Mexico and Puebla-Tlaxcala. This situation ultimately made him liable to pay tithe in both dioceses. A suit over his tithe obligation reached the royal courts in 1587, when the two dioceses came to loggerheads.[97] The suit continued until 1591, when the Mexican cathedral chapter decided to drop it, reasoning that the costs of continuing the suit were well known while the possible benefit was uncertain.[98]

In 1587, Rodrigo Morán won the rental of the tithe on goats and pigs.[99] His bondsmen for the rental were Bartolomé Palomo, a pork, bacon, and sausage seller/maker (*tocinero*), and Francisco Hidalgo, a merchant. Lamentably, Morán's occupation is unknown. Clearly Palomo and Hidalgo agreed to post the bonds in the hopes of utilizing the pigs and goats collected in the tithe in their own businesses, the one processing the animals, the other selling the cured products. Ultimately, Morán stepped out of the agreement and transferred responsibility for the collection to Palomo. The contract amounted to nearly 2,000 pesos, an impressive sum for a pig butcher.[100] Morán and Palomo also rented the *excusado* for 1597, along with Antonio Gutiérrez. As noted earlier, the contract cost them just over 2,000 pesos.[101]

The participation of merchants in the tithe rental, already seen, was quite common. Their role often consisted of serving as bondholders, since many had enough cash to guarantee the contracts. This surfeit of cash also allowed them to participate as the principal renter. Often the very largest rentals involved merchants. In 1597 one of the largest tithe rental obligations was issued by Francisco de Solís Bristos (Bristol?), as principal, and Juan de Torres de Loranza, merchant, and Cristóbal Jiménez de Narváez, royal notary, as *fiadores*. The contract was worth 7,100 pesos and covered the collection of the tithe on wool, fleece, cheese, milk, and butter.[102] The potential sales generated by this large a supply of foodstuffs and raw materials clearly was an incentive for the bidders. Solís may have been either a relative of the encomendero of Acolman, Francisco de Solís Orduña, or the man himself, since from time to time he used different surnames.[103] Solís continued to rent the tithe in 1600 and 1601 on the same commodities. In the 1600 rental he paid nearly 8,800 pesos for the contract. A marginal note indicated that by 1602 he had paid off the 1601 contract. In 1601 he also rented the collection of the tithe on lambs and successfully paid it off a year later.[104] His prompt fulfillment of the obligations must have endeared him to the church officials and indicates the ability of the truly wealthy to speculate on the rental of the tithe.

Other members of the elite also participated in the speculation on tithe collection. Diego Mexía de la Cerda served as alcalde mayor of Zacatecas from 1579 to 1582, alguacil mayor of Mexico City, 1582–85, administrator of tribute corn for the Valley of Mexico, 1587, and from 1596 as alcalde mayor of the province of Coatzacoalcos. In 1593, he rented the king's ninth in the diocese of Puebla, as already seen, for 5,600 pesos.[105]

Many of the tithe renters, however, were not wealthy or powerful. Many were minor lights in regional or provincial systems. Finding biographical data on these men is nearly impossible. In fact the only indication of their activity and residence is the brief mention in the tithe rental documents. But in many instances, year after year, the same individual rented the same tithe in the same province. Such a case was Juan de Galarza, who served between 1592 and 1601 as the tithe renter-collector for the province of Tulancingo.[106] In a similar vein, Domingo Núñez consistently held the right to collect the tithe on grain and livestock from the province of Chalco from 1592 to 1600.[107] Unlike Galarza, who was a resident of the province in which he worked, Núñez was listed as a resident of both Mexico and Tepotzotlan.

Within the economy, the tithe rental attracted two basic types of investors. One type could immediately use the goods to be collected; he purchased the tithe collection as a means of acquiring the goods at less than the going rate and thus invested his own labor and management. This category includes the estate owners, butchers, bakers, and candlemakers who collected the raw materials for their various enterprises. The other type of tithe rental involved individuals with available capital looking for a good return on their investment. If the tithe on the royal ninth in Puebla is any indication, these speculators could look forward to a gross profit of 100 per cent. Nevertheless, both types of renters had one common fear, a disaster in the agricultural economy. Severe drought, floods, heat, frost, and a host of other natural disasters could quickly destroy whatever margin of profit existed between the rental and the actual collection. Thus the tithe rental must be considered as a highly speculative investment. The large number of suits concerning the collection of delinquent tithes and delinquent tithe contracts attests to this.

The tithe in general played an even more important role in the overall economy. As a flat 10 percent tax, the tithe represented a major cost of production. When an estate owner calculated fixed costs of equipment and labor, the tithe had to be figured in last to determine the success or failure of the enterprise. The tithe obligation placed every Spanish and mestizo farmer at least partially into the larger economy, since everyone had to deal with the institution. Surely some abuses must have resulted from the collection, especially through renters and from clerics who could keep a percentage of the total.

The best way to maximize income was to overcollect from nearly everyone to assure that the initial investment was paid off and resulted in a comfortable cushion. In this context, the efforts of the renters to collect must have been even more furious in bad years, especially where the tithe rental was based on past years' crops and not on current conditions. This was more true at mid-century than later. There was a general shift from renting the tithe before the crop was in, to renting after harvest. Thus, by 1600, the fluctuations in the tithe must have been more representative of actual conditions of the harvest, while earlier they might have been merely reflections of the best guess.

Within the Spanish and mestizo community, then, the tithe touched nearly everyone directly or indirectly. Estate owners, farmers, and sharecroppers, or tenants who rented fields all felt the immediate impact of the tithe in their net income. The residents of towns and cities felt the tithe through its effect on market conditions, as either the church or the tithe renters speculated with the goods received. By controlling one-tenth of the annual production, the church could easily make the market for the products. In reality, the church controlled more than just 10 percent of the market, since it collected the tithe on all agriculture, both subsistence and market oriented. Within the socioeconomic realm many persons from all levels of society participated in the tithe rental. Low-status groups attempted to make money to increase their social standing and quality of life. The elite used the system to receive tremendous return on their investments. Thus, for better or for worse, the tithe affected all.

Tithe Collection

2. Tithe Distribution

The collection of the tithe was only part of the overall problem posed to the church. Equally difficult and complicated was the division of tithe revenues among the various individuals and institutions signaled to receive a share. The tithe was the major source for the salaries of chapter members, and it provided the cathedral with operating expenses. The method of tithe division was so complicated that it often aggravated the cash flow problems of the church. Tithe rental procedures, already seen, sought to provide the church with the ready cash, but this money had to be divided among the legal recipients before any one of them could use it. As the tithe was the major source of income, church operations could be slowed or halted until the revenue it provided came through. The church in the sixteenth century lived at the edge of its resources, thus there was a great competition among the recipients of the tithe each for their fair share.

The cathedral chapter shared responsibility for the collection and distribution of the tithe with the bishop or archbishop of the diocese. Nevertheless, because the prelate concerned himself with the more pressing judicial and administrative decisions of the see, the major effort of oversight usually fell to the cathedral chapter. The papal bull that erected the Mexican dioceses established the principle that the prelate and his chapter receive equal portions of the tithe. In reality, the distribution became far more difficult and complex as it evolved from this simplistic beginning. Canon and civil law, based on the papal bull and royal decrees, closely regulated the division of tithe revenues.¹ Traditionally in Spain the tithe had been divided into three equal parts. One part was for the support of the bishop, cathedral chapter, and beneficiaries in the cathedral. The second part went to the local churches and their priests. The last third was used to build and maintain the churches and purchase equipment for them. The royal share, a ninth of the whole, consisted of one-third of the final third.²

Tithe Allocation Funds

In the New World a significantly different method was instituted. The gross tithe revenues, after the expenses of collection were removed, were called the *grueso* (see Fig. 1). The *grueso* was first divided into two halves. The prelate and cathedral chapter equally shared one of these halves. Thus, from this first division the bishop or archbishop received one-quarter of the whole tithe, called the *mesa episcopal*. The chapter received the other quarter, the *mesa capitular*, which provided the prelate with both his salary and the operating expenses for his household and administrative staff. He had complete freedom regarding the allocation of his share among those recipients. The *mesa capitular* served as the fund from which the salaries of the chapter members came. Its allocation among them was a very complex process, as will be seen later.

The remaining half of the gross tithe was divided into ninths, to be allocated to four funds. Two of these ninths (11.1 percent) went to the king as patron, a question discussed in Chapter 1. Four of these ninths (22.2 percent) were earmarked for salaries for local parish priests. The remaining three-ninths of the second half (16.6 percent) were divided equally between the fabric of the cathedral and the hospital affiliated with the cathedral. Thus, of the gross tithe there were six recipients: the prelate (25 percent), cathedral chapter (25 percent), the king (11.1 percent), the local curates (22.2 percent), the fabric of the

Figure 1.
Tithe Division

Tithe Distribution

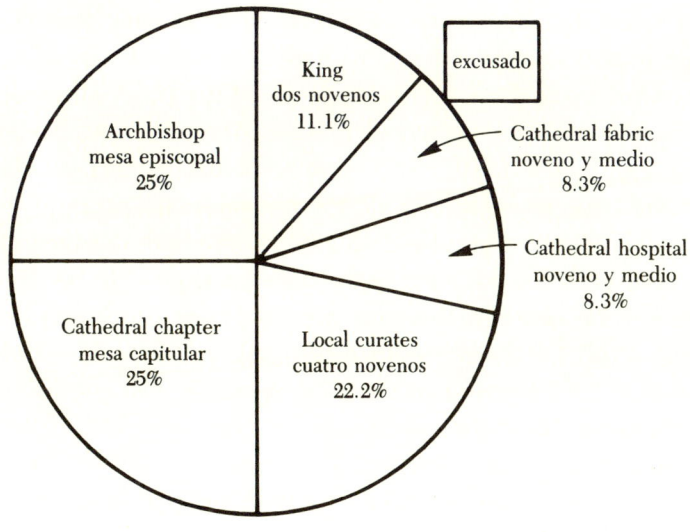

cathedral (8.35 percent), and the cathedral hospital (8.35 percent).

One of the major questions facing the church in the first decades following the conquest centered on the means of support for the activities of local parish priests. Although a distinction was drawn between the upper and lower clergy in Spain, the constitutional bull made no specific provision for priests outside of the cathedral parish. Thus, of the various funds receiving incomes out of the tithe, all except two, the royal and episcopal, financed the cathedral. Nevertheless, by the 1540s, the crown resolved that at least part of the tithe revenues should go to support the work of the church beyond the cathedral. In 1541 the king significantly modified the distribution of the tithe revenues.[3] In his royal decree he ordered that the curates' share be distributed among all the local parish priests, such that each would receive 22.2 percent of the tithe generated in the parish he served. Nevertheless, this order, like many others, was generally ignored for practical reasons.

Early local tithe revenues could in no way support the local clergy. In 1538, for instance, the tithe for the province of Pánuco was 210 *pesos de minas*.[4] The curas' share of this amounted to only 47 pesos with which to support the four priests of the area. By 1530 the annual base salary alloted to a curate in Pánuco had already reached 100 *pesos de minas*. The situation did not improve greatly with time. In 1583 the Pánuco tithe amounted to 860 *pesos de minas*, possibly the highest level of the century. From this, the curates might have enjoyed 190 *pesos de minas*. Divided among the four who served the region, the tithe would have provided less than 50 *pesos de minas* a piece, at a time when most annually received 200 *pesos de minas* from the royal treasury.[5] In some regions, at some times, local parish priests did receive at least part of their annual stipend from the tithe. In the province of Coatzacoalcos, four curates did enjoy some of the locally generated tithe revenue. Nevertheless, it constituted only a small fraction of their overall salaries. Likewise, in New Galicia, five parish priests received about half their salaries from the local tithe. In general, local parish priests did not receive any salary from the tithe, in spite of the royal decree to the contrary.

Since the crown finally decided that local priests would be paid from tribute revenues, the curates' tithe fund reverted to the cathedral, as had been implied in the papal bull that created the diocese. The money alloted to the curates, in fact and according to the bull, paid not only the cathedral curates' salaries but those of the choirboys, various chaplains, the herald, secretary, organist, sacristan, janitor, and others on the staff. Any money left over from the curates' fund was added to the *mesa capitular*. This surplus, called the *superavit*, was the source of much discord within the cathedral, as will be seen.

The fund allocated to the fabric (8.35 percent) was used for the purchase of ornaments and vestments and to pay some salaries and maintenance. As noted in the section on tithe collection, the fabric often had its own mayordomo, who kept strict accounts of the income and outlay of the fabric's fund. In addition to the money received from the division of the gross tithe, the fabric also enjoyed all the revenues of the *fondo excusado*, as seen in the previous chapter.

The hospital fund, (8.35 percent) provided the hospital affiliated with the cathedral with its working capital. In the case of the cathedral of Mexico, this hospital was the Amor de Dios (Hospital de Bubas) founded by the first bishop of the see, Fr. Juan de Zumárraga.[6] In the case of Michoacán, this money formed part of the complex hospital system organized by Bishop Quiroga.[7] In Guadalajara, the money was directly applied to the foundation of a cathedral hospital, Hospital de San Miguel, although some monies were also invested in rural estates to provide added income to the hospital.[8] In Puebla, the cathedral hospital was founded by the first archdeacon of the cathedral, D. Francisco de León, under the advocation of San Pedro.[9]

The various funds allocated from the gross tithe fall into two basic categories: those providing salaries and those providing capital. Unfortunately, the fund dedicated to the bishop cannot be fully studied here because of an almost total lack of information on its disposal and use.[10] The funds providing salaries included the chapter's fund and the curates' fund; the funds providing capital were the hospital fund and fabric fund, with the king's fund being a case apart. Although the king's portion was to be handed over to the royal treasury, as we have seen, throughout most of the century it was actually added to the fabric account. The funds that provided salaries were subject to further division in order to pay each official his fair share.

Allocation of Cathedral Salaries

To understand how the salary funds were allocated, one must study the distribution of the chapter's fund throughout the sixteenth century. The cathedral chapter consisted of clerics appointed by the king to lifetime benefices.[11] These priests were organized into four ranks. The highest rank consisted of the *dignidades* (dignitaries), each of whom carried a title of office, enjoyed the honorific *don*, and dealt with specific matters for the chapter as a whole. The most important of these was the dean, who acted as the presiding officer of the chapter. The next rank was that of the canons, followed by the *racioneros* and *medio-racioneros*. The constitutional bull for all of the Mexican dioceses stipulated that there be five dignitaries, ten canons, six *racioneros*, and six *medio-racioneros*, for a total of twenty-seven. Nevertheless, the king did not fill all of these seats initially.

Just as the general allocation of the tithe fell under royal jurisdiction, so the salaries paid to all ecclesiastical personnel became subject to royal interpretation. Specifically the bishop and chapter members received guaranteed annual incomes, defined in the constitutional bull and in royal decrees. The bull provided for a basic salary of 150 *castel-*

Figure 2.
Cabildo Salaries
Mexico
(oro comun)

	Erection	1545	1564	1566	1576	1577	1588	1594
Dean	276	392	655		1530	(1141)*	(1151)	1293
Dignitary	232	357	600	633	1484	1106	1116	1120
Canon	178	267	450	475	(1113)	(851)	(858)	862
Racionero	124	178	299	316	(742)	(596)	(601)	603
Medio-Racionero	62	89	149	158	(371)	(298)	(300)	301

*Figures in parenthesis were calculated
Sources: Erection, Galvan Rivera, *Concilio*, xxviii; 1545, Carreño, *Desconocido*, 109, 162, 197, and ACTAS, 5 Jan. 1545; 1564 and 1566, AGI, Justicia, 209, Num. 1; 1576, AGI, Contaduria, 697, Data—Salarios; 1577, Lilly Library, Latin American Manuscripts, Mexico II; 1588, AGI, Contaduria, 690, Data—Salarios; 1594, ACEM, 12, exp. 25.

lanos for the dean, 130 for each of the dignitaries, 100 for each canon, and 70 for each *racionero*. *Medio-racioneros* received 35 each, half that of a *racionero* (see Fig. 2). The bull also called for six choirboys and six chaplains and an undetermined number of curates. These positions enjoyed salaries from the tithe, but the bull did not specify minimum levels. This important document did, however, provide for an organist at 16 *castellanos*, a secretary at the same rate, a *pertiguero* (herald) at 16, a sacristan or *ecónomo* at 50, and a *perrero* at 12. The *perrero* literally removed all dogs that entered the cathedral. The *pertiguero* acted as an adjutant or herald for the chapter, announcing meetings, posting notices, and doing other odd jobs.[12]

In 1532, before the arrival of the actual constitutional bull, the royal audiencia, at the insistence of the king and cathedral chapter, created an interim document to establish pay scales and other administrative matters. Based on the papal bull that created the diocese of Tlaxcala, the audiencia's creation differed in several ways from the final bull issued by the pope. While the salaries for prebends did not differ between the two, the provisional document allowed 50 *castellanos* to the curates, 30 *castellanos* and up to 30 *pesos de minas* more to the sacristan, and to the organist 16 *castellanos* and up to 30 *pesos de minas* more. The interim agreement also designated no less than 30 *pesos de minas* to one of the cathedral chantries, and up to a total of 60 *pesos de minas* for the *sochantre* (subchanter). The differences in salaries between the two documents reflect the opinion of the audiencia that the stipends outlined in the papal bull just could not support the staff.[13]

The first record of the distribution of the tithe comes from 1530, before the arrival of the constitution or the creation of the provisional one, and thus followed neither pattern described above. Almost all the money went to pay the salaries of the bishop, cathedral curates, and the curates of the other major Spanish towns in New Spain.[14] By 1538 the papally mandated system had finally begun. At that time the Mexican tithe revenue was 9,261 *pesos de minas*. The *mesa capitular* equaled 2,315 *pesos de minas*, and after all salaries had been paid, including a host of others not listed here, a total of three pesos remained.[15] At this time, the curates' fund paid the local parish priests and not the cathedral staff. The chapter's fund provided for all the personnel of the cathedral. Another important feature of this distribution was that each official received specifically what was ordered in the constitutional bull. But the distribution system still had serious flaws, and the salaries paid did not reflect the cost of living in Mexico. The king, under pressure from the chapter, granted pay increases, but all raises depended on the growth of the tithe. In 1536 and 1540 cédulas authorized higher salaries for the organist, *pertiguero*, and secretary. In 1545 the chapter drew up a new pay scale. The decision, made on January 5, 1545, called for 200 *castellanos* to the *dignidades*, with the dean receiving the usual twenty more, 150 *castellanos* for the canons, and 100 for the *racioneros*. This revision received royal approval in May of the same year.[16]

There were two basic methods for dividing up the chapter's fund. The original allocation followed the proportions reflected in the bull of erection. Thus, considering a canon's individual pay as one unit, the dean received 1.5, the other dignitaries 1.3, the *racioneros* 0.7, and the *medio-racioneros* 0.35. In the 1545 decision noted above, the chapter abandoned this system in favor of another. In the new scale a *medio-racionero*'s salary represented one unit. Thus a *racionero* received twice as much, a canon three times, and a *dignidad* four times as much. The dean's portion equaled that of the other dignitaries, plus the traditional twenty *castellanos*.[17] The second system gave the higher-ranking prebends a greater proportion of the *mesa capitular* than the system based on the erection. In the years following 1545, while the chapter had a full complement of *dignidades* and most of its canons, the new system favored them over the one or two *racioneros*. When, by the 1590s, it had finally filled out its ranks, the distribution system reverted to the formula based on the erection. Thus, once the number of *racioneros* increased to a point where they played an important role in the life of the chapter, their pay came up to the higher proportion indicated in the constitutional bull.[18]

In 1548 the cathedral chapter made a basic decision regarding the distribution of salaries. They resolved to divide the chapter's fund proportionally among the members, but to continue to pay the other employees only the salary specified by the bull and royal decrees. Thus for the rest of the century the chapter members' salaries tended to rise, while the others' remained constant.[19] The question probably arose at this time because the tithe had grown enough to pay all the salaries fully, with some surplus remaining.

The proportional distribution method of the chapter's fund was certainly in place by 1564. This method had an important impact on the staff of the cathedral. To use that year as an example, the gross tithe amounted to 15,720 *pesos de minas* (see Fig. 3). The chapter's fund, 25 percent of the gross, amounted to 3,805 *pesos de minas*, after the removal of the costs of collection. The 3,805 pesos were then divided among all the members of the chapter on a proportional basis. Nevertheless, the constitutional bull stipulated that if money was left over from the curate's fund the surplus, or *superavit*, could be added to the chapter's fund before distribution to the prebends. Therefore, the chapter began paying the cathedral staff only the minimum salary stipulated by the papal bull. Those salaries amounted to only 1,162 *pesos de minas*, out of the 3,082 *pesos de minas* in the curate's fund. The remaining 2,219 pesos constituted the *superavit* and were added to the chapter's fund. In this manner the chapter members enjoyed a distribution of 6,024 pesos rather than the original 3,805. This had a tremendous impact on the individual salaries of the chapter members. A canon who would have received 178 *pesos de minas* from the chapter fund alone, now received 281 *pesos de minas*. Since the chapter controlled all aspects of the administration of the cathedral, it was to their advantage to keep the staff's salaries low, in order to keep their own salaries high.

The preceding discussion assumed that each of the chapter members and curates had a perfect attendance record. One of the major canonical obligations of the cathedral chapter members was the corporate celebration of the Canonical Hours, or Divine Office. These daily offices are collections of prayers, psalms, lessons, and other texts that every priest should celebrate. Members of religious orders and other corporate bodies celebrate them collectively, while individual priests, or priests unable to attend corporate services, recite them alone. The canonical hours consist of eight offices: matins, lauds, prime, terce, sext, none, vespers, and compline.

The *Breviary* contains the liturgy for these services, which are celebrated at specific times of the day. Matins and lauds

Figure 3.
Division of the Tithe, 1564–66
Archdiocese of Mexico (pesos de minas)

		1564	1566
Total		15320.1.10	16427.6.7
Cost of collection		499.7.7	523.4.10
Total for distribution		15220.2.3	15904.1.9
1/4		3805.0.7	3976.0.5
1/2		7610.1	7952.0.10
1/18 [1/9 of 1/2]		745.4.6	883.4.6
Royal Ninth		1691.1	1767.1
Cathedral Fabric Fund		1268.2.9	1325.2.9
Hospital Fund		1268.2.9	1325.2.9
Curates' Fund		3082.2	3534.2
Salaries from Curates' Fund (all in *castellanos*):			
sacristan	60.		
secretary	40.		
choir boys 2 @	16.		
2 @	12.		
2 @	8.		
perrero	12.		
Total	394. =	424.5.1	411.5.7
herald	100.		
organist	80.		
apuntador	20.		
sacristan #2	40.		
6 chaplains @ 50 each	300.		
vestuario	198.		
Total	738.	738	737.3.6
Total expenditures		1162.5.1	1149.1.1
Surplus from Curates' Fund [*Superavit*]		2219.4.1	2385.0.11
Mesa capitular		3805.0.6	3976.0.6
Total available to chapter		6024.5.5	6361.1.4
Salaries for each chapter member:			
5 Dignitaries		375.1.4	396.1.8
10 Canons		281.3	297.1.3
6 Racioneros		187.4.6	198.0.10
6 Medio-Racioneros		93.6.4	99.0.5
Salaries without the *Superavit*:			
Dignitaries		237.6.4	257.1
Canons		178.2.9	185.2.9
Racioneros		118.7.2	123.4.6
Medio-Racioneros		59.3.7	61.6.3

Source: AGI, Justica, 209, Num. 1

are part of the nighttime vigil; prime marks daybreak; terce comes between 8:00 and 9:00; sext was celebrated at midmorning between 11:00 and 12:00; none is the historical equivalent of noon between 2:00 and 3:00; vespers occurs in the afternoon, between 3:00 and 4:00; and compline at day's end.[20] In the sixteenth-century Mexican cathedrals lauds, matins, and compline were counted together as a unit.[21] Thus, for accounting purposes, the chapter recognized six or seven of the ceremonies.

All chapter members, and many of the cathedral staff, had to attend these services and participate in them as part of their ecclesiastical duties. Absences were penalized. Since the salary system for the prebends was on a proportional basis, the penalty for absence depended upon the attendance of others. The accounting system behind the distribution of chapter salaries became complex in the extreme. In later centuries scores of books and manuscripts would be written on the method of accounting the absences.[22]

Only fragments of the account books detailing chapter attendance have been found for sixteenth-century Mexico. Without them, the only example to help illustrate part of the complex attendance accounting procedure is the case of D. Sancho Sánchez de Muñón. Sánchez de Muñón was appointed the *maestrescuela* of the Mexico cathedral in 1559. He served in that post for the remainder of the century. During that period he spent one long period in Spain as the agent to the royal court for the cathedrals and churches of New Spain from 1568–75. During that time he succeeded in winning for himself a royal pension of 2,000 ducats annually for extraordinary service to the crown. He had been one of the major informants during the so-called Cortés Conspiracy. Upon return to Mexico he ultimately became the governor of the archdiocese during the vacancy of the see upon Archbishop Moya de Contreras's elevation to president of the Council of the Indies. In the *sede vacante* which followed Moya's death, Sánchez continued as governor. He also took on the duties of *comisario sub-delegado* of the

Bula de la Santa Cruzada, the chief officer of the sale of indulgences in the form of the Bull of the Holy Crusade. Both of these posts surely netted him an adequate income. Moreover, as part of his cathedral office he also served as chancellor of the local university, a position high in honor but low in remuneration.[23]

Because of his multiple interests, Sánchez de Muñón was unable to attend cathedral services regularly. Starting in 1584 his absences outnumbered the times he was present. To demonstrate the excessive number of absences, in 1597 the Inquisitor Lobo Guerrero ordered that Sánchez de Muñón's attendance records be copied and sent to the king.[24]

To understand the attendance records better, one must be aware that each chapter member enjoyed two types of leave from services. One was the standard vacation, *recle*. The constitutional bull called for a minimum attendance of eight months per year. If a prebend attended less, his seat could be declared vacant and he could be replaced.[25] Reflecting the changing attitude brought about by the Council of Trent, the *Statutes* of the cathedral, collected in 1585, declared that no prebend might be absent more than three months per year. Within that the statutes allowed each chapter member to take seventy days of vacation without fear of losing his seat on the chapter. Nevertheless, on certain days every priest had to serve his office, some forty-two in all, not counting all the days of Lent.[26] Beyond the vacation leave was the *patitur*. This was the sixteenth-century equivalent of sickleave. The bull that created the diocese did not make specific mention of leaves for illness, but the 1585 *Statutes* did. Perhaps in recognition of the era and its illnesses, the *Statutes* allowed unlimited absence for illness as required by the individual prebend. In all such cases he could collect his full salary. At the same time the regulations called for each prebend to examine his conscience to determine if he was truly ill, or merely attempting to avoid services. If the suffering priest should leave his home for some location other than the church, he would lose his leave.[27]

To keep track of this complex system of attendance, the chapter employed an attendance taker, *puntador,* to be in charge of the comings and goings of the chapter members. As noted, each prebend had to attend all of the divine offices each day. Nevertheless, certain guidelines were established in order to get the business of the church done, since celebration of these services could occupy the better part of the day. For the purpose of administration, the cathedral chapter was divided into two choirs. During the actual services each choir sat on a different side of the choir loft. The dean headed one choir, while the second highest chapter officer, the archdeacon, led the other. Each choir contained half of each rank of the chapter. In order to provide at least half the choir with some free time occasionally, it was resolved that matins and vespers be said on a rotational basis. One week one choir would say both, the next week the other choir would take over the responsibility, and so on.[28]

In addition to the divine offices, the chapter celebrated a corporate, capitular mass everyday, as mandated in the bull erecting the diocese. This mass occurred immediately after terce. Attendance at the mass automatically gave the prebend the right to collect terce and sext, even if he did not attend. Likewise, if a priest attended terce and the mass, he could then celebrate at another mass and still collect sext. Conversely, if a priest missed terce and the mass, he automatically lost sext, even if he attended it. Thus, certain daily offices were intimately linked to one another.[29]

As if this were not enough to worry about, each prebend could also be penalized a fraction of an hour. For minor infractions there was a series of penalties called *puntas*, or points. The largest penalty was four points, which implies that an hour was probably six or eight points. Examples of these infractions were: if a prebend did not follow the instructions of the precentor or subchanter while serving in the choir, he lost a point;[30] horseplay, joking, or games in the choir cost four points penalty.[31] It is possible that each point represented an hour. For example, if upon entering the choir area the priest stopped along the way to talk, not going directly to his seat, he would lose the whole hour. Likewise, if during the service he left his seat to chat he would lose only one point. Also, by saying the wrong prayer during the service he lost credit for the entire hour. In these examples, to maintain an equality of punishment for similar crimes, one can reasonably assume that a point equaled an hour. A remaining example of the accounting procedure does not clarify the matter any further. The end-of-the-year records contain integers representing days and fractions, expressed in sixths, which one assumes represented the six hours credited during the day.

To cite the example described earlier, of D. Sancho Sánchez de Muñón, the year 1576 might serve as a normal attendance pattern. Of the 366 days that year, a leap year, he attended 281, used 61 1/6 days of *recle* or vacation, 4/6 day of absence, 21 2/6 days of *patitur* or sick leave, and he lost 5/6 day in penalties.[32] Although not specifically explained, the penalties were probably subtracted from the days present rather than from the vacation days. In the career of Sánchez de Muñón, 1567 ranked as his best year for attendance, the eighth year after his appointment to the chapter. In that year he attended 332 5/6 days, took 26 days vacation, was absent 3 2/6 days, ill 2 1/6 days, and lost 1 3/6 days in penalties. As noted above, his attendance became more irregular in the late years of the century, primarily because of his other duties. Furthermore, since he enjoyed a 2,000-ducat pension from the crown, he clearly was not overly concerned about his cathedral salary.

A wide variation could develop between the salaries of various cathedral chapter members in any given year. In 1577 the chapter treasurer D. Esteban del Portillo was exiled from New Spain when the audiencia found him guilty of *lése majesté* for exercising his power as ecclesiastical judge in a case they ruled belonged in the royal courts. As a result of this action, Portillo was stripped of his cathedral seat and its revenues and exiled to Spain. The revenues of the dignity were divided among the other chapter members. As it turned out, the Council of the Indies in Spain exonerated Portillo of any wrongdoing and ordered his back pay returned. Some of the accounts of this process have survived.[33]

The variation among chapter members at the same level was quite wide (see Fig. 4). The table consists of the money to be returned to Portillo, for the period April 4–December 31, 1577. The dean and precentor were actually Inquisitors who also received cathedral salaries. According to various royal decrees, they were to receive their full salaries without regard to attendance, and so the figures for them should represent full attendance. The base rate for canons in this accounting must have been about fifty pesos, as demonstrated by the large number receiving about that much. To take the case of Sánchez de Muñón again, his low portion in this example doubtless resulted from his failure to attend services regularly. Lastly, the whole event demonstrates how the other members of the cathedral chapter could benefit from the absence of one individual since money lost by one was divided among the others.

Just as chapter members had to attend the daily observance of the divine offices, so did other personnel in the cathedral. The bull that created the diocese mandated that the curates of the cathedral and the chaplains also participate. In the case of these priests, however, a different allocation system determined their salary. As noted above, they received a simple salary ordered by the papal bull. This salary did not rise with time, nor was the division of the curates' fund converted to a proportional system, as the chapter had done for itself. Yet these priests were equally penalized for failing to attend services. The result of this practice dictated that the curates and chaplains often re-

Figure 4.
Division of Revenues
Cathedral Chapter of Mexico
1577 (partial)
(oro comun)

Tithe Distribution

Dean D. Alonso Hernandez de Bonilla	87.1
Arcediano D. Juan Zurnero	60.3.5
Chantre D. Alonso Avalos de Granero	87.1
Maestrescuela D. Sancho Sanchez de Muñon	13.1.5
Tesorero D. Pedro Garces	50.4.3
Can. Pedro de Nava	45.4.9
Can. Juan Cabello	50.3
Can. Gaspar de Mendiola	3.0.6
Can. Diego Lopez de Agurto	48.0.6
Can. Alonso Lopez de Cardenas	48
Can. Melchor de la Cadena	44.4.6
Can. Alonso de Ecija	38.4.5
Rac. Pedro de Peñas	22.4.7
Rac. Manuel de Nava	26.5
Rac. Rodrigo Muñoz	35.7.7
Rac. Juan de Aberruza	18.0.9
Rac. Antonio de Salazar	24.1.5
Rac. Claudio de la Cueva	27.4.3
Rac. Pedro Osorio	14.7.1
Rac. Juan Hernandez	2.3.6
Rac. Lorenzo de Sola	10.7.2
Rac. Servan Ribero	11.4.3

Source: Lilly Library, Latin American Manuscripts, Mexico II.

ceived annual salaries far below those actually outlined in the bull.

Again, a few examples remain to demonstrate the system. One is the case of Juan de Ortega, a chaplain in the cathedral who received his salary from the tithe. Pay records for him cover the period 1592–98. This includes ten biannual pay receipts. His official salary by this time had reached 80 *pesos de minas* a year, or 129 *pesos de oro común*.

Nevertheless, although his six months' pay should have been nearly 65 pesos, the amount he actually received ranged from a low of 18½ pesos for the first six months of 1595 to a high of 57¾ pesos for the first half of 1593, owing to deductions for absences.[34]

A similar situation occurred with Diego de Vivero, one of the curates of the metropolitan cathedral. Like the prebendaries of the cathedral chapter, he received his appointment from the king and essentially had the right to serve the benefice for life, unlike the chaplains who served at the pleasure of the chapter. He sued the cathedral for his back pay in 1591, alleging that he had not received all of his official salary. In the records of the suit several of his pay receipts appear. They show that the official salary served merely as a basis upon which further calculations were made. In December 1589 Vivero received his pay for the period August 1, 1588–November 3, 1589. His annual salary was sixty *pesos de minas*. Although he had served for sixteen months, according to the attendance record he was present only twenty-six days, which netted him slightly over eight pesos in pay. Furthermore, he had been penalized for failing to bless the congregation with holy water on those Sundays that fell to him as a cathedral curate. The fine amounted to thirty pesos. Thus, after serving for sixteen months, Diego de Vivero owed the cathedral twenty-one pesos, plus change.[35]

The question of sickleave and vacation time for the curates and chaplains was a common topic of discussion for the cathedral chapter. The chapter members often vacillated in their opinion on the matter. Ultimately the chapter granted the employees sick leave under several conditions. Basically, the illness had to be severe enough to prohibit the priest from serving his post and be known to others in the cathedral, and the employee had to send in a physician's certificate to verify the illness.[36]

Between 1577 and 1583 the question of the curates' fund,

the *superavit*, and the proportional salary system rose to the forefront. By this time, the tithe collections in the various Mexican dioceses had reached all-time highs. The cathedrals were relatively well provided for, and some concern could be shown toward various cathedral staff members and the parish clergy. The bishops began to suggest to the king that the *mesa capitular* was sufficient to pay the cathedral chapters, and that the *superavit* was no longer necessary to supplement their income. Thus, all of the curates' fund could be used for the cathedral staff in a proportional distribution. Likewise, perhaps some of the curates' fund could go on to support the parish clergy, thus relieving the royal treasury of some obligations.[37]

Needless to say, the cathedral chapter opposed these suggestions vehemently, showing how necessary the *superavit* was to augment their paltry incomes. Various suits had already been in the courts since 1566, and the decision had been to continue using the *superavit* for the cathedral chapter.[38]

After considering all of this, the Council of the Indies and the king issued a ruling in 1583. In a cédula addressed to all of the Mexican bishops, the king summarized the arguments, expressed a desire to see the constitutional bull enforced and the cathedral staff receive proportional salary allocations from the curates' fund, and then left the question up to the individual bishops, with the advise and consent of the viceroy.[39] Thus, the bishop of Michoacán interpreted the ruling to favor strict salaries over proportional distribution, while the bishop of Puebla-Tlaxcala came to the exact opposite decision. In 1585, when all of the bishops convened for the provincial council, they resolved that the issue be governed strictly by the constitutional bull, thus denying proportional distribution to the cathedral staff and continuing to authorize that the *superavit* augment the *mesa capitular*.[40]

Fabric Account

The other fund of the tithe distribution that paid salaries was the fabric account. As noted earlier, in the first decade or so of the cathedral, all of the cathedral staff's salaries came from the fabric account. By the 1540s, the fabric account supplied the salaries for only some of the staff, with the curates and chaplains enjoying the curates' fund. The fabric account ultimately became an important source for miscellaneous salaries within the cathedral yet also served the more immediate purpose of purchasing supplies and ornament for the cathedral. Detailed records of the income and expenses of this account exist thanks to a royal inquiry into the use of the royal ninth, which, along with the *excusado*, was added to the fabric account. The records of the account have been saved in Spain. The copy includes both income and outlay from the mid-1540s to 1575.[41]

By the mid-1560s several cathedral employees received their salaries from the fabric account. They include the *obrero mayor* (supervisor of works), the *maestro de capilla* (chapel master), the cantors, choirboys, and various musicians. The fund also provided money to purchase ornaments, vestments, wine, wax, and wafers. The important works of art added to the cathedral usually were purchased from this fund, along with organs, bells, and other costly items.

The musical staff was headed by the chapel master. In 1564 the *racionero* Lázaro del Alamo served as *maestro de capilla,* collecting a salary of 165 *pesos de minas*. His official salary was 150 *pesos de minas;* the additional 15 pesos came from enjoying certain *obvenciones* (perquisites), the right to receive fees for special services. In 1566, however, he collected slightly less than 130 *pesos de minas*. This implies that these employees also suffered salary reductions as a result of absences. While they were allowed sick leave, under the conditions described earlier, they were not given vacations. In general, the cathedral singers were all priests

Figure 5.
Salary Cuts
Musical Staff
Cathedral of Mexico
6 July 1582

	Salary		
	Old	Cut	New
Can. Alonso de Ecija	100 m	50 c	115.3.6 c
Rac. Fernando Franco	600 c	300 c	300 c
Rac. Juan Hernandez	300 c	100 c	200 c
Cura Alonso de Trujillo	200 c	50 c	150 c
Marcos Tello	200 c	50 c	150 c
Agustin Diaz	50 m		50 c
Bartolome Franco	300 c	50 c	250 c
P. Pedro Lopez	100 c	30 c	70 c
Luis de Toro	50 m		50 c
Pedro Martin	50 m		50 c
Antonio Ortiz	100 c	20 c	80 c
Ministriles			200 c

Source: ACTAS, 6 July 1582.

or had at least entered holy orders. In 1564 there were ten singers. They collected from 15 to 100 *pesos de minas*. The odd amounts paid to several of the singers probably indicates that they had been penalized for absences. The lowest members of this particular hierarchy were the choirboys. The minutes of the cathedral chapter indicate that there was a relatively fast turnover in choirboys.[42] In addition to their stipends, the boys received a cassock and elementary education. The stipend ranged from 8 to 16 *pesos de minas* a year. They actually collected from 3½ to 17 pesos, again suffering absences and enjoying perquisites.

By 1582 the salaries of most cathedral employees had increased somewhat[43] (see Fig. 5). Nevertheless, in that year the chapter embarked on a cost-cutting program aimed primarily at the musical staff paid from the fabric account. By this time the cathedral began to feel the economic impact of the 1576 epidemic, combined with the fact that the king had not donated the royal ninth to the fabric since 1578. Before the measures were enacted, the highest-paid musician was the *maestro de capilla*, *racionero* Fernando Franco, who received 600 pesos per year. The chapter slashed his pay in half. One of the singers, the *racionero* Juan Fernández had received 300 pesos per year but saw his income plummet to 200 pesos. Some of the changes were so minor as to be almost cosmetic; Agustín Díaz suffered a pay cut from 50 *pesos de minas* to 50 *pesos de oro común*. The pay cuts were short-lived, however. By February of the next year, the *maestro de capilla* received 400 pesos annual salary. This was later raised to 450 in 1584.[44] Thus, although some of the loss was recouped, the old level of 600 pesos was not reached again in the sixteenth century. The other musical employees of the cathedral also saw their salaries fluctuate in much the same manner as did the *maestro de capilla*.

The miscellaneous employees paid from the fabric account included a laundrywoman, an organist, and a teacher for the choirboys. The laundrywoman, Mari Jiménez, received 60 *pesos de minas* for her work. The teacher for the choirboys earned 20 *pesos de minas* for teaching them to read and write. The system of primary education given to the choirboys must have been a good one, since several chapter members began their careers as choirboys. The organist enjoyed a salary of 39 *pesos de minas* in 1564. It is difficult to determine the fixed salary for the position. Each organist seemed to have received a different sum. The organist who took over in 1566 was authorized a 200–peso stipend. In addition to the official organist, each year outside organists were hired either to augment the staff or to inspect the functioning of the organ. Other individuals employed by the cathedral and paid from the fabric account included Indian musicians, *indios chirimias*, who served the cathedral for 120 pesos per year. The mayordomo himself was paid from the fabric account for his work on the fabric. He received 90 pesos from the fabric and 160 directly from the tithe.

The fabric account is perhaps best known because of the works of art and other capital purchases made from it. The year 1564 is a particularly good one to use as an example. The expenditures that year were somewhat higher than others because preparations were being made for the Second Provincial Council to be held in the fall of 1565. Some of the expensive items purchased that year included new seats for the choir, where the cathedral chapter sat, and for the archiepiscopal throne or *cathedra*. The construction of these items took longer than just the calendar year 1564. During that year, however, 250 pesos were spent on the archiepiscopal throne and 536 on the choir stalls. The chapter also ordered a new organ made for the church. In this year, a total of 600 pesos was given to Agustín de Sotomayor and Gerónimo Hernández for work on the organ. The cathedral was also being refurbished in 1564. The *obrero mayor,* Canon Pedro de Nava, and the treasurer D. Francisco Rodríguez Santos, presented a bill for 1,176 pesos spent on that project. Specific items purchased also included a gilded chalice for 534 pesos, 432 for brocaded vestments, 78 for thirteen breviaries, 130 for more vestments, and 27 pesos for binding several other books. Thus the fabric account disbursed money for salaries, capital improvements, equipment, and ornaments.

The ornaments and implements of the cathedral carried the generic name of the "treasure." While many of these items were purchased with tithe money, donations constituted a major source of both money and articles. Four inventories of the fabric and the sacristy date from the sixteenth century.[45] Using these one can reconstruct the growth and change of the physical holdings of the cathedral. The earliest of the inventories dates from 1541. Although many items were included, the descriptions were brief. Only one item still in existence can be identified from this list, a *gremial* owned by the first bishop, Fr. Juan de Zumárraga.[46] Even in the early years the cathedral had much decoration. Included in the inventory were eight tapestries which adorned the walls, plus another thirty-five in storage, all purchased from Garrido, a merchant. These plus scores of chasubles, and other vestments, chalices, platens, lamps, candelabra, reliquaries, and crosses all reached the cathedral through purchase with tithe revenues.

The existence of these inventories resulted from the custom of checking the possessions of the cathedral whenever a new sacristan took office. As the mayordomo was responsible for the monetary wealth of the cathedral, the sacristan guarded its moveable property.

By 1588 the inventory of the treasures of the cathedral had expanded greatly. One of the most impressive pieces by that time was a silver monstrance weighing 500 marks. It was square at the base and in two tiers. The first tier rested on eight nude figures holding pyramids. Within was a figurine of St. Michael vanquishing a demon. The second tier rose above twelve columns grouped in threes, supporting angels carrying the symbols of the passion. Within this grouping was the gold frame that held the consecrated host, topped by a miniature bell tower. Further ornamentation surrounded the main base upon which all the others stood. This base included the papal insignia, the crest of Archbishop Pedro Moya de Contreras, and a figure of the virgin. This piece was made by order of Moya de Contreras for the cathedral. It was paid for either out of his fourth of the tithe or from the fabric account, since Moya had almost no wealth other than his episcopal income. Again, from this inventory only a very few items have survived to the present, including another *gremial*.[47]

There were great changes in the fabric account from year to year, depending on specific purchases and other expenses. In 1561 a total of 23,575 *pesos de minas* was in the account.[48] Much of that, 18,934, had been carried over from the previous year. In turn, 18,260 remained in the account after expenses, to be applied to the next year. The days of tremendous reserves did not last forever, however. Between 1569 and 1571 the surplus dropped from 24,793 to 14,013. Then in 1572 only 6,499 remained to carry over. After that, at least until 1576, nothing remained at the end of the year, even though this was a period of increasing tithe income.

It just so happened that during this period no fine works of art were purchased, but rather the cathedral began to feel the pinch of pressures beyond its control. Several contracts for tithe collection had gone into arrears, and the difference was drawn from the fabric account, for repayment later. Furthermore, if the tithe renters did not have the cash necessary to put up the king's ninth for the royal treasury, rather than find a new renter, the cathedral loaned them money for that purpose. Because the fabric tended to accumulate surplus cash in times when no major purchases came along, it served as a slush fund to balance the other accounts. For instance, between 1567 and 1574 the *maestrescuela* Dr. D. Sancho Sánchez de Muñón was in Spain as an agent at court for the cathedrals of New Spain. Part of his pay was regularly advanced out of the fabric account until the Mexican cathedral could collect the shares coming from the other cathedral chapters.

Pressures on Tithe Division

Although used for different purposes, all of the tithe receiving funds faced similar problems. Major among these was reconciling the need for cash with a desire to capitalize on the large quantity of grain and other goods received in kind, with which they could speculate. The church did store and speculate with these goods, as seen in the chapter on tithe collection. When the time came for the distribution among the various funds, however, actual goods posed a problem. Guarantees had to be made to ensure that each fund received its fair share of the goods. This meant that not only the quantity but the quality of the goods distributed had to be taken into account. Grains were separated—the good from the spoiled, frozen, soaked, or infested—for distribution and to prevent further deterioration. To ensure the equitable distribution of the goods, each of the funds had a representative present at the allocation.

Once the major division had been made into funds, the chapter's fund was further subdivided for each chapter member. For all of the other accounts, the portion could then be sold, used, or further divided. In the case of the fabric account, the wheat received from the tithe was often milled and used by the church for the hosts in the mass. After the goods had been distributed, the tithe administrators no longer had the responsibility of storing the grain. Each of the accounts had to remove its portion from storage to dispose of it as it pleased. Often tithe officials became upset with the tardy collection of the distributed goods. In 1590, for example, the chapter ordered all interested parties to collect their grain immediately or pay storage costs.[49]

The sale of tithe grains was an important feature of the entire system. Individuals often chose to sell their portion of grains collected from the tithe. In 1583 both the archbishop and the archdeacon sold at least part of their grain. The archbishop sold thirty bushels of wheat to Bartolomé García, a farmer from Tepotzotlán. The same day the archdeacon, Dr. D. Juan de Zurnero, sold eighteen bushels to Pedro Ramírez Becerra, a farmer from Tacuba.[50] In both instances the price was $2^{1}/_{2}$ pesos per bushel, considerably above the going rate of $1^{1}/_{2}$ pesos. These sales probably provided the farmers with seed grain.

This practice became so successful that by the early years of the seventeenth century, Canon Antonio de Salazar traveled from one farming community to another selling the tithe grain for seed grain. In 1602 Salazar signed sixteen contracts in the region from Texcoco to Tlalmanalco selling tithe grain to farmers. The largest of these was for 500 bushels of wheat at 1³/₄ pesos a bushel, an 875-peso contract, while the smallest was for 36³/₄ pesos for 6 bushels of wheat at 2 pesos a bushel and 18 bushels of corn at 1³/₄ pesos. Similarly in 1602 the archbishop sold part of his tithe income to Gerónimo de Lamarilla, 250 bushels of wheat. The dean of the chapter even gave a blanket power of attorney to Salazar to dispose of his share in the best manner possible.[51]

As seen, by the end of the century, part of the tithe was distributed in kind. This had a threefold purpose. These goods provided each recipient with food and daily necessities. Secondly, they could also speculate with the goods they did not use, waiting until the market had peaked before selling. Lastly, the cathedral chapter could defraud the royal treasury better. If the tithe had been distributed in money alone, ascertaining the king's portion would be simple. But when it was distributed in money and five or six commodities, it was difficult to guarantee the equitability of the portions. This would be far more true in the suffragan dioceses than in Mexico and Guadalajara, since in these capitals a royal treasury official could attend every distribution, of which there were several each year. But in the other dioceses, except for the local royal magistrate, there was no treasury officer competent to oversee the division. As the bishop of Puebla-Tlaxcala explained in a 1597 letter, "Wheat, wool, corn, sugar, and other trifles [*menudencias*] are given to each one of the interested parties in kind, so that they can sell or speculate with them as best they can, and thus one cannot know how much it all was worth. . . ."[52]

Just as the tithe collection had a great impact on the economy of the colony, so did the distribution. Because the church acted as a speculator in grains and other goods, its activity directly affected the general price in the market. Probably after the crown it was the largest grain seller, and in terms of wheat and secondary grains other than corn, it was the leader. Furthermore, the practice of selling the tithe grain for seed grain was very important, especially in specific rural areas. For the church it allowed an almost immediate benefit, selling the highest quality grain at a considerable premium over the market. For the buyers, it further strengthened their dependence on the church, or at least tightened the relationship. Not only was 10 percent of the crop handed over to the church, but then the seed grain was purchased back.

As will be seen in the last chapter, fluctuations in the general economy had an eventual effect on the tithe income. As noted earlier, the epidemic of 1576 was felt by the 1580s, and in response to that, the church had to make certain decisions concerning not only the collection of the tithe, but its distribution as well. The cuts to the musicians' salaries, the denial of proportional distribution to the cathedral staff, and application of the *superavit* to the chapter's fund were all measures taken in the realm of distribution to respond to the general economic conditions.

Considering tithe revenues from collection through distribution, the process occupied an enormous amount of time for church officials. Yet the tithe clearly ranked as the single most important source of church revenue, and in spite of annual fluctuations, its most constant. Consequently the energies expended on the tithe were in direct proportion to the profit received. Beginning from exceedingly small returns in 1523, the tithe grew to mammoth dimensions by century's end.

Since the tithe financed the ongoing work of the church, especially within the cathedral and the prelate's office, the prompt collection and distribution of it were imperative. But as seen, the process was fraught with delay and complications. The unwieldy nature of the tithe dictated that more flexible sources of revenues be found for the administration of the church. As will be seen in later chapters, this change ultimately came after a major crisis of revenues and the development of a new popular piety willing to support the efforts of the church.

3. Parish Revenues

In early colonial Mexico, the regular orders held primacy over the secular clergy. The first organized groups of missionaries sent out after the conquest were made up of regulars: first twelve Franciscans, then Dominicans, and finally Agustinians. Because of this organizational primacy, the regular orders were able to consolidate these early missionary efforts, and by the middle of the sixteenth century controlled most rural Indian parishes.

The secular clergy lack this organizational advantage, and although some of the first priests in Mexico were seculars, they operated as independent agents in the immediate post-conquest society. Not until the first dioceses were founded was there any institutional supervision of their activities. The seculars tended to acquire urban parishes serving the Spanish population, along with some rural parishes and parishes in mining districts. The slow growth of the secular clergy in the second half of the sixteenth century ultimately set the stage for conflict between the seculars and regulars over the control of the parishes.

Canon law recognized the secular clergy as the proper parochial clergy. The orders were, in general, to remain cloistered and practice other vocations. Nevertheless, the regular orders received special papal concessions, which allowed them to develop and maintain parishes. Under the *Patronato Real*, however, the monarch was also granted papal concessions giving him authority over the parish clergy. The king, desirous to increase and maintain his power, saw the regular clergy as a threat, since it did not fall under the normal ecclesiastical hierarchy of bishops and archbishops, having instead an internal order ultimately headed by the pope. Thus, as the secular clergy grew and sought greater control over the parishes, the king sought to diminish the regulars' control and allow the seculars to take over. By the 1570s the regulars had lost some of their early missionary zeal and thus found themselves coming into conflict with the king. This conflict ultimately signaled the end of regular dominance in the parishes, although centuries would pass before they were finally removed. Control over the parishes in many ways was an economic conflict, since each parish represented both a minimum annual stipend and the potential for gifts and alms. Thus, parochial duties and parochial revenues were intimately linked.

Within the ecclesiastical hierarchy, the local parish priests had the most frequent contact with the laity. As noted, the regular orders administered many parishes. Even in the absence of specific parochial obligations, many monasteries served as de facto parish centers because of popular support, as was the case of San Francisco in Mexico City. This arrangement caused constant friction between the regular and secular clergy because of the limited sources of parochial income. While there were great differences between individual parishes, in general, all were poor. The question of how best to support the parish clergy occupied both royal and ecclesiastical officials. The following description will trace those decisions. While the tithe financed the upper clergy and episcopal hierarchy, other sources of revenue had to be found for the parish curates. The experience of the sixteenth century set the trend for the rest of the colonial period, and many aspects reflected at that time continued on into the modern era.

Within the framework of the secular clergy, one could find three basic types of parishes. The richest and most prestigious were the urban parishes of major cities, and parishes of Spaniards in general. Examples of these are the cathedral parishes of each diocese, the other parishes of cities like Mexico, and the parishes of Spanish towns like Toluca, Colima, or San Ildefonso de los Zapotecas.

The next type of parish was the mining district. In these areas the actual parochial structure was often quite complex, since Spaniards, Indians, slaves, and mixed groups all concentrated near the mines. These parishes required several priests, each with specific obligations. One could serve the Spanish community, another the laborers, and a third could minister to the surrounding Indian villages.

The last category of parish was the common *partido de indios*, or Indian parish. Although the most numerous, they varied greatly in wealth and size. Priests serving these parishes usually had to command at least one Indian language and had to be prepared to ride circuit among the suffragan villages.

These three categories also reflect the financial differences between parishes. In general, priests serving the first two, Spanish towns and mines, received their pay from their parishioners, directly through ecclesiastical fees and levies or through the tithe. On the other hand, priests serving Indian parishes collected their salary from the local encomendero or the royal crown. On the one hand, priests ministering to Spaniards could, and did, collect fees from their parishioners, while on the other, clerics in the Indian parishes were forbidden from collecting any fees.

Spanish Parishes

The cathedral parishes of each diocese stood as the most wealthy and prestigious within New Spain. In keeping with this, the cathedral parish of Mexico City clearly ranked as the most important of all. Nevertheless, this power and seeming wealth did not exempt the curates there from seeking to increase their income. As seen in the chapter on tithes, the cathedral curates enjoyed the four-ninths allocated to parish priests, either wholly or in part. They also collected common fees for the performance of ecclesiastical duties, baptisms, marriages, and burials. One remarkable fact of this period is that there are no surviving *aranceles*, printed fee schedules, outlining the proper emoluments for various services. What information on fees has reached us comes by way of various lawsuits and other court documents.

From the provincial towns and mining districts, the metropolitan cathedral loomed like a beacon to the parish clergy. Lamentably we do not have the account books for the cathedral parish, nor any other clear indication of the exact fees they charged for the administration of the sacraments until the seventeenth century. However, some evidence indicates the general level of income which these provided. In 1570 when a general investigation of the clerical establishment was under way, the cathedral curates indicated that in addition to the salary mandated by the bull of erection, each curate received about 20 *pesos de tipuzque* each month from burials, baptisms, weddings, and other remunerative activities. Over a year this could reach 240 pesos, over and above their 112-peso base salary.[1]

The cathedral curates guarded this source of income jealously. Because of the large number of religious establishments in downtown Mexico City, the potential for conflict was omnipresent. The greatest threat came from the religious orders and the various chaplains in the city. As early as 1564 the cathedral *curas* won an injunction against the cathedral chapter, which prohibited chapter members from exercising the duties of curate in burials. This prohibition had had the effect of denying the curates the revenue.[2]

Over the course of the rest of the century the curates maintained their vigil over the ecclesiastical community in Mexico, guarding their rights to certain revenues. In 1583 they filed suit against Bachiller Blas de Bustamante, the chaplain of the Hospital of Nuestra Señora de la Purísima Concepción. The final injunction prohibited him, and any other chaplain or priest, from usurping the duties of parish priest. The court order defined these as the normal parochial duties of baptisms and weddings, plus sung requiem or burial masses. Since part of Bustamante's canonical duties included singing requiem masses for the indigents who died in the hospital, he was allowed to conduct those, but only those, and no others.[3]

In the wake of the successful litigation against Bustamante, the cathedral *curas* pressed their suit against all chaplains and priests in the city, prohibiting others from usurping parochial duties, and, consequently, parochial revenues. This suit too proved successful, and in 1589 they won a total injunction on the practice. There is no indication in the papers of the suit if the injunction was ever lifted.[4]

Meanwhile, the cathedral chapter, chafing against the rising power of the curates, decided to reassert its traditional supervision of the administration of the sacraments in the cathedral. In 1585 the chapter ruled that the curates had exceeded their power by performing funerals and requiem honors in the cathedral. While this was within their right and duty, the curates had been and were limited to the exercise of their functions in the Chapel of the Santíssimo Sacramento and not at the main altar of the cathedral itself.[5] The curates immediately protested and appealed the ruling. Although a judge was appointed to hear the case, no final ruling appeared.[6]

Suits between the cathedral chapter and the cathedral curates dragged on for the rest of the century. They are a clear indication of the extreme tension created when two essentially different groups shared the same physical structure. Moreover, the tension between the chapter and curates inevitably reached such a high level of acrimony because they competed for the same sources of revenue. As late as the 1590s the cathedral curates still protested the chapter's allocation of the four-ninths or curates' fund of the tithe. The curates argued that rather than be paid strict salaries, based on attendance at the canonical hours, they should divide the fund equally among themselves. Furthermore, they complained that their primary duty, as curates in the cathedral parish, was to minister to the parishioners residing there, and not to be members of the choir. Thus they argued that attendance at the canonical hours should not have been mandatory.[7]

By the early seventeenth century printed fee schedules (*aranceles*) appeared in Mexico. The cathedral chapter of Mexico drew one up in 1638.[8] The fees were assessed by caste and by type of service. The schedule recognized four castes: Spaniards; blacks, mestizos, and mulattoes; Indian laborers; and village Indians. The *arancel* covered the following services: burials, requiems, and related ceremonies; marriages, including vigils; and baptisms. The bulk of the revenues generated by these services came from the Spaniards. The schedule noted that the fees listed were above and beyond "those contracts made with Spaniards for the administration of the other sacraments." The most expensive services were a memorial mass, including vigil, vespers, and offering, for twenty pesos; and a novena of sung masses, which cost six pesos each mass, plus one peso per mass to the Indian singers, making a total of sixty-three pesos.

The parish of the cathedral was by no means the only parish in Mexico City. Even smaller diocesan seats, such as Puebla, had a large enough population by the end of the century to support other parishes in the capital. In the late 1560s and 1570s Mexico City had three parishes served by the secular clergy. As a result of a territorial dispute with the regulars, one of these, San Pablo, was subsequently lost to the Agustinians.[9] The two parishes that remained under the control of the seculars were Santa Catalina and Santa Vera Cruz. After the cathedral parish, these two were the most highly prized in the archdiocese, although the parishes of Iztapalapa and Huitzilopochco (modern Churubusco), because of their proximity to the capital, were also eagerly sought after by priests wishing jobs near the center of power.

Endless conflicts broke out between the regulars and the

seculars over the administration of these urban parishes, like the parish of San Pablo, which began under the seculars and was successfully won by the Agustinians, and the parish of Santa Vera Cruz, which fell within the territory of the major Franciscan house. Many residents preferred to go to San Francisco for everyday religious services. The archdiocesan hierarchy saw this as a direct violation of their parochial authority. Needless to say, a major concern of the secular clergy was the loss of vital revenue to the religious orders. If the seculars could not enjoy a monopoly over the rural Indian parishes, they at least expected to control the largely Spanish urban parishes without contest.

A long petition to the crown from the Congregación de San Pedro, a cofradía made up largely of secular priests, summed up these notions. The first item on their list complained that in the archdiocese alone there were 200 secular priests without occupation.[10] The petition pointed out that members of the religious orders had no incentive to do well in parochial administration, since their livelihood was guaranteed by the order. Many of the cofradia's other arguments cited excesses of the regulars in rural Indian parishes. In short, the Congregación de San Pedro feared loss of position and revenue for its members as a result of the power of the orders.

Although parishes in Spanish towns were generally seen as being superior to Indian villages, in fact the salary and emoluments hardly constituted a living wage by sixteenth-century standards. The 250 to 300 *peso de oro común* range acknowledged as a minimum wage was barely exceeded by the cathedral curates in 1569. The availability of chantries in the cities, as opposed to the provinces, greatly improved clerical incomes.[11] Likewise some curates of the cathedral augmented their parochial wages by serving on the general staff of the cathedral as singers or musicians. In a similar fashion, while parish priests in the mining districts seem to have enjoyed relatively low wages, the wealth of the area provided them with ample opportunity to augment their incomes from outside sources. As long as their extraclerical activities remained discreet and did not intrude on the exercise of their ecclesiastical functions, there were few official restrictions on priests.

Two examples deal specifically with the question of clerical fees in other Spanish regions. The first comes from the resolution of the will and estate of the *beneficiado* of the town of Colima. In 1581, two years before his death Rodrigo de Vargas began to keep an account book of the income and expense of his ministry. Upon his death this book formed part of the papers of his estate and aided his executor in fulfilling the will. Among his various sources of income the most important was the fees collected for burials. In the period covered by the book, Vargas received thirty-two pesos for burials; the fee varied from one-half peso to five pesos. In fact, according to the record, he collected no other ecclesiastical fees. His other sources of income came from the revenues of several chantries which he served, and they were worth more than the burial fees.[12]

A similar case comes from the mining area of Zaqualpa. In 1600 the *beneficiado*, Alonso Martínez de Zayas, had to go to Mexico City for medical reasons. He left a substitute in his place, Br. Gerónimo Rodríguez de Paz. As part of their agreement, Rodríguez de Paz would share whatever fees and emoluments he collected with the *beneficiado*, to whom they legally belonged. When Martínez de Zayas returned, Rodríguez was loath to live up to his part of the deal, and a lawsuit ensued in which Martínez sought the fees collected in his absence.[13]

As opposed to the Colima example, in Zaqualpa the parish priest received gifts and fees for at least three different activities. On one occasion he collected three *reales* for a baptism. He said several memorial masses with the average fee being two pesos. He also performed several burials ranging in cost from one and one-half pesos to three pesos each. While the total revenue from these sources was very small, they provided some important additional income.

Yet these fees often had to provide the priest with a minimum income, while in most rural areas the Spanish population was insufficient to support a priest. Thus, alternate sources of income were important.

The degree to which a *beneficiado* possessed his parish cannot be overstated. In the case of an absence of whatever type, the *beneficiado* had the primary responsibility to find a substitute. Legally the *beneficiado* continued to collect his pay, even while absent, and paid the substitute out of his own pocket. Thus the ecclesiastical courts acted only as arbitrators in the suit between Rodríguez de Paz and Martínez de Zayas. Another example can be seen in the testament of Bartolomé Becerra, the *beneficiado* of Tempoal. Becerra, the son of Bernal Díaz del Castillo, became ill the last part of his life and went to Mexico City for care. During his absence from the parish, Diego de Ribas served as a substitute with the title *vicario*. In his will Becerra ordered that his salary be collected from Ribas, who had collected it from the royal treasury. Ribas would then receive his pay from the estate of Becerra.[14]

Mixed Populations

Very few towns in colonial Mexico qualified as purely Spanish, especially in the outlying provinces. The mining districts, towns with large Spanish populations contained or coexisted with large Indian and black populations. This constituted a major problem in providing a living income for parish priests. As will be seen in greater depth later, Indians were relieved of having to pay for the administration of the sacraments. Nevertheless, Spaniards had an obligation to pay. Thus, in areas with a mixed population different systems evolved to provide for the parish priests. These systems fall under two categories: royally mandated, and ad hoc or extraordinary. In several regions local curates enjoyed some of the local tithe revenues. In the diocese of Oaxaca, the province of Coatzacoalcos eventually supported four *beneficiados*. These priests received their pay from a combination of the local tithe and the royal treasury. According to the formula the four-ninths of the provincial tithe was divided equally among the *beneficiados*, initially two, later growing to four. Royal tribute supplemented that income until each cleric had a minimum salary of 300 *pesos de oro común*.[15]

A similar arrangement continued in the northern reaches of the archbishopric of Mexico. The *beneficiados* of Pánuco and Tampico both received their pay from the local tithe, via the royal treasury. In this case the curate's salary was guaranteed by the crown. When the tithe revenues for the district did not reach the level necessary for the parochial salaries, the royal treasury made up the difference.[16] The four curates in the diocese of Guadalajara who received their salaries from the tithe did not collect any other salary, and if the tithe proved insufficient, they went without their full pay.[17]

The mining districts presented a very complex system of remuneration for the parochial clergy. As noted, often the various priests were charged with ministering to different ethnic groups in the district. In the case of Taxco, the salaries came from three sources. One priest received his pay from a levy placed on all Spanish mine owners. Another priest collected 150 *pesos de minas* from the royal treasury for ministering to the Indians working in the mines. A third priest collected his salary partially from the royal treasury and partially from the local encomendero for serving the Indian communities surrounding Taxco. Nevertheless, four priests were assigned to serve the parish. In this case, all the money from all sources was combined and equally distributed among the four.[18]

A somewhat different system controlled the salaries in the Pachuca mining district. Here the three curates had distinct territorial obligations. One served the Indian villages and the mines of Pachuca, assisting the other *cura*, who served the Real del Monte and Tlilquauhtla. The third ministered to the Real de Arriba and the Real de Atotonilco. The three received pay from different sources. Local encomenderos paid the first priest for ministering to the Indians, and the miners paid him a bit more for the church services. The other two priests were paid totally out of levies imposed on the miners. Unlike Taxco, not all of this money was shared. Only the first two priests shared their income. The third enjoyed his alone.[19]

In the Zaqualpa mines, where Alonso Martínez de Zayas served as one of the two *beneficiados*, a similar system of shared income was the rule. Nevertheless, in 1600, Martínez suggested to his colleague and to the archiepiscopal administration, that they change the manner in which they divided the income. Rather than both priests serve fulltime, pool their income, and then divide it equally, they should alternate from week to week. One week one *beneficiado* would be responsible for the services that incurred fees and dues, while the other would conduct routine services. Then the following week they would alternate. They could plan ahead for major seasons such as Easter and Holy Week so that they could alternate from year to year to guarantee equitable distribution of the income. It also meant that rather than have two men working all the time, one could pick up any slack and redouble his efforts, while the other had a somewhat easier load, every other week. Neither his partner nor the archiepiscopal authorities greeted the plan with approval. For the latter, the idea of one priest taking it relatively easy probably conjured up fears of reproach from the regular clergy and royal officials.[20]

Indian Villages

The ecclesiastical hierarchy and the royal government in general rejected the notion of Indians paying for the sacraments on the same grounds that they opposed the Indian tithe. Since the natives already had to pay tribute, other taxes and levies would be both redundant and oppressive.[21]

Rather than subject the Indians to many different forms of taxation, the government preferred collecting one large payment in the form of tribute. Likewise, the encomienda had originally served as a means of providing the Indians with spiritual training without direct cost to the crown. It was the obligation of the encomendero to pay the local priest.[22] Of course, the crown, as encomendero, found itself in the position of having to pay many of the local parish priests.

In terms of salary, then, Indian parishes can be divided into three types: those in encomienda, those under the crown, and mixed crown and encomienda. Following the implementation of the Ordenanza del Patronazgo in 1574, each appointment to a parish clearly stipulated the salary to be paid to the parish priest.[23] In the mixed parishes the amount falling to each party was outlined. An example of this from the 1580s is the parish of Tlacozautitlán, in the diocese of Puebla, in which the *beneficiado* received 100 *pesos de oro común* each, from the royal treasury and the encomendero Lorenzo Porcallo.[24] Apportionments could become quite complex. In the case of Mizquiahuala, in the archdiocese, the *beneficiado* received 50 *pesos de oro de minas* from the royal treasury, 35 from the encomendero of Mizquiahuala, 40 from the encomendero of Tecpatepec, and 25 from the encomendero of Tezontepec.[25]

Priests serving in parishes partially or fully under the crown collected that part of the salary from the royal treasury in Mexico.[26] These salaries were paid every four months if the priest so desired. He needed certification from his ecclesiastical superiors that he had in fact fulfilled his obligations. When duly certified, the viceroy, as vice-patron, would draw up a *libramiento*, ordering the treasury officials to pay the cleric the stipulated monies. The treasury office would then issue a *libranza* good for the amount of salary. Clearly not every priest traveled to Mexico City three times annually to collect the pay. Many never appeared in person. The most common procedure was for an *apoderado* to collect the salary for the priest. The recipient, be he priest or *apoderado*, then signed a *carta de pago* signifying receipt. The *libranza* was in fact a pay order, which was presented to the treasurer, or an assistant, for cash. These *libranzas* drawn on the royal treasury often circulated in the economy like money, subject to discounting. In short, the procedure was complex, but the priest was relatively sure of ultimately receiving his stipulated salary.[27]

Priests serving villages in encomienda, however, did not face such an easy task in receiving their pay. If the amount of legislation is any indication, many priests were hard pressed to collect their pay. As the sixteenth century progressed, the value of many encomiendas declined. In some instances encomenderos were caught in the middle between fixed costs and declining revenues. Logistically it made sense for the local curate simply to take his salary out of the tribute before it was sent on to the encomendero. This, however, gave the priest too much local coercive power and opened the door for abuses.[28] Thus the crown preferred to have the encomenderos actually pay the priests. Sometimes, it was impossible for the priest to collect his pay from the encomendero, and so exceptions could be and were made.[29] Ultimately the exceptions became the rule. In recognition of this, in 1594 the crown allowed the curates to collect their salaries directly out of the tribute in the town they served without having to go to the encomendero.[30] This rule, although applied to the royal treasury too, did not seem to affect that office.

While the base salary for the majority of *partidos* in the sixteenth century was 150 *pesos de minas* per year, several *partidos* carried only 100 pesos, while several others had 200. Usually the salary accurately reflected the actual labor involved in the administration of the parish.[31] While no records indicate that the salary of any parish ever decreased, several increased.

Juan de Mesa, one of the few candidates for sainthood among the early seculars, worked in the province of Pánuco for years. Born sometime around 1530, Mesa came to Mexico with his parents as a child. He supposedly inherited a small fortune from his uncle, an encomendero and hacendado of Tempoal. While accepting the legacy, Mesa gave most of it to the Indians of the Pánuco area, keeping only enough to support himself. From the middle 1550s he began administering the sacraments in the province. Royal treasury records indicate that he began collecting a salary in 1558, having begun work in October 1557. He rode circuit in the Huasteca and Pánuco, with an annual salary of 200 *pesos de oro común,* although most other priests were paid in *oro de minas.* The treasury accounts noted that the stipend was a special grant from the viceroy in recognition of Mesa's missionary efforts.[32] In 1576, Juan settled down a little, becoming the *cura vicario* of Tempoal, in the center of the district. When the *partido* became a *beneficio,* he applied for the position, entered the *oposición* and won.[33] The newly created *beneficio* carried a salary of 150 *pesos de minas,* so Juan enjoyed an increase in pay upon taking the post.[34]

Upon becoming the *beneficiado,* Mesa redoubled his missionary efforts. His labor did not go unnoticed. During a *visita* conducted in the province by Archbishop Moya de Contreras, the prelate decided that Mesa deserved a much higher salary than he received. Accordingly, as of March 9, 1585, Mesa began collecting 200 *pesos de minas* for his *beneficio.* The official grant explained the increase by saying that it reflected the tremendous work required and the roughness of the territory.[35] Mesa's hagiographer, Fr. Gerónimo de Mendieta, O.F.M., maintained that Mesa actually gave most of his pay to the Indians, just as he had given most of his uncle's legacy to them. Furthermore, Mendieta asserted that Mesa never accepted anything from the Indians without paying for it first. The Franciscan wrote that Mesa retired to a little house in nearby Tampico shortly before his death. Nevertheless, he drew up his last will and testament before a Mexico City notary and died in Mexico.[36]

While most clerical salaries did not increase with time or length of service, in several instances they did rise, generally reflecting the difficulty of administering a given *partido*. The pay increases also occasionally resulted from administrative reorganization of the *partidos*. Any increases in pay probably cannot be ascribed to inflation, since so few salaries did change.

Both the First and Third Provincial Councils strictly prohibited curates of Indian parishes from collecting fees for their services.[37] Royal decrees to the same end further bolstered this prohibition.[38] Nevertheless, the Third Council did mandate the creation of *aranceles*, fee schedules, for parochial use, but undoubtedly these were for use in Spanish parishes.[39] The *arancel* written in 1638 carried the notation that it was written in accord with the council. Thus the curate in Indian towns was legally limited to collect his salary and nothing more.

A great deal of confusion centered on whether or not the Indians were obligated to give their priests food. In the middle decades of the sixteenth century there seems to have been no hard and fast rule. The First Council merely prohibited curates from receiving more food than allowed.[40] Several of the tribute levies seem to include a provision for food. In Tempoal in 1564 the *tasación* ordered that 100 *fanegas* of corn be kept in the village for the sustenance of the curate. But in 1567 the *tasación* for Tlatlauquitepec ordered that everything having to do with the support of the clergy be paid from the royal treasury. In one village there was a shift in this period. In 1560 the village of Tepeucila was ordered to hold back the 100 *fanegas* of corn, as in Tempoal, but two years later the *tasación* was changed to place everything in the hands of the treasury officials.[41]

Even within the secular and ecclesiastical hierarchies there was disagreement over whether or not the Indians had to provide curates with food. Writing in 1575 and complaining of the poverty of rural Indian parishes, Archbishop Moya de Contreras declared that few priests desired to serve the rural area, since they had to depend on the Indians for food over and above their paltry 150 *pesos de oro de minas* wages.[42] Yet one year earlier the *oidor* Dr. Arteaga de Mendiola, wrote that unlike the system in Guatemala, in the archbishopric of Mexico the Indians did not provide the local curates with food.[43] Slightly later, the bishop of Puebla-Tlaxcala, writing to the king, indicated that there had been a change in policy: "Formerly they [parish priests] were paid 200 *pesos de minas* and the Indians gave them food; later it was reduced to 150 pesos, also *de minas*, and they ordered that the Indians not give food."[44]

In actual practice, before the 1560s Indians commonly provided food for the local priest. In the famous Codex Sierra, drawn as an account of income and expense in the Oaxaca village of Texupa, yearly entries describe the food given to the parish priest. These ranged in value from 206 pesos for 1559 to about 40 in 1562 and 1563.[45] The practice seems to have been perfectly legitimate at the time. No complaint was raised. The bishop conducted a visitation in 1562, with an outlay on the part of the village of 32 pesos in refreshments for the prelate and his retainers, and no objections entered the public record.

Later in the century the practice of giving food to the parish priest became illegal.[46] Several suits appeared as early as the 1570s against the practice. In the diocese of Puebla, a local curate, Luis Hidalgo de Montemayor, was indicted during a visitation for having demanded excessive foodstuffs from the natives without paying for them. According to the charges, drawn up in the summer of 1572, Hidalgo had collected 81 pesos worth of food in seven months, including 110 Spanish chickens and 74 local poultry, plus 35 *fanegas* of corn for himself and his animals. The complaint said that he had demanded 20 fowl each week. The ecclesiastical judge conducting the visitation found him guilty and fined him 32 pesos in court costs, and made him pay 40 pesos for the food.[47]

In a similar case in the diocese of Michoacán, the curate

of Turicato, Diego de Mendoza, found himself accused of taking food illegally from the Indians. While the time period over which the infraction was supposed to have taken place is not clear, the totals are. He allegedly took 400 fish, 400 eggs, 200 chickens, 20 *fanegas* of corn, plus butter and Spanish bread from the Indians in his charge.[48] The case occurred in 1574, and the papers of the suit contain no sentence. Nevertheless, it clearly indicates that the Indians no longer had to give food to curates without remuneration.

A growing body of legislation governed these suits. In the records of executive orders coming from both the viceroy and the audiencia the practice of giving food to curates was clearly a problem which both decided to eliminate. Viceregal orders from as early as 1575 outlawed the practice, demanding that Indians not provide any foodstuffs to the curate without first receiving proper payment.[49] In the case of Tepeucila, mentioned above, in 1580 the viceroy ordered that the *beneficiado*'s salary be embargoed until he had paid for food he had received from the Indians.[50] The general philosophy on this question was that since the food payments were not mandated in the *tasaciones*, they were not legal. Many curates argued, and perhaps quite rightly, that the food gifts had been well established by tradition. Nevertheless, as the century wore on, the curates lost this additional source of maintenance.

In spite of its illegality, not all curates gave up the custom. In 1597 the *beneficiado* of Iztapa and Tonatico in the archdiocese of Mexico was investigated for a long list of charges drawn up by the Indians of his parish. These charges, written in Nahuatl, claimed that every year for ten years, 1587–97, the *beneficiado* Rodrigo de Robles Porras, had received seventeen pesos worth of chickens, bread, wine, and fruit from the Indians. While the papers of the investigation do not include a sentence, pay records from the royal treasury indicate that Robles Porras was absent from the parish for five months following the investigation, perhaps as a result of having been fined and exiled from his post.[51]

100

Chapter 3

Figure 6.
Codex Sierra

In spite of executive orders, law suits, and punishment, the tradition of taking food from Indian parishioners did not die easily. In 1601 Francisco Rodríguez Tejada, the *beneficiado* of Tlalchichilco, a *sujeto* of Hueyacocotla, found himself charged with many wrongdoings. The Indian leaders of the community raised the complaints against him based on his four years of service in the post.

Prominently among the other charges levied against Rodríguez Tejada, the Indians alleged that he demanded food. Specifically, they accused him of having required them to provide forty fish every Friday and Saturday, three turkeys and six chickens every day of Holy Week, some 5,600 eggs a year, daily butter and cooking fat valued at seventy pesos a year, plus tallow and honey worth thirty pesos annually, and four *botijos* of wine costing forty-eight pesos. Clearly many of these items had to do with specific religious feasts: the fish and eggs for fast days, the chickens and turkeys for Holy Week, and the wine for Christmas, Easter, Corpus Cristi, and San Agustín, the town's patron. Consequently one cannot be sure that Francisco used the wine for personal consumption. Perhaps part went to the celebrations. Only the butter and honey do not correspond to special festivities. Nevertheless, by the strict letter of the law, Rodríguez could not ask for any of these goods. He could accept them as freely given alms, but he could not requisition them. Although the royal prosecuter entered the case, no formal charges appeared. Quite possibly the suit never reached court, for no sentence accompanies the documents. Four years later, in 1605, Rodríguez still served the *beneficio* of Tlalchichilco, when he entered the *oposición* for the post at Teoloyuca.[52]

The tradition of giving food to the parish priest clearly originated in the early years of the colony, perhaps out of a generalized system of tribute in which encomenderos and Indian nobles also received food. This pattern is certainly true of labor services. Labor and its allocation served as one of the basic principles behind the encomienda. The early institution, before the New Laws of 1542, made great labor demands on the tributary population. The laws sought to reduce and eliminate the labor service, among other goals, and to convert the institution to a purely tributary relationship between Indian and Spaniard. After 1551, then, labor service disappeared as a component in the tribute scene in New Spain.[53]

One of the normal recipients of this labor was the local parish priest.[54] The labor consisted of personal service. Indians also were compelled from time to time to provide other labor services of a more generalized nature, such as construction labor for local churches and the like. The history of these services closely parallels that of the food grants. While in the first fifty years the tradition held, by the 1570s it had passed into illegality. In their opposition to the collection of fees for the sacraments from Indians, the bishops of New Spain included labor service and goods as equally forbidden means of payment.

Several law suits demonstrate the degree to which labor services functioned in parish life. The case of Luis Hidalgo de Montemayor in Chicontepec, noted above, is equally applicable here. In addition to having taken food from the Indians, according to the suit he received two different types of personal service. He demanded the labor of nine Indians to fulfill general functions in his household. Beyond that he had three Indian women to grind corn, three men to cut firewood, three to provide fodder for his horses, two to guard the horses, and one to keep watch on all the others. The Indians valued this labor at 36 pesos for the seven months. The other type of labor which he enjoyed was far more specialized. In the absence of beasts of burden, the Indians of Mexico had used porters, *tamemes*. Even after the conquest and the introduction of European animals, the tradition of using human bearers continued. The crown made several attempts to outlaw the practice, or at least to regulate it to protect the Indian porters.[55] Nevertheless, the system continued. Hidalgo de Montemayor used three such bearers to carry fish from Tulancingo to Chicontepec and to carry goods on to Puebla. He ultimately was forced to pay for both types of Indian labor. The court levied ten pesos specifically for the *tamemes*.⁵⁶

In executive orders after 1575, the viceroys reasserted the illegality of demanding service from the Indians in case after case. For many years suits appeared to be declining until the turn of the century. In the last decade of the sixteenth century the question again arose. When Rodrigo de Robles Porras was accused of taking food from the Indians, they also demanded that he pay for the labor they had provided him. The complaint stated that over the ten-year period he had, on an annual basis, used the labor services of six Indians. One male served in his household, while a woman ground his corn. Two men guarded his flocks of goats, while two boys guarded his home. In addition to that, he took two *cargas* of firewood and ten *fanegas* of corn for his personal use, above and beyond the other foodstuffs. The total value of these goods and services, according to the Indian complaint, was thirty-two pesos per year.⁵⁷

In 1599, though, something odd happened with reference to personal service. It made a comeback. Three executive orders that year granted labor services to parish priests. Specifically the *beneficiados* of the Pachuca and Taxco mining districts were each granted the use of one Indian. The *beneficiado* of Pátzcuaro received the labor service of two Indians and one Indian woman to grind the corn.⁵⁸ Nevertheless, the use of Indian labor without specific permission remained against the law.

Without the possibility of receiving income from either personal service or gifts of food, the parish priest in Indian villages was left with his simple salary. Just as food gifts and personal service were outlawed but continued, in spite of royal and ecclesiastical orders to the contrary, local curates did collect fees for their services. Again the case of Luis Hidalgo de Montemayor is illustrative. The leading Indians of Chicontepec accused him of forcing them to pay for special religious services. Specifically they claimed that he collected one and one-half pesos for each wedding, one *real* for each baptism, and as much as he could garner for burials.[59] He did not make many of the collections himself but rather ordered his Indian assistants, the alguacil and *fiscal*, to extort the parishioners. Similarly, in the early years of the seventeenth century, in much the same area as Hidalgo, Francisco Rodríguez Tejada allegedly collected fees for special church services, including marriages, baptisms, and burials. In his case he demanded three *reales* for a baptism, six for a wedding, and a full peso for a funeral.[60]

One must imagine that these two cases constitute merely the ones who were caught, for whom trial records remain, and that the practice was very widespread. Part of the explanation lies in the fact that royal law prohibited only the collection of fees for the mass itself, not for other sacraments.[61] Nevertheless, the Third Provincial Council very clearly stated that "nothing having any temporal value be given for the administration of the sacraments."[62] Yet when dealing with priests who served without a clearly defined stipend or salary, the council mandated the collection of fees for the sacraments and the writing of an *arancel* in each diocese for that purpose.[63]

There is evidence for legally mandated fees for the sacraments. In 1590 in the parochial instructions directed at Bernabé López, *beneficiado* of Tequisquiac in the archbishopric, the *visitador* left clear authority to receive emoluments for certain services. While the instructions prohibited fees for confession and baptism, they allowed the curate to collect the customary right for burials and marriages.[64] This permission, coming as it did five years after the Third Provincial Council and granted in an Indian village, casts some doubt on the total illegality of collecting fees. As a result, perhaps, of the confusion inherent in the laws, when one does find priests collecting for their ministry, the sacraments usually involved are baptism, marriage, unction, and the service of burial. Almost never does one find a priest collecting for the eucharist itself.

This confusion continued throughout the sixteenth century, as seen in the cases studied. At some point in the seventeenth century the decision was finally made to begin collecting fees from all parishioners, Spanish and Indian. With this change the *arancel* became a very common part of parish life.

Fees Outside the Parish

The king foresaw the collection of special fees as additional ecclesiastical income for some levels of the clergy. In 1532, when the royal audiencia drew up the cathedral's provisional erection, it included a ten-peso fee for the chapter for attending burials.[65] When it arrived a few years later, the actual bull lacked such specific approval for these fees. Nevertheless, it did allow the collection of fees and duties, noting that they could be allocated to the chapter members in the proportions ordered in the tithe distribution. Likewise the erection gave blanket approval for all ceremonies and customs used in the cathedral of Seville, to which Mexico was suffragan, probably thereby giving tacit approval to the collection of fees.[66]

By mid-century, fees became a prominent subject in the chapter meetings. The arrival of Archbishop Montúfar in 1554 enlivened the discussion, since he felt that the chapter should not levy any special fees. The chapter members debated the question for almost three years. At first the group wanted to charge 100 *pesos de minas* for full funeral services, a vigil and requiem mass, outside the cathedral, and sixty pesos inside the church. Celebration outside the cathedral entailed proceeding en masse to another church, and thus greater expense. The chapter also offered a simple celebration of requiem honors for 30 pesos outside the cathedral and 20 within. After much argument over the propriety of leaving the cathedral to celebrate funeral honors in some other church, the chapter decided to limit the offer to services in the cathedral. In the final decision the chapter voted to assess 100 *pesos de minas* for the full celebration in the cathedral and 60 pesos for simple requiem honors. In addition to these fees, the client had to pay one and a half pesos to the celebrant priest, a half peso to the assistant, and three-quarters peso to the *pertiguero*.[67]

These special services, such as funerals, could only help increase the income of the prebends, and thus few chapter members opposed them completely. In addition to funerals, many of the *capellanias* founded in the cathedral put aside 20 percent of the annual income for the celebration of an anniversary mass, on a date chosen by the founder. By 1578, the total value of these anniversaries reached 273 pesos.[68] Although not a king's ransom, these funds did add to the income of the chapter. In 1577 the additional income from all these special fees and services added about 240 pesos to the value of a *dignidad*.[69] This constituted a 22 percent increase over the base pay from the tithe. These items represent only the additional income that might accrue through simple membership in the chapter.

In the diocese of Guadalajara, the cathedral chapter similarly decided to collect burial dues for those services in which they participated and for burials within the cathedral. Their schedule of fees recognized only the location of the burial, indicating that perhaps not the full chapter would be in attendance. Beginning at the front door, burials became more expensive as one approached the main altar. Using the seven side altars as points of reference, at the first range, near the door, burial cost two pesos. The price increased by two pesos with each range as one moved to the altar. In the sixth range the cost jumped from ten to twenty pesos, with the seventh range costing fifty pesos. This is the area in which the royal audiencia of New Galicia sat while attending the cathedral.[70]

Other Sources of Income

Priests had other means of augmenting personal income. Many followed several careers at the same time. Curates near Mexico City could both serve their parish and teach at the university, as did Dr. Hernando Ortiz de Hinojosa. In the diocese of Oaxaca the salaries of the cathedral chapter members were so low that several chose to forgo the privilege of participating in the chapter and took parishes instead. These clerics enjoyed the title and prestige of their prebend but not its salary or any other privilege within the cathedral.[71] These were the legally sanctioned means of supplementing one's income.

Several methods of varying degrees of illegality found practice among curates of the sixteenth century. A variation on labor service, as in the case of Robles Porras, the curate used the labor of parishioners on his estates in the district. While parish priests were discouraged from holding land in their parish, the injunction was pretty much a dead letter. In the late sixteenth century many viceregal orders prohibited the use of Indian labor on these estates without just payment.[72] Another method was the *repartimiento de bienes*, known as the *derrama*. This was the forced sale of goods, a practice which reached a peak in the eighteenth century at the hands of local magistrates. In the sixteenth century the practice was still being developed and was illegal. It involved purchasing items in bulk from wholesale merchants at a low cost, then forcing the Indians of the district to buy the goods at inflated prices. In 1575 Juan de la Cruz, the curate of the Guatinicamanes villages of the Zapoteca, was enjoined from conducting this abuse.[73]

There is no doubt that clerical income in the rural parishes was far higher than the stipend awarded in the appointment to the parish. The colonial government recognized this and merely attempted to curb the most flagrant abuses. In 1590, in fact, the audiencia began to evaluate parishes in terms of their gross income. This came about when priests requested permission to raise testimony concerning their career and service, *relación de meritos y servicios*. At this time the audiencia mandated several questions to be included in all such testimony. The points covered included investigation into the value of the parish, whether or not the priest engaged in business activity, whether Indians had died without confession and infants without baptism, and if the priest had received food or service without just payment. The practice of including these questions, however, lasted less than a year.

Three of these *relaciones* from 1590 give some insight into the actual worth of an Indian parish. In testimony for Diego Bravo, the *beneficiado* of Iztlan in Michoacán, testimony valued the parish at 400 pesos, although the salary paid was 248.[74] The parish of Teutila, administered by Esteban de Alavés in the diocese of Oaxaca, was similarly valued at 800 pesos, although the official salary was 248. One witness even placed the value as high as one thousand pesos, as did the audiencia in its final evaluation.[75] Almost exactly the same result occurred in the *relación* for Miguel de Cervantes, *beneficiado* of Ocelotepec in Oaxaca. Testimony revealed that his parish provided him with from 800 to 1,000 pesos annually, although the audiencia reported the lower figure. In addition to the parish, Cervantes also had a horse ranch, which reportedly gave him an additional 5,000 pesos annual income. To his credit, the estate was outside the parish.[76]

When assessing the level of clerical income in both Spanish and Indian parishes, then, the stipulated salary should be taken as a minimum. Priests had many methods, legal and not, to increase this level. Incomes in urban parishes could be augmented by serving chantries and working for other institutions, such as the university or the Inquisition. As shall be seen, there were many sources of alms and other income for the urban priest. In rural areas chantries were limited, but the priest could accept alms for services, if he did not use coercion. Thus while even the gross incomes were generally low for Spanish professionals, they were certainly adequate.

Although some forces tended to limit the number of ways a parish priest could legally supplement his income, other trends helped to stabilize the official income. As will be seen in a later chapter, the royal government, while curtailing the abuses practiced by the curates, guaranteed that they would ultimately enjoy a living wage. Thus, the overall income of the corps of parish priests probably remained uniform throughout the century. The extra-legal methods used to augment income clearly continued, since they became a source of acrimony in later centuries. The establishment of chantries and other pious works helped to stabilize the income of the parish priests. As well, the creation of local ecclesiastical institutions, such as religious sodalities, provided a means whereby a parish priest might augment his income. The growth of both of these institutions falls beyond the scope of this study. Consequently, one concludes a view of parish revenues in the sixteenth century with a vision of priests earning marginal salaries, not so low as to leave priests in poverty but not so rich as to rank them among the economic elite. Later in the colonial period, the use of *aranceles* became ubiquitous even in the rural parishes. Various types of coercive practices by parish priests also provided suplementary income, not only through the *derrama* but through obligatory alms and labor. In the end, in spite of royal law, the parish priests augmented their incomes in the traditional manner.

4. Pious Works and Alms

In sixteenth-century Catholic thought, pious works occupied a very important place. It was upon this specific issue that Luther based much of his opposition to the Catholic church. For Luther, justification came through faith in God alone. For the Catholic church, at that time, justification was intimately linked to merit, or that property of a good work which entitled the doer to receive a reward. Thus, the creation of ongoing agents of good work, such as the institutions generically called pious works, granted the founder a similarly ongoing merit and with it grace, heavenly glory, and other rewards. While justification and salvation are not synonymous, in this context they can be taken as such. Justification is the process through which something is made just. Thus, in questions of faith, justification is the transformation of the sinner from a state of unrighteousness to a state of holiness. Salvation is a gift of God which cannot be merited. Justification creates a receptivity within the individual for that gift. Because of the centrality of good work in the Catholic opposition to Luther, the institution of pious works surged in importance as a clear refutation of Luther in the later sixteenth century.

Pious works included a very wide range of institutions in sixteenth-century New Spain. Under this general heading fell endowments for chantries, funds to provide dowries to poor girls, and the founding of hospitals and monasteries. The one thing all pious works had in common was a reliance on invested capital to supply the income necessary to carry out the patron's or benefactor's will. The growth in the number and size of pious works in the sixteenth century was rapid. While the earliest endowments date from the two decades after the conquest, following 1575 there is a dramatic expansion. The growth of the institution is closely linked to the spread of popular piety during the Counter-Reformation. The spread of pious works had the added benefit of offering a penurious church an almost unlimited supply of operating capital. While the pious works did not provide an immediate financial benefit to the diocesan administration itself, they did help to support the rapidly growing priesthood.

The endowment of all these institutions originated in one of three ways. The simplest form consisted of a pure cash donation. The money would then be loaned out, and the interest that was paid back provided the working income. The principal for the pious work could also take the form of real property, such as land, houses, or sugar mills. The administrators then had the decision of renting the property out and using the proceeds, or selling the property for cash and investing the money, as with the first type. The third form of endowment was an encumbrance placed on a piece of property not otherwise encumbered. The interest generated by the encumbrance was the income for the pious work. In this last case, in essence, new capital was created where none had existed before.

Chantries

The most widespread form of pious work was the *capellanía*, or chantry. There were four general types of *capellanias* in sixteenth-century Mexico. The most common included pious works established by individuals for the perpetual celebration of memorial masses, privately administered. The next type was the same but under corporate administration. The third type consisted of endowed posts in monasteries, convents, churches, and hospitals. These posts also had as their central obligation the saying of memorial masses but entailed some quasi-parochial duties. The last type of *capellanía* included posts ancillary to other corporations. The *capellán* oversaw the spiritual obligations of the group. This category included the *capellanes* of the municipal council and the audiencia, among others. In any given church one could usually find several of these types of chantries coexisting.

Within the metropolitan cathedral, by 1569, there were nineteen *capellanias* endowed by private persons under the patronage of the chapter.[1] The *capellán* of each had to say the masses personally in the cathedral. One could establish a private *capellanía* in any church and under almost any patronage. The most common private *capellanias* served as the fixed income upon which a priest received his ordination. If a priest could not win a benefice or if he knew no Indian language he could have a *capellanía* established which would guarantee him a minimum income, usually 300 pesos per year, and thus qualify him in this respect for the priesthood. As in the case of the *benefice*, the endowment of the chantry had to be perpetual. The *capellanias* in the cathedral, however, could not serve as a *congrua* or *título* for ordination, since the *capellanes* served at the pleasure of the chapter and did not receive canonical institution for them.

Privately Endowed Chantries

The papers of some seventy-five sixteenth-century *capellanias* are held in the Mexican national archive. The government confiscated the wealth of the church in the nineteenth century and thus acquired the papers of the chantry court, *Juzgado de capellanias*.[2] Because some of these papers were initially catalogued according to the date in which the court last revised them, undoubtedly there are more sixteenth-century *capellanias* than just these seventy-five, but they appear under the last date in which the court had to intervene in their administration, making a search for them difficult. This collection, augmented by others found in notarial and ecclesiastical archives, presents a fairly good cross section of the institution.

As noted earlier in the general considerations of pious works, there were three means of providing the capital for the endowment. The group of sixteenth-century *capellanias* reflects all of these means. The two most common forms of endowment were cash grants or gifts of property. Whether or not the money was invested or the property rented, the endowment provided the basis for a censo. Strictly speaking a censo was a mortgage. Nevertheless, the term also referred to long-term rental agreements on properties which formed the principal for pious works and to encumbrances and liens placed on property. In general, two types of censos appear in the documents. The *censo redimible* was, as the name indicates, redeemable periodically, such as annually, but in effect on demand. The censo could be redeemed merely by paying back the principal with whatever accrued interest. Likewise, the renter could return the rental property, but the *censo redimible* was almost never used for rental property. Rather, the preferred form of long term-lease property was the *censo perpetuo*. This censo was not really perpetual but certainly could be. Usually it ran for any number of specified lifetimes, often two or three. The church seldom loaned out money in *censo perpetuo*. Thus, property was rented in a *censo perpetuo* but money loaned in a *censo redimible*.

Almost universally in the sixteenth-century the interest was 7.14 percent, figured annually (*catorce el millar*). For an endowment of 1,000 pesos, the annual interest would be 71 pesos 3 *tomines* 2 *granos*. An endowment of 1,400 pesos accrued 100 pesos interest. While this rate was fairly common, some censos rented for as much as 10 percent, to as little as 5 percent.[3]

The third form of endowment imposed an encumbrance or lien on a previously clear property. In order to accomplish this the founder of the pious work, or someone he designated, would pledge to begin interest payments as if a mortgage had been imposed. This created new capital where none existed before. In a cash-and-capital-poor economy this device was exceedingly important in order to allow sustained growth. By this means, once the pious work was established, it functioned as if it had a cash principal, imposed on whatever property the founder indicated. To add to the confusion, however, this lien was also called a censo.

One further method existed for the endowment of a pious work, as a variation on the cash endowment. Rather than put up a large sum of cash, one could merely present the revenues from an already established censo. In the sixteenth century the loaning of money between individuals was relatively common. These loans could then serve as the basis for a chantry or other pious work.

The endowment of chantries could only be cash or real estate. Furthermore, the principal in a cash endowment had to be secured by real property. In general, when an individual borrowed the money of the chantry, a mortgage lien was placed on all his property, rather than on a specific piece. Thus the records of the censos include good sources of information on the ownership of real estate. If by chance the debtor chronically failed to pay the interest on the censo, the administrator of the pious work could confiscate the encumbered property and sell it at auction to recoup the principal and accrued interest.

In the administration of these pious works, the most difficult moral problem was the distinction between the mortgage and the simple borrowing of money at interest. The former was legal, the latter was not. Simple loans for a fixed, usually short, term could not generate any type of interest. To do so would constitute the sin of usury. For the mortgage to be legal, and to allow interest to be collected, it was viewed not as a loan but as a purchase of capital. There were several conditions placed on the mortgage: (1) It had to be secured with productive real property. (2) The principal had to be delivered in cash before a notary.

(3) The property that served as the security could not be alienated. (4) The principal could not be increased by unpaid interest; they were to be kept as two separate things. (5) If the property lost value, the mortgage likewise had to be decreased. (6) If the security was lost through fate, the principal could not be collected. (7) The mortgage could always be redeemed for its initial value.[4]

Private chantries normally were founded for one of two basic, not mutually exclusive, canonical reasons. The most common was to demonstrate piety in a desire to gain the spiritual benefits offered by the chantry, namely justification through good work. The chantry had as its end the lessening of the soul's torments in purgatory. The perpetuity of the chantry guaranteed that forever in the future masses would be said for the redemption of one's soul, and for those of one's family and others stipulated in the foundation. The second major reason for establishing a chantry was to provide a canonical income for a young cleric seeking to enter the priesthood. The income of the chantry could be applied to the *congrua* necessary for ordination.

In addition to these two ecclesiastical reasons for chantries, others had a more mundane social and economic basis. On an obvious level, the chantry provided sons in the priesthood with a minimum wage. Control over the capital or property used to found the chantry could remain in the family. Furthermore, because the money and property were dedicated to a canonical end and formed part of a mortgage, they were inalienable. They could not be sold or transferred without specific permission from the ecclesiastical authorities. In this sense they acted as a mini-*mayorazgo*.[5] Spanish inheritance laws called for the equal division of parents' estates among their children, regardless of sex or condition. In order to prevent the fragmentation of family wealth, some sons entered the priesthood, women the convent, and others remained unwed. This tended to limit the number of second-generation offspring. The share in their parents' estate of the clerics, nuns, and unmarried children could then be diverted back to the limited second generation. Moreover, in the case of the *capellanía* it could be used again to provide the *congrua* for young men in the next generation.

As the economy of New Spain grew in the sixteenth century, more capital was available for investment in the church. The *capellanía* in specific, and pious works in general, offered a number of spiritual and financial benefits, as noted above. In addition, the religious climate of the times also supported the creation of pious works. The general missionary feeling prevalent in the New World, coupled with the encouragement of public demonstrations of piety of the Counter-Reformation stressing good works, also spurred the wealthy to establish these institutions. Thus, the number of chantries grew rapidly in the closing years of the sixteenth century, establishing a precedent for later periods.

Within the group of private *capellanias*, two subgroups existed. One consisted of privately endowed chantries which had a corporate patron. Examples of this type were the *capellanias* established in the cathedral by private citizens yet under the patronage of the chapter. The other type was the simple private *capellanía* in which the patronage was reserved either to the founder or to a person he designated.

In the sixteenth century the number of private chantries that fell under corporate patronage was rather small. As noted earlier, in 1569 there were nineteen such chantries in the cathedral of Mexico. Less than a decade later the number had increased to twenty. Three of the earlier ones ceased to exist as chantries because their revenues could no longer support masses. Nevertheless, new chantries were added in the same period, including four endowed by the same individual.[6] The cathedral chantries enjoyed, on average, slightly lower incomes than privately administered ones. The most common chantries ranged from 100 to 150 pesos in annual rent. The cathedral *capellanias* averaged 116 pesos per year. Since they fell under the patronage and administration of the cathedral chapter, the priests appointed to serve them invariably came from among the cathedral staff and members of the chapter. The chapter oversaw all appointments, and, unlike other chantries, the appointment was *ad mobile ad nutum,* or at the pleasure of the chapter, rather than *ad titulum perpetuum.*[7]

The private chantries established in the cathedral under chapter patronage often had three constituent parts. From the interest on the endowment, the largest portion went to pay the priest for saying the masses. In the case of the *capellanía* founded by Juan Jiménez, the annual interest was 167 pesos. From that total, 106 went to pay for the 107 masses said per year. Ten percent of the amount for masses was then deducted and given to the fabric to pay for supplies of wax, wine, and wafers, and to cover wear and tear on vestments. The chapter kept another 47 pesos to pay for an anniversary service, celebrated corporately on the date on which the founder, Jiménez, died. When the founder did not mandate an anniversary, the annual interest paid only the priest and the ten percent to the fabric. As seen, the cost of each mass was one peso. These chantries provided a good source of additional income for the chapter members and the cathedral staff.

In 1580 the cathedral of Michoacán also reported the chantries it administered. In all, thirteen appeared on the list. The founders of these pious works differed from those seen in the Mexican cathedral in that most were priests. Of the thirteen, only three were founded by the laity. These chantries were even poorer than those in Mexico, averaging only eighty-five pesos each in annual rent. Of the group, seven included anniversary masses, worth twenty pesos each. The listing does not indicate who served the *capellanias,* but one can assume that the staff of the cathedral did since the document does say that the dean and cabildo said the masses.[8]

Other basic features of the chantry are the number of masses to be said and the schedule. Since the masses cost

Figure 7.
Chantries in the Cathedral of Mexico, 1570 and 1578

	A	B	C	D	E	F	G
Mari Quijada	81.	56.1.6	101.	167.0.9	116.8.9	16.6.8	33.4.4
Catalina Hernandez	81.	56.1.6	81.	134.	94.	13.3	26.6
Can. Palomares	40.	22.	40.	66.1.6	36.3.3	3.2.6	26.3.9
Ana Morales	25.	22.5.4					
Geronimo Frago	50.	30.	35.5.8	59.6	41.2.9	5.7.6	11.6.6
Rodrigo Gomez	87.1	61.87.1	87.1	144.0.9	100.7	14.3.3	28.7.6
Francisco de Hoyos	100.	70.	100.	165.3.6	115.6.6	16.4.4	33.0.8
Rui Diaz	80.	56.	80.	132.3	92.5.6	13.1.10	26.3.8
Juan Jimenez	107.1.2	71.3.5	107.1.2	167.2	106.1.6	11.6.6	47.1
Benito del Nero	40.	36.	40.	66.1.6	59.4.6	6.5	
D. R. de Cervanes	71.3.5	64.1.5	71.3.6	118.1.6	106.1.6	12.	
Juan de Cabra	100.	95.		71.1.2	67.4.6	3.4.6	
Luisa Lopez	12.						
Garcia de Vega				200.			
Diego Hernandez				120.	108.	12.	
Diego de Trejo				143.	109.	14.	
Br. Ortega			406.3.1	602.2.8	145.3.6		
					145.3.6		
					100.		
					180.		
					80.		

A. 1569 Total income, oro de minas
B. 1569 Chaplain's salary, oro de minas
C. 1578 Total income, oro de minas
D. 1578 Total income, oro comun
E. 1578 Chaplain's salary, oro comun
F. 1578 Cathedral expenses, oro comun
G. 1578 Anniversary, oro comun
Source: ACTAS, 18 Mar. 1578; Ledesma, *Descripcion*, p. 1–7.

Figure 8.
Chantries in the
Cathedral of Michoacán
(oro comun)

	A	B
D. Fernando de Tapia	53.4.8	48
Lorenzo Yañez	24	24
Leonor de la Peña	107.1	87 + anniversary
Canon Geronimo Rodriguez	71.3.5	72
P. Juan de Zorita	57.1*	72 + anniversary
P. Alonso Rodriguez	28.3*	2 anniversaries
Canon Lic. Juan Marquez	214.2.4	196 + anniversary
P. Juan de Mesa	35.5.8	36
P. Francisco de la Cerna	91.1	72 + anniversary
D. Lorenzo de Alvarez Salgado	100	80 + anniversary
Canon Antonio de Ayala	200	200
Canon Juan de Velasco	107.0.6	108
D. Pedro de Yepes	20	anniversary

*Oro de minas
A. Revenue
B. Number of masses
Source: AGI, Mexico, 374.

one peso each, the annual rent dictated the number of masses to be celebrated. Normally the founder stipulated the days on which the masses would be said. Thus an endowment of 1,400 pesos netted 100 pesos interest, for 100 masses per year, or just under two per week. In fact this was a common relationship, 100 pesos for 104 masses. The founder could then request that the masses be said on specific days of the week for specific purposes, such as to Our Lady of the Immaculate Conception on Wednesday, or to the Passion of Our Lord on Friday. Beyond this, each *capellanía* had to be located in a religious institution. The founder could indicate any of the churches, convents, monasteries, hospitals, or even jails of the city, as the place in which to say the masses. Some money went to the host institution to cover the costs of materials, as seen in the cathedral. Generally the specific religious institution had to give permission before the chantry could begin to operate. The records of the cathedral indicate that the chapter was loathe to accept any privately administered chantries, preferring to allow only those over which it also received patronage. Furthermore, many convents and monasteries would not accept patronage of some *capellanias* if they felt that the cost of administration would outweigh the benefits, since patrons and administrators did not necessarily receive anything for their expenses.

Several examples will help to demonstrate the features of the chantry in action. In the realm of privately endowed, privately administered *capellanias*, there were great variations. Two subtypes appeared: those chantries founded in wills and those founded during the initial patron's life. They shared several features basic to all chantries. As noted, each had a founder and a patron. The patron or administrator was responsible for investing the funds, seeing that the interest was collected, appointing the chaplain, and paying him for his services. Often the founder reserved the right of patronage in an in-life endowment. Next most common was the selection of a close relative, usually a son, to serve or succeed as patron. In some cases the right of patronage fell to the priest who served as chaplain.

Each chantry had a chaplain. Often the chaplain was a relative of the founder or patron, especially in the case of chaplaincies endowed for ordination. A common stipulation in endowments mandated that the chaplain be a direct descendent of the founder, thus assuring that the pious work stayed in the family. Most chaplains seem to have taken over the responsibilities of investing the principal and collecting the interest regardless of the patron, since they had a directly vested concern.

The case of Lic. Luis de Espinosa demonstrates how a *capellanía* was utilized for ordination. In 1596 Espinosa's mother, Catalina de Godoy, established a chantry for his ordination. The endowment had a principal of 1,400 pesos. The money went into a mortgage on two pairs of houses in the Santa Catalina neighborhood of Mexico. Jacome Vela, Espinosa's brother-in-law, owned the houses and paid the interest on the mortgage. This interest served as the fixed income for the *capellanía*, roughly 100 pesos yearly. The obligations of the *capellanía* included saying 100 masses annually for the souls of Espinosa's parents at the standard rate. Lic. Espinosa served as the patron of the bequest, along with his brother. In the event of Espinosa's death, or in the case he no longer needed or wanted the income, the *capellanía* was to go to Catalina de Godoy's nearest male relative who desired to enter the priesthood. Thus the *capellanía* passed perpetually to male descendents needing a *título* for ordination. This particular case demonstrates how much control the family could keep over the bequest. Espinosa and his brother administered the principal for the chantry, while their brother-in-law borrowed the money using his home as collateral.[9]

By naming a male heir as patron, the chantry remained in the family. In the absence of direct descendents, however, questions of succession could result in court cases. In 1597 a protracted legal suit sought to determine the nearest male heir of Francisco de Lara and Doña Juana de Rebolledo, who had founded a chantry of three masses per week, having an endowment of approximately 3,000 pesos. No fewer than six parties claimed the chantry. One was the Monastery of San Agustín, the ultimate heir in the case no other claim was valid. The others included all of Doña Juana's brothers, sisters, and their children. The court finally ruled in favor of the children of one of Doña Juana's brothers, rather than the grandchildren of another brother. Nevertheless, the court case took five years to resolve.[10]

In the absence of any other patron, the archbishop could take over *capellanías*. He was often granted the patronage outright by the founder. When Cristóbal Miguel, a miner in Zultepec, founded a chantry in 1570, he gave the patronage to the archbishop along with the right to determine the place where the masses were to be said. The endowment was substantial, property valued at 2,000 *pesos de minas*, with responsibility for only two masses per week.[11] The archbishop did not oversee these matters himself but appointed an administrator.

Two officials on the archiepiscopal staff dealt with pious works. One of these was the *provisor-vicario general*. The *provisor* dealt with most administrative matters for the prelate, and, as *vicario general*, he was the judge of the archiepiscopal court. Nevertheless, cases involving pious works were not heard in the first instance in that court but in a special probate court called the *juzgado de capellanias y bienes de difuntos*. This court had its own presiding judge. Cases went on appeal to the *vicario general*. In questions of the appointment of chaplains, once the *juzgado de capellanias* had decided the legality of an appointment and suitability of the priest, the *provisor* endowed him canonically with the chantry, in the *colación* and canonical institution.

Cosme García founded a chantry naming his nephew, of the same name, as patron. The founder was a priest, and the chantry had been created to allow his nephew to be ordained. The elder García also appointed the nephew as chaplain. Nevertheless, the boy was too young, and so Juan de Ayllón became interim *capellán* until young Cosme came of age. Something happened in the meanwhile. Between the founding in 1586 and 1595 the *juzgado* began to administer the chantry and to regulate Ayllón, who, it claimed, had violated the specifics of the endowment.[12]

In another case, the archbishop took over a chantry when the founder died intestate without having named a patron. In 1582 Francisco Ramírez Bravo, a miner in the Taxco mining district, founded the pious work as an in-life endowment. He established the chantry in the *hermita* of San Antonio Abad on the Iztapalapa road in Mexico. Ramírez

Bravo appointed the son of friends as chaplain, with the chantry serving as the boy's *congrua* for ordination. In the foundation papers, Ramírez Bravo reserved the patronage to himself, saying that he would appoint a successor later but never did. Thus, when he died in 1619 the *juzgado* took over the patronage in the absence of a clear successor.[13]

If the donor founded a chantry in his life, he could reserve most powers. If he mandated it in his will, he likewise could make stipulations, but the final foundation and execution of the will fell to his executor, albacea. Often the executor became patron of the chantry and appointed his own relatives to serve it. This was the case of the chantry mandated by Juan Pérez in his will in 1578. Pérez had requested that his illegitimate son, Juan Pérez Loaisa, benefit from the chantry. The endowment of 2,000 pesos would generate enough to pay a chaplain and provide an additional small income to Pérez Loaisa. Dr. Pedro López, the famous Mexico city surgeon, served as executor of the will and patron of the chantry. He appointed his own son, Br. Joseph López, as chaplain for the purpose of ordination.[14] The chantry records do not indicate if Pérez de Loaisa actually received anything from the endowment.

Patrons had great power in the administration of chantries. Hernando Rebolledo, a resident of Veracruz, was the executor of the estate of Nicolás Cazano, an export-import merchant who died at sea. In his will Cazano requested that a chantry be created in the Colegio de Donceles in Mexico City. Although Cazano named the cofradía of the Santísimo Sacramento as patron, Rebolledo took on the position. The testament called for a daily mass to be said, giving a hefty endowment of 3,000 *pesos de minas*. Nevertheless, when Rebolledo established the chantry in 1567 he reduced the number of masses to four per week, on a stipend of 150 *pesos de minas*, with an additional ten *pesos de minas* going to the colegio for overhead. The income of the lien should have reached 214 *pesos de minas*. Thus, either Rebolledo kept some of the revenue for himself, or the full 3,000 pesos could not be collected from the estate. Finally in 1586, almost twenty years after the foundation of the chantry, the cofradía took over administration.[15]

It was not uncommon for chantries to lose capital slowly. The problem was much more grave in those pious works that had an endowment of property. This occurred in the abovementioned chantry founded by Cristóbal Miguel. Even though the property upon which the chantry was founded had been valued at 2,000 *pesos de minas* in 1570, twenty-four years later it had become dilapidated, run down, and not worth much at all. The patron of the *capellanía* requested that the real estate be sold at auction and that the proceeds invested in censos. The court approved the petition. When the houses reached the auction block they raised only 750 pesos. The patron, Gonzalo Menéndez, then requested permission to place the mortgage lien on his own property, which the court also accepted.[16]

Some very interesting inheritance patterns occurred in chantries with a priest as patron. In 1557 Beatriz López of Puebla founded a chantry based upon some houses. She named D. Francisco de León as patron and chaplain. He was the archdeacon of the cathedral chapter of Puebla. The chantry was poor, paying only twenty-six pesos per year for one mass per week, far below the going rate. León first handed over the patronage to Pedro Moreno, also of Puebla, and in 1565 León retired as chaplain. Moreno then appointed León's nephew, Br. D. Fernando Pacheco, as chaplain. Pacheco also succeeded his uncle as archdeacon on the Puebla cathedral chapter. In 1599 Pacheco renounced the chantry, and his nephew, D. Alonso Pacheco de Alarcón, in turn was appointed chaplain. The chantry continued on well into the nineteenth century.[17]

The succession of priests and patrons was not always a clear-cut matter. The *juzgado* had the responsibility to see that the masses mandated by the founder were actually celebrated. D. Beltrán de la Cueva served two different chantries in Mexico. The notary Antonio Alonso founded one. Doña Juana de Ribera ordered the other in her will, but Cristóbal de Vargas Valadés actually founded it and was patron. When Cueva left Mexico for a protracted length of time, the *juzgado* appointed two priests to serve the chantries. Alonso Cornejo was appointed to the Ribera-Vargas Valadés chantry and Juan de Torres Ronquillo to the Alonso. When Cornejo applied to the court for his pay as chaplain, the court discovered that Cristóbal de Vargas Valadés no longer served as patron. Vargas Valadés testified that his brother, Hernando de Vargas, had become patron and had already appointed a new chaplain: Gonzalo de Villalobos. Nevertheless, Villalobos said he was appointed by Vargas Valadés acting for Hernando de Vargas. In the end, the court had one chantry with two patrons and two chaplains. To prohibit the loss of any money during the court action, the judge embargoed the property upon which the principal had been placed until the resolution of the case. In the final judgment, the court upheld its own appointment of Cornejo and found Hernando de Vargas liable to pay him for the services.[18]

The patrons of *capellanias* could specify exact conditions for the chantry. The founder-patrons Andrés Merino de Meneses and Inez Sánchez, his wife, placed very precise requirements on almost all aspects of their chantry. They established the chantry in the church of Santa Catalina in Mexico. Of the three masses per week, they requested that one be on Saturday for the Virgin Mary. Furthermore, they ordered additional masses on the five feasts of the Virgin, and on the following saints' days: S. Miguel Angel, S. Francisco, S. Juan Evangelista, S. Andrés, Sta. Inez, Sta. Anna, the Santas Virgenes, S. Gerónimo, and Santiago. They reserved the patronage, but upon their deaths it would pass to their daughter, Inez de Meneses, beata of S. Domingo, and then to their other daughter, Francisca de Meneses, wife of Antón Martín, and then to Francisca and Antón's children. Furthermore, the chaplain had to be "the closest and most direct relative in our lineage."[19] When their nephew claimed rights as chaplain eight years later, they further modified the chaplaincy to admit only direct descendents–children or grandchildren.

Similar to this, Juan Bautista Duarte founded a chantry for Melchor Pérez Simal. In his will, Pérez Simal had allocated one-fifth of a hacienda as the endowment for the chantry. Duarte stipulated that the seventy-two masses per year be said in the following manner: nine on the feasts of the Virgin, sixteen to the Five Wounds of Christ (on Wednesdays), sixteen to the Passion of Our Lord (on Fridays), fifteen to the Blessed Virgin (on Saturdays), and the remaining fifteen however the chaplain saw fit. He then transferred the patronage and the rights of chaplain to his own son, Br. Pedro Duarte.[20]

The chaplain had a close tie to the investment upon which the chantry was based, since his livelihood depended on it. In a clause in his will, Miguel Benítez of Mexico City ordered a chantry founded. His executor, Diego Baena, drew up the papers for the institution fourteen years after Benítez's death. The delay occurred because the chantry would have taken more than half the estate, and Benítez's wife survived him. She finally gave her consent to the reduction of her dower interest, but the process still took ten more years. Finally in 1590, after both Benítez and his wife had died, Baena appointed the first chaplain, Br. Jusepe de Texadillo. The endowment for the chantry, 1,080 pesos, was placed in a censo on the houses of Cristóbal de Texadillo Basante, Jusepe's brother. None of these people seem to be related, except for the Texadillo brothers. The association merely helped to serve their own ends.[21] The chantry allowed Jusepe to be ordained, and his brother helped by accepting the censo. Four years later, once he no longer needed the chantry, he resigned and another chaplain was appointed. One further interesting aspect of the chantry was that its seventy masses per year were to be said in the jails of the city.

Titular Chantries

As noted, *capellanias* called for the celebration of a certain number of masses in a stipulated church or religious establishment. One should not confuse, however, the *capellán* of the Hospital de Nuestra Señora de la Purísima Concepción, for instance, with a *capellán* in the hospital. Each major church, hospital, convent, or monastery in Mexico had several private *capellanias* founded in it. All the hospitals and colegios also had at least one titular *capellán*. These priests fulfilled some parochial-like duties within those institutions. In the case of the Hospital de Nuestra Señora de la Purísima Concepción, for several years the titular *capellán* was Blas de Bustamante. The son of a university professor, Bustamante received the appointment to the post from Don Martín Cortés, the patron of the hospital. Don Hernán Cortés, the first marqués del Valle, founded the hospital. As patrons the Cortés family held powers of appointment to the institution and in 1569 placed Bustamante in it. In a hospital, the chaplain had to see to the spiritual needs of the patients. He lived in the institution, said a daily mass for the patients in the hospital chapel, and remained on call at all times to administer extreme unction to the dying and celebrate a sung requiem mass after their death. He also had other obligations, mostly pertaining to the celebration of masses for the Cortés family.[22]

Mexico City suffered no shortage of titular chaplains. As seen in an earlier chapter, the *curas* of the cathedral parish filed a suit in 1582 enjoining all clerics who held posts as chaplains in hospitals or colleges from singing mass or participating in any funeral services. The cathedral curates asserted that these privileges specifically pertained to them. They allowed the chaplains to say masses according to the obligations of their *capellanias* and to administer the last rights. The final judgment favored the rights of the *curas* of the cathedral parish.[23] The whole incident demonstrated that although the titular chaplains of the various institutions around the city performed quasi-parochial duties, the actual parish priests would not allow them to operate beyond certain limits. A clear distinction was drawn between the obligations of a chaplain, as stipulated in the foundation of a *capellanía*, and the rights and obligations of curates as outlined in canon law.

The cathedrals of New Spain had similar titular chaplains, in addition to those serving the private chantries within the cathedrals. These more institutional chantries were mandated by the bulls of erection. As noted earlier, the priests serving them received their pay from the tithe revenues of the diocese, specifically the curates' fund. But like other private chantries under cathedral administration, the appointments to these were at the pleasure of the cathedral chapter, and thus they could not be used as a *título* for ordination.

Some of the chaplains to the various churches, monasteries, convents, and schools had administrative responsibilities in addition to their canonical duties. The Canon Álvaro de Vega, chaplain and *vicario* of the Convent of Nuestra Señora de la Purísima Concepción, was empowered to act on the behalf of the convent in many legal issues, including loaning money in censos. Similarly Fernando de Cuevas, the chaplain of the Convent of Santa Clara in Mexico, received power of attorney from that convent to act in conjunction with the mayordomo in all administrative matters.[24]

The salaries of these institutional chaplains fell within the regular range of about 150 *pesos de minas*. Nevertheless, they could easily augment this basic stipend by taking on privately endowed chantries administered by the religious institutions for which they worked. The relationship between these chaplains and the convents and colleges had additional financial advantages. Canon Álvaro de Vega received a reduced rate when he placed his niece in the convent for which he worked. The admission papers clearly noted that the 400 pesos that Vega provided fell far below the standard donation for entrance. When the girl was ready to profess into the order, Vega did not have sufficient cash to pay the dowry, 1,400 pesos in addition to the entrance fee. He then obligated the revenues from the titular chantry he served in the convent toward the dowry.[25] Vega also had his friends help in paying both the dowry and maintenance fee for his niece. Alonso de Vargas Sotomayor, the master of ceremonies in the cathedral, assigned part of his salary to the convent for this purpose.[26] Thus, although the chaplains of the institutions could receive various benefits, they could not have certain requirements waived altogether.

Free room and board constituted one further perquisite which could accrue to these titular chaplains. In the case of the chaplains of hospitals, in order to be available to administer the last rites to dying patients, they had to be near and on call. They often lived in accommodations in the hospital with the right to eat in the hospital kitchen. This aspect appeared in a suit against Blas de Bustamante. In 1572, he was tried for sexual incontinence with Ana de Cisneros. One of the allegations posited that Bustamante would leave the hospital by night for secret rendezvous with Cisneros. Furthermore, on weekends the two of them would retire to his family's estate in the gardens west of the city. His conviction on these charges demonstrates Bustamante's failings for having violated the vow of chastity and his shortcomings in his duties as chaplain.[27]

Corporate Chantries

The last type of *capellán* was the priest attached to a corporation or other legal body. This included the chaplains for the municipal council and the audiencia. Such corporate chaplains had to celebrate mass for the body that employed them. They led prayer services and fulfilled other ecclesiastical duties for the corporation. In the case of both the city council and the audiencia, the *capellán* had the additional obligation of seeing to the spiritual needs of the prisoners in jail. In this manner his duties approached those of the titular chaplains of the hospitals or colleges. Likewise the corporate chaplains fell under the injunction against funeral services and sung masses along with the others. They received fairly high salaries and had few duties. Nevertheless, since the various corporations appointed them, the posts usually went to sons or relatives of the members.

Perhaps the most important of these institutional chaplains served the royal audiencia. The priest who filled the position also had the duty of saying mass and ministering to the prisoners in the royal jail. The salary came from the royal revenues, along with the salaries of other court officials. By the end of the century it was worth 300 ducats of Castile, or about 485 pesos.[28] For many years Canon Alonso López de Cárdenas held the post. He was the son of the *oidor,* Dr. Cespedes de Cárdenas.[29]

The next important institutional chaplaincy was that of the municipal council. The post was curious in that, beginning in about 1560, the responsibilities included serving as parish priest for the town of Iztapalapa, which the council held in encomienda, up until the late date of 1582. Starting in 1540 the chaplain received 40,000 *marevedises* annual salary, equal to 133 pesos.[30] By 1560 the salary had not changed and was 80 *pesos de minas,* approximately the same. Up until this time the chaplain had been responsible only for saying masses in the municipal jail and serving for the town council. But in that year, as a result of pressure from the Indians of Iztapalapa, the town council resolved to have their chaplain administer the sacraments in the encomienda town as well.[31] With this added obligation, the council doubled the salary, to 160 *pesos de minas.*

The stipend remained at the new level for six years. As part of his remuneration, the Indians provided the chaplain with food on the days when he administered the sacraments in the town. This practice died out, and the chaplain found himself without a source of food. In recognition of this, and the travel inherent in serving both the public jails and the village, the city council again raised the salary of the chaplain to 200 *pesos de minas*.³² The office of chaplain to the municipal council and curate of Iztapalapa were finally split in 1575–76 when the *oposición* system of filling curacies came into effect. At that point the post of *cura beneficiado* of the village went to Francisco de Loya, who won the job in the competitive exams. The new system took the patronage of the curacy out of the hands of the Mexico City Council and gave it to the viceroy, although the city still had to pay the salary, now established at 150 *pesos de minas* for the village alone. Ultimately, on December 23, 1582, the village of Iztapalapa passed fully under the control of the crown, and all ties to the municipal council of Mexico ended.³³ After 1575, the chaplain of the municipal council had only the immediate duty of saying mass in the jail and serving the council.

The municipal council had control over other chantries. The chaplain of the church of Nuestra Señora de los Remedios also was appointed by the municipal council.³⁴ In 1586, the chaplain to the council received the added post of chaplain of the Church of San Hipólito.³⁵ These two chaplaincies ranked highly within the Spanish community, for both harked back to the immediate postconquest period. The standard that Cortés carried into battle was Nuestra Señora de los Remedios, and she was looked upon as the patroness of the city. The Aztec capital, Tenochtitlan, fell on August 13, 1521, the Feast of San Hipólito, and thus that saint became the patron of the Spanish community.

Another important institutional chaplain in Mexico City was the chaplain of the Holy Office of the Inquisition. Like the previous two studied here, this chaplain had responsibility for saying masses for the prisoners of the Inquisitorial jail. By the end of the century, three secular priests served as chaplains.³⁶ In addition to the salary, the Inquisition chaplains enjoyed other benefits, not the least of which was their status as employees of the Holy Office and their right to its *fuero*, along with the *familiares* and others. All three of the chaplains held down other positions. One was the night curate of the cathedral, another the sacristan of the cathedral, and the last the chaplain of the Church of Nuestra Señora de Monserrate. Like other chaplains, they also owed their posts to social and political connections. One was the son of the *contador* of the Inquisition while another had come to New Spain as the confessor of an inquisitor.

Thus, there were basically four types of chantries: privately endowed, privately administered; privately endowed, corporately administered; titular, of hospitals and convents; and institutional, of the audiencia and others.

Other Pious Works

The number of other pious works was indeed large, since any bequest that provided for ongoing support was a pious work. The foundation of colleges and convents, burial funds, and dowry funds all constituted pious works. The most important types of pious works for the secular clergy included the endowments for dowries and hospitals. Only a few colleges were founded or administered by the secular clergy.

There were several funds to provide dowries to orphaned Spanish girls. The one that appeared most in the records of the secular clergy of Mexico was the fund established by the alguacil mayor of Mexico City, García de Vega.[37] In his will in 1555, Vega divided his estate into two parts. One part went to his daughter, Ana de Vega; the other was to be invested in censos, the revenues from which went to his sister, Mayor de Vega. Upon her death the revenues from her half of his estate would become the income for a fund for marrying orphan girls. If by chance his daughter died without heirs, her share would also go into the fund. The patron of the fund was the cathedral chapter of Mexico. In 1569, after the death of Ana, the pious work achieved official foundation, also after a long suit between the cathedral chapter and García de Vega's other heirs.[38]

Legal battles continued, and only in 1575 did the chapter begin to organize the procedure for implementing the pious work. Finally, the chapter received 8,000 *pesos de minas* for the endowment. They resolved to give out the dowries on August 15, 1576, and thereafter annually on August 15, the feast of the Assumption of the Virgin.[39] The first selection was delayed until the first week of September 1576. Each of the eight girls received a dowry of 300 pesos.[40] The chapter also decided to pay 50 pesos a year to the cathedral for the administration of the endowment. The pious work continued to provide dowries for the rest of the sixteenth century. The girls competing for the award were interviewed annually by the members of the cathedral chapter. There were two basic qualifications: the girls had to be of pure Spanish ancestry and be orphans. The definition of orphan in this instance did not require the loss of both parents, merely the father.

The relationship of the chapter to the pious work was further strengthened by the presence of Álvaro de Vega, the nephew of García, who worked on the archdiocesan staff as *visitador general*, in spite of holding a prebend on the cathedral chapter of Puebla. Ultimately, in 1577 Álvaro became a canon on the Mexican chapter and took an active part in the endowment founded by his uncle. García had ordered that a chantry be established in the cathedral in conjunction with the dowry fund. Because of the family tie, the chapter named Álvaro as chaplain.

Hospitals

The endowment of hospitals was also a type of pious work. There were many hospitals in sixteenth-century New Spain. In Mexico City some of the more famous included the Hospital Amor de Dios, the Hospital San Lázaro, Hospital de la Concepción, de San Hipólito, de los Desamparados, and others.⁴¹ With the exception of the Hospital Amor de Dios, each of these had an endowment established by a patron, following the norms already seen for other pious works. The Hospital Amor de Dios, or Hospital de Bubas, was in fact founded by the first bishop of Mexico, Fr. Juan de Zumárraga, but it became institutionalized with the erection of the diocese of Mexico, and thereafter drew its revenues from the tithe, as well as its private endowment.⁴²

The epithet "de Bubas" recognized that the institution specialized in venereal and other skin diseases. The hospital had a varied endowment. As part of his episcopal revenues, Zumárraga had received the town of Ocuituco in encomienda. He transferred the income from this grant to the hospital, with royal approval in 1540. The encomienda was lost in 1544, following the promulgation of the New Laws.⁴³ To make up for the revenue lost to the hospital, the crown accepted partial patronage over the hospital. In the wake of these actions, a new constitution was drawn up for the hospital, a result of agreements between Viceroy Mendoza and Bishop Zumárraga. For his part, the bishop further donated several houses he had purchased in Mexico City to support the hospital.⁴⁴ As the actual administrators of the patronage, and a joint power with the bishop, the cathedral chapter formally recognized all the above. In a subsequent dispute with the diocese of Michoacán, three of the houses were confiscated and sold at auction to repay an alleged debt to the other diocese.⁴⁵ The loss of these possessions placed only a momentary pinch on the operating budget of the hospital, although continued royal support was requested to guarantee the financial strength of the hospital. Certainly the share the hospital received from the tithe was always an important source of income.

The Hospital Nuestra Señora de la Concepción (La Concepción de Nuestra Señora) was founded by the conqueror Hernán Cortés.⁴⁶ His endowment formed the major source of revenues for the institution, based on the tremendous wealth of income from his estate in the modern states of

Morelos, Mexico, and Oaxaca. The Cortés family, as seen, continued to participate actively in the patronage of the hospital throughout the sixteenth century.

The two hospitals, San Lázaro and the Desamparados, were founded by one of Mexico City's important early medical doctors, Dr. Pedro López. Upon his death, his heirs sought to have the institutions placed under royal patronage, to ensure their financial stability over and beyond the endowment. Dr. López's son, Dr. Jusepe López, a curate of the cathedral of Mexico, became mayordomo and administrator of the hospitals after his father's death.[47]

The Hospital of San Lázaro dealt specifically with caring for lepers while the Desamparados served as the Mexican capital's first foundling home. The exact source of the revenues for San Lázaro is unclear. Surely the family of Dr. López continued to support its work up until the early eighteenth century. The physical structure was large, including four wards, offices and rooms for the administration and workers, a chapel, and garden. In the case of the Desamparados the administration of the hospital fell to the heirs of Dr. López along with the Cofradía de Nuestra Señora de los Desamparados (del Tránsito de Nuestra Señora). The initial endowment reached only 2,700 pesos, placed in censos. Dr. López and the cofradía provided the remaining operating expenses. Upon his death the hospital fell under the administration of his son, as noted, although in 1599 the king accepted patronage. This arrangement lasted only until 1604, when the hospital was disbanded and passed to the control of the order of San Hipólito.[48]

The Hospital de San Hipólito had an interesting background in that a private ciitizen founded it. He had such concern over helping the ill in New Spain that he was instrumental in creating a religious order or brotherhood (Order of San Hipólito or Hermanos de la Caridad) to carry on this ministry. The founder, Bernardino Álvarez, wealthy from the trade with Perú, dedicated himself to curing the sick in 1556. Ten years later he began the hospital using his own wealth and donations of others.[49] The church of San Hipólito, however, belonged to the city of Mexico, as noted, since that saint was the patron of the city. The hospital grew up around the earlier structure, soon overtaking it. In 1584 the church was demolished to build a new one. The brotherhood founded by Álvarez went on to establish and acquire hospitals throughout New Spain, as seen in the case of the Desamparados.

These mark only some of the successful hospitals to be founded in the capital. Several of the most important foundations were not located in the capital city. The work of D. Vasco de Quiroga in endowing hospitals is well known.[50] Made famous by its location was the Hospital de Perote, located in the hills beyond the coastal plain behind Veracruz. It was a major center, curing travelers leaving the disease-ridden coastal region for the more healthful highlands. It was founded either by D. Francisco Rodríguez Santos, a canon, later treasurer, of the Mexico City cathedral chapter, or by Bishop D. Julián Garcés, first prelate of Puebla-Tlaxcala.[51]

Both Rodríguez Santos and D. Vasco de Quiroga demonstrated the close ties between one type of philanthropy and others. These men also used their private funds to endow educational facilities in addition to hospitals. Quiroga founded the famous Colegio de San Nicolás in Michoacán, while Rodríguez Santos founded the Colegio de Omnium Sanctorum in Mexico City.

Because these types of pious works were larger than the simple chantries, they required a much more complex endowment and administration. In his endeavors, Don Vasco de Quiroga established the Colegio de San Nicolás and his pueblo-hospitals as interlinking parts of a large system.[52] The pueblo-hospitals produced goods which they sold for income. The pueblo of Santa Fe de Mexico annually generated from 3,000 to 4,000 pesos at the time of Quiroga's death.[53] This income was then funneled into the colegio to provide for the education of young men to enter the priesthood. These young priests would then go back out into the pueblos to minister to the Indians.

Quiroga's endowment also had a complex patronage system of overlapping and ranked patrons. He requested that the monarch become the superior patron and ultimate defender of the pious works, administered through the viceroy and audiencia. Beneath the level of royal administration, the cathedral chapters of Mexico and Michoacán acted as patrons at the more immediate level. Finally, the rector of the colegio was the lowest patron, envisioned by Quiroga as deciding most of the day-to-day affairs of the system.[54]

At this point very little is known of the early years of the Perote Hospital. Some sources place its founding in 1541 by Bishop Garcés. Certainly by 1555 the hospital existed under the leadership of Rodríguez Santos. Viceroy Velasco also supported the work of the institution. Velasco and Rodríguez Santos finally agreed on a formula whereby the hospital would fall under royal patronage, with an annual grant of 1,000 *ducados*. Rodríguez became the administrator of the hospital.[55] Nevertheless, this was merely a temporary action and required royal approval, which by 1566 still had not arrived.[56] In the meantime the Hermanos de la Caridad, which had supported the institution under the guidance of Bernardino Álvarez, vacillated in its support. The day-to-day existence of the hospital was secured by 1568 when the Hermandad took over the operation.

The major work of Rodríguez Santos's philanthropy was the foundation of the Colegio de Santa María Omnium Sanctorum (Todos Santos). He began his efforts to create the college in 1565 but had to wait eight years before seeing them reach fruition. The school opened officially on August 15, 1573, the feast of the Assumption of the Virgin, patroness of the school. In addition to building the physical structure of the school, Rodríguez Santos provided an endowment which granted scholarships to ten students. The source of the endowment for faculty and operating expenses quite possibly also came from Rodríguez Santos. Up until the great flowering of the Jesuit schools, later in the century, the Colegio de Todos Santos was the best school in the realm, continuing even after the rise of the Jesuits.[57]

Although this study has focused on pious works founded or administered by the secular clergy, often the lines between the orders and the seculars were not so clear-cut. One example of this is the foundation of the convent of the Recogidas de la Encarnación. The founder and first patron of the house was the *maestrescuela* of the cathedral chapter of Mexico, Don Sancho Sánchez de Muñón. Don Sancho built his life in Mexico having served there for nearly half a century. His brother and family had even come out to join him. In return for services to the crown during the aborted Cortés Conspiracy, the king awarded Sánchez de Muñón an annual pension of 2,000 *ducados* from the tributes of Tehuacán, as noted in an earlier chapter. In addition to his position on the chapter, and the concomitant role as chancellor of the University of Mexico, Sánchez de Muñón also served as comisario general of the Santa Cruzada, with responsibility over thousands of pesos of revenue. One of his major pious works was the convent of La Encarnación. By the end of the sixteenth century the endowment was reputed to approach 20,000 pesos, mostly from Sánchez de Muñón's largesse. Nevertheless, he died suddenly, and in the subsequent battle over his estate, the convent lost most of the endowment.[58]

Pious works, considered as a whole, provided the church with some income. For most chantries, the overall sum going to the church hierarchy was about 10 percent of the revenues, to defray costs of materials. The rest of the annual interest went to clergy. In the case of the larger pious works, it is difficult to assess the degree to which the church and clergy benefited monetarily. In the colleges, young clerics could gain scholarships from the endowment, and these endowments helped to offset the cost of the education. One priest might also serve as chaplain to the institution. But the important function of the colleges was to improve the quality of priests in the region to the great benefit of society. Similarly, in the case of hospitals, the benefit to the church hierarchy was not so much financial as spiritual and physical. Outside of providing an income for the titular chaplain, the endowment usually paid the cost of medical treatments. Thus, although pious works involved huge sums of money, taken as a whole, the net proceeds to the hierarchy of the church were very low. What these institutions did, rather, was to provide a framework of charity, spiritual concern, and moral example within which the church operated and to create perpetual endowments for the support of priests. Thus, as time went by, priests did not have to rely as heavily on the tithe and parish revenues for a living income. The basic salary might come from these sources, but it would be augmented by income from pious works, especially *capellanias*.

Alms and Extraordinary Income

At present it is difficult to determine what percentage of priests did not serve an ecclesiastical post. The number was usually quite large, especially in the cities. By the end of the sixteenth century there were numerous chantries, and regulations on ordination sought to see that all priests had a regular income, yet there were still priests who did not hold a normal clerical post. For them, and for all levels of the heirarchy, the realm of alms, gifts, and outside occupations provided a significant source of income.

The most common source of additional income was the celebration of memorial masses, as distinct from masses in a perpetual chantry. Nearly every testament mandated that a series of these masses be said for the soul of the newly departed, his family and relatives, the souls in purgatory, and others. The stipend carried by these masses ranged from one-half to one peso. In addition to these simple masses, often the testator would ask that sung requiem masses be performed. These carried a much higher price, often as much as five pesos if all the vigils and responses were included.

Small estates might call for as few as a dozen memorial masses to be said in commemoration of the burial. Antón Jiménez, a *vecino* of Coatepec, ordered a total of seventy-eight masses said for his own soul and for others. In addition to these he requested one sung requiem mass with deacon and subdeacon. He was a small estate owner, listing six *caballerias* of land near Coatepec, his home in Coatepec, other houses in Chicolapa, and rights to two freshwater springs. He had outstanding debts of under 200 pesos, while others owed him 422 pesos. He was clearly a man with enough wealth and sense of social standing to draw up a will. Therefore his case may be taken as a low minimum for these masses.[59]

An example of an average bequest for memorial masses comes from the testament of Cosme García, mentioned above. In his will he ordered over 400 incidental masses. The records of the administration of the estate indicate that fifteen different priests said the masses, including two regulars. The largest single sum was 100 pesos to Maestro Francisco Gómez Ronquillo, *cura* of the cathedral. The price paid for these masses was one-half peso each. Subtracting the one large payment to Gómez Ronquillo, the average collected by each of the others was slightly less than eight pesos.[60]

It was not uncommon to find testaments that called for even greater numbers of masses to be said. In his will, Antonio Freire, first hermit of the sanctuary of Nuestra Señora de Guadalupe and founder of the Congregación de San Pedro, called for 1,000 masses to be said for his soul, those of his relatives, and for the souls in purgatory. He further ordered, as did most people, that the masses be said at those altars where they would receive additional indulgences.[61]

Individuals requesting these mortuary masses could be very specific in their demands. Common requirements were that the masses be said before particular altars, or for particular individuals in addition to the benefactor. Often, because of close ties to a religious order, or the secular clergy, the individual might ask that all masses be said by one order, or a special combination of priests. For example, Pedro López de Proano, a secular priest, who lived as an estate owner rather than practice his clerical profession, asked that eight hundred masses be said upon his death: six hundred for his own soul, one hundred for the souls in purgatory, and another hundred for those people to whom he was obligated. Furthermore, he mandated that these masses be said only by poor secular priests and not by members of religious orders.[62]

Other ecclesiastical revenue came from testaments, such as simple gifts to particular churches. These gifts did not go toward paying individual priests but rather were used to purchase and maintain ornaments of the church. Nearly every will granted several of these gifts, ranging in value from a few pesos to thousands. Every testament recognized the *mandas forzososas*, bequests ordered by law. These gifts were a pittance but had to be given to make the will legal. In the accounts of the division of the estate of Cosme García, the *mandas forzosas* came to only five pesos, paid to Dr. Pedro López. One assumes that the money was then used in the Hospital of San Lázaro, the project of Dr. López.[63]

Some of these bequests provided the funds for the acquisition of the monumental works of art in Mexican churches. Nevertheless, the number of these in the sixteenth century was limited. This type of gift was credited to the account of the fabric of the church. This source of income was usually so inconsequential that it represented one of the smallest entries in the yearly fabric accounts. In the cathedral in 1557 the gifts to the fabric amounted to half again as much as the income from the 10 percent on chantries, 157 *pesos de oro de minas* as compared to 105 *pesos de minas*.[64] But the alms could fluctuate greatly from year to year. In 1574 the total alms reached 11 *pesos de oro de minas*. Two years later it was 51 pesos. Nevertheless, even this latter amount is relatively insignificant in an account that had 4,610 *pesos de oro de minas* annual income.

Churches other than the cathedral received tokens of largess from the dying. In the case of Antonio Freire, noted above, his will ordered that 2,000 pesos be given to the sanctuary and hermitage of Our Lady of Guadalupe. The gift was earmarked for improvement of the physical structure, to make it more sturdy and sumptuous, *"de cal y canto."* To assure that his will would be carried out, Freire stipulated that the construction had to begin within three years and not last over twelve.[65] It might be pointed out that four years before his death, in testimony before the Inquisition, Freire claimed to be 102 years old, thus making him 106 at his death.

Pious works and alms, then, served the church in numerous ways. The major difference between them was the scale, in terms of both endowment and duration. The pious work served as a continual and perpetual example of the religious piety of the founder. It likewise served the church in an on-going fashion. Alms, on the other hand, constituted a far smaller portion of the total clerical income. The money provided by them served individual priests and specific churches. They had no inherent perpetual nature and were meant to be utilized in the short term. Yet for many unemployed and underemployed priests in the urban areas, alms must have been an eagerly sought after source of needed income.

The growth of the church in the late sixteenth and early seventeenth century came as a result of the increase in the number of pious works. The administration of the works offered revenue and employment to the church and to priests; the capital with which the institutions were endowed went to benefit the economy as a whole by providing investment capital for the further growth of the economy. The requirement that the capital be loaned in a mortgage placed on property limited the extent to which any group other than the elite could participate. Nevertheless, all the forces within the society pressed for the further expansion of pious works because the institution as a whole provided benefits for all.

In modern Latin America the church has often come under attack for its extensive holdings in capital and real estate. Much of this wealth has been acquired through various pious works established over the centuries. Possession of this tremendous wealth was viewed by the liberal politicians of the early nineteenth century as being contrary to the economic well-being of the nation, since wealth tied up by the church was not productive.[66] The assumption made at the time was that all church wealth was held in mortmain, and was thereby inalienable, and furthermore that once the church acquired wealth, the capital it represented could no longer be used to improve the economy.

After very humble beginnings in the sixteenth century, the number of pious works created in later centuries was tremendous. By the end of the colonial period it has been estimated that as much as half of all land and capital was held by the church. Likewise, through the use of capital from pious works, the church dominated the financial market of the colony. When the endowments of the chantries and other pious works were taken over by the royal government in 1804, the total value was estimated at 44.5 million pesos, the bulk of which was in land and credit, rather than cash.[67] Nevertheless, in the diocese of Guadalajara at the same time, loans made by the church accounted for only about one-third of the total mortgages issued annually. This demonstrates a marked decrease over the century. During the twenty years from 1721 to 1740 mortgages from the church represented 71 percent of the total mortgage market value. By the last twenty years of the colonial period, 1798–1820, this figure declined to 24.6 percent of the market.[68] The decline confirms data for the district of León, where in the decade 1780–90 church loans provided

32 percent of the loan capital, while miners and merchants loaned out the remaining 68 percent.[69]

Using these figures to extrapolate backward, the general trend indicates that in the late sixteenth century the church must have provided the largest share of credit in the economy. Before studying global credit figures further, one must take into consideration that pious works could have any of three types of endowment: land, cash, and liens or encumbrances. Within the church records these types were noted as only two categories, land and censos. Nevertheless, for the founder there was a considerable difference between an endowment in cash and an encumbrance. In the case of the former, he actually had to put up cash or other instruments which could be redeemed for cash. In the latter he merely pledged his own real property as the basis for an encumbrance. The church had to loan out the cash it received, usually placing an encumbrance on the property of the recipient. Thus, for the church the two endowments ultimately became encumbrances.

Global figures for the reserves in endowment for the church seldom distinguish between the three types. In discussing the period after 1765, Arnold Bauer has concluded that most chantries and pious works were founded on encumbrances and not on cash donations or land.[70] Nevertheless, when one looks at the fragmentary data available for the sixteenth century, a different picture emerges. Of fifty-one chantries for which foundation documents exist, nineteen were founded on cash, sixteen on land, and only eleven on encumbrances. Even if all the cases of uncertainty are taken into account, an equal number of pious works were established on cash as on liens.

The economic function of the pious work was very important. Rather than being a nonproductive investment in terms of the overall economy, the pious work helped to provide badly needed investment capital for the economy. The provision of investment capital is clearest in the case of the cash endowment, which the church would in turn loan out at interest, secured with real property. But in the case of the encumbrance a similarly important phenomenon was at work. To the initial mortgagee, an obligation was created where none had existed before, and he did not enjoy receipt of cash; yet in terms of the economy as a whole capital had been formed. The lien placed on the property could, at some future date, be repaid and when that occurred the capital created with the institution of the encumbrance would enter into the immediate credit market.[71]

While the bulk of obligations studied in the sixteenth century were placed on urban real estate, much evidence shows that rural real estate was equally encumbered.[72] The combination of the tithe and the foundation of pious works made the church become intimately involved in the agricultural sector. Large estate owners could participate in pious works in three ways. They could receive the capital from the foundations of others and pledge their land as security. They could merely use their own land as an endowment, either in free gift or as security for a lien. Lastly, they could use the profits from the land to provide a cash endowment. In all these cases, the pious work financial complex meant that production on the estate would in one way or another pass to the church credit market. The tithe, as a simple 10 percent tax on production, had a similar effect in draining production from the estates. In the end, then, the church represented a major recipient of production, in cash and goods, of the agricultural sector.

In spite of the drain that the church placed on the agricultural sector, estate owners also benefited. Because church loans required security based on land, the landowners were essentially the only ones who could borrow from the church. The church provided a source of capital available for expansion and development of the land. Of course, not all of the loans went to rural estates. As noted, much was invested in urban real estate. In general, however, the same group of individuals tended to benefit—members of the elite who owned land, be it urban or rural. In terms of the other two sectors of the economy, mining and commerce, in order to benefit from the capital available for speculation, individual miners and merchants had to have access to land upon which loans could be secured. Thus, either they had to diversify their own holdings, or they had to enter into credit arrangements with individuals who did own land. These requirements tied the three sectors of the economy even closer and played into the process of the formation of the great estates. This question will be dealt with in the last chapter.

Certainly capital acquired by the church reentered the colonial economy to continue to be productive. Likewise lands owned by the church did not necessarily fall into mortmain. In the chantries studied here, of those founded on land, half saw the property endowment sold within a score of years, either for cash to reestablish the chantry or to acquire a better piece of property upon which to base the pious work. Indeed, in general the church bought and sold land to a greater degree than its critics in the early nineteenth century recognized.[73]

In one sense, the institution of pious works took excess capital from the economy and then recycled it. Profits from any of the three sectors might be put up as the endowment for a pious work and then be loaned out to the agricultural sector. But through the use of diversification by miners and merchants into real estate, or by contracts between miners and merchants and landowners, the capital could then flow back into the general system wherever it was needed. The encumbrance can be viewed as a long-term removal of excess capital, to reenter the economy later. Moreover, the revenues from all types of pious works helped to fuel the economy since priests used their incomes to support themsevles and pay living expenses. Thus, within the family and within the economy as a whole the pious works played a tremendously important role in the late sixteenth century.

5. *The Critical Decade*

The decade 1575–85 was a watershed for the church in Mexico. Changes occurred on a wide range of fronts, leading to a sweeping transformation of the institution. The forces of change pressed on the church internally and from many different directions including the crown and the economy. The ways in which the church reacted to these stresses and reforms would dictate the patterns that would characterize the institution for the rest of the century and up to the recent past. This chapter will study several of these pressures that affected the church in the decade and focus on the modifications that ensued.

The Epidemic of 1576

Within the colony as a whole, perhaps the major event of this period was the devastating epidemic of 1576, striking Indians more than Spaniards. The pestilence probably continued to vex the native population until 1581. Several scholars have studied the tragedy, both for its demographic implications and as an episode in medical history.[1] Between 1568 and 1580 the native population declined from 2.6 million to 1.9 million or by over a quarter. In the period from 1568 to 1595, the drop reached 48 percent.[2] The extent of the pestilence has led some historians to posit that the colony underwent a drastic reorganization. The loss of Indian population, which provided the bulk of the work force, created the need for either new technologies or new sources of labor. When neither fully resolved the crisis, the colony entered into a period of depression, according to the argument.³ In recent years others have questioned both the extent and nature of this depression, since some industries, such as mining, reached record levels of output before the end of the century.⁴ Yet the church certainly felt the full impact of the epidemic.

Even with a wide range of sources of income, the church in the sixteenth century faced a financial crisis in the decade following the Indian epidemic of 1576. Since Indians provided a significant portion of the labor for the agricultural sector, mortality directly affected overall production. In turn, the church relied heavily on agricultural production for its major source of income, the tithe. The net effect was that Indian mortality caused a serious shortage of clerical revenues after 1576.

Given the complex system of tithe collection and distribution, and all its vagaries, one would assume that there would be minor fluctuations in total receipts from one year to the next. Nevertheless, from 1550 to 1574 tithe collections in Mexico, Michoacán, and Guadalajara climbed at a fairly steady rate, doubling or even trebling in the quarter century (see Fig. 9). This trend reflected both the increasing Spanish agricultural production and more efficient tithe collection. In the diocese of Oaxaca the pattern of tithe revenues was somewhat different. From 1562, when the record begins, until 1568 the gross income actually declined. Then in 1575 the tithe income reached a new peak, only to decline again slightly and remain stagnant until 1582 when it began to rise again. In quite a different fashion, in Puebla the earliest revenues were terribly small, with a slow steady growth until 1556, a decline of one year, and then a meteoric rise, with some fluctuations until 1579. The tithe dropped off but rebounded by 1582. Then the tithe data are missing until the early years of the seventeenth century.

While no distinctive pattern emerges from the rise and fall of the tithe receipts of these five dioceses, several trends

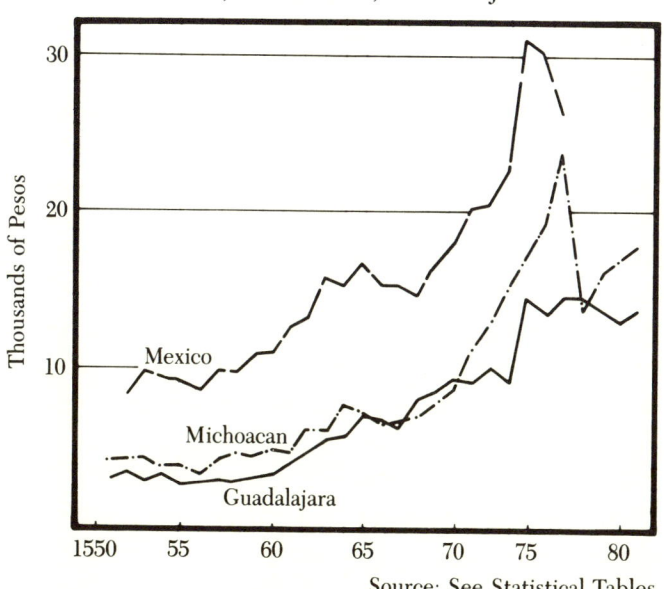

Figure 9.
Gross Tithe Revenues:
Mexico, Michoacán, Guadalajara

The Critical Decade

Source: See Statistical Tables

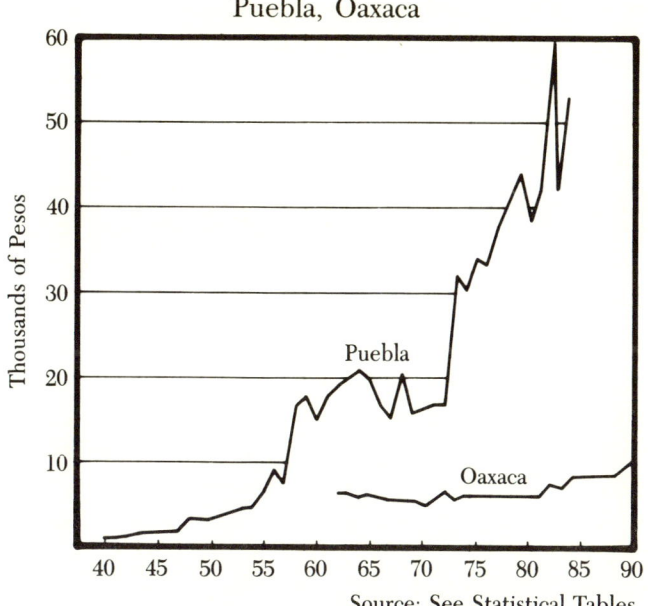

Figure 10.
Gross Tithe Revenues:
Puebla, Oaxaca

Source: See Statistical Tables

were in effect. In Mexico, Michoacán, and Guadalajara the tithe rose before 1576, dropped off sharply, and remained depressed for approximately ten years. In Oaxaca there was no sharp drop in 1576, but the tithe did stagnate. In Puebla between 1576 and 1582 the tithe remained relatively stable, with a drop in 1580. Thus in Oaxaca and Puebla one would not expect to find any major disruption of ecclesiastical activities because of tithe revenues. In Mexico, Michoacán, and Guadalajara, on the other hand, cost-cutting action must have been taken, for a true fiscal crisis seems to have been in effect.

The exact chronology of the crisis may never be known. Detailed tithe and pay records for the cathedrals no longer exist, and what documentation does remain comes from disparate sources, inhibiting comparison. The earliest extant documentary indication of financial difficulty is from 1578. Either the chapter or the archbishop of Mexico wrote to the king predicting large-scale dismissals of the staff unless cathedral income rose.[5] This may have been an attempt on the part of the Mexican church to speed up royal largess in the redonation of the royal ninth. The last grant had lapsed in 1571. Furthermore, between 1574 and 1578, the king had been reorganizing the basis of the royal patronage over the church, as will be seen later, and investigating the use of the donated ninth. At this time, information was also sought on the nature and extent of chantries in the cathedral, and the use of the *excusado* and fabric fund of the tithe. In short, the crown was clearly attempting to reevaluate the financial operations of the cathedral.[6] At any rate, predictions of financial doom were not uncommon in correspondence from ecclesiastical authorities to the king. Thus, complaints of poverty would not prove the existence of fiscal problems.

In 1581, the cathedral chapter of Mexico continued its complaints of poverty, humbly requesting the redonation of the king's fund, now in abeyance for a decade. They wrote:

It is a great pity that in a land where many of the rivers flow with gold, hills and mountains are of silver, and in the cliffs and ridges one finds precious stones: that there should be for Him the Creator of all things, and Who made Your Grace the King and Lord, a house of adobe, falling down and without ministers nor ornaments with which to be honored.[7]

The next rumblings of serious financial straits came in early July 1582. On the third of the month, the chapter resolved to prohibit all cathedral staff members from filing suits to collect back pay. All employees had to swear to abide by the ruling as a requirement for their further employment. In the minutes of the meeting the secretary copied the resolution:

If you wish to serve this Holy Church in your offices it will be with the conditions imposed: that they have to wait to collect their salaries until the Holy Church has enough to comfortably pay them, and they will drop any action or proceeding against this Church, and will not have and do not have any right against this Church.[8]

At their next meeting, the chapter members voted to cut back the majority of the singers' and musicians' salaries by 50 per cent, acting out the threat sent to the king four years earlier. The chapel master's pay suffered a cut from 600 pesos to 300. Several cantors who had enjoyed salaries of 200 pesos ended up with only 50.[9] In so doing, the chapter managed to trim the annual music budget from 2,310 pesos to 1,665, a savings of 645. All that, however, equaled the salary loss from the tithe of just one dignitary. In the wake of these cuts, almost all of the singers and musicians resigned their posts, including those chapter members who had taken on additional duties in the musical ensemble. Several weeks later the chapter continued the program of fiscal restraint. It resolved to distribute each member's share of the tithe in kind and not in money, thus guaranteeing each prebendary with a supply of food and the opportunity to sell his goods at the higher Mexico City price. The accountant was fired, or he resigned, and the chapter drew up the proper papers for excommunicating all persons who still owed the tithe from 1577.[10]

Archbishop Pedro Moya de Contreras became personally involved in the situation in late August 1582. He called on both the chapter and the musical staff to get together again and return to the status quo ante. He expressed the hope that a grant from the king to the cathedral would arrive in the fall, on the next fleet. The king had continually donated his percentage of tithe funds to the church in Mexico for varying periods since 1534.[11] Moya indicated that the money in the grant would pay the back wages, among other things. He made that supposition based on the knowledge that the king usually allocated his share of the tithe for a set period running from when the previous gift had ended. Thus Moya counted on the redonation not only beginning in 1583 but filling in the past gaps. With this, the musical confrontation ended, although no mention of it appeared in the meetings of the chapter. By the next year, 1583, the chapel master had returned to work, and the chapter had granted him a pay raise, back up to 400 pesos, although still below his previous high of 600. Yet financial concerns still occupied a major part of the chapter's time. In April 1583, for instance, the cabildo renewed a suit against the diocese of Michoacán over the tithe rights to the Querétaro region, a suit that had lain dormant for years, in fact since the postepidemic year of 1577.[12]

All these events lead one to the inevitable conclusion that something went awry with church revenues. The tithe, as the major source of income, appears the logical culprit. The cathedral chapter expended an enormous amount of energy at increasing tithe income, appointing new accountants and administrators, and even renewing the suit against Michoacán. Judging from the actions on the part of the Mexican *cabildo eclesiástico* and the contemporary records of the Michoacán and Guadalajara tithe collection, a serious stagnation of the tithe revenues seems evident. Whatever problems there were with normal tithe collections, the situation must have been aggravated by the king's refusal to grant the two-ninths since 1571.

It would appear that the Indian epidemic of 1576 had a devastating effect on agricultural production in Michoacán. While the tithe return for 1576 itself manifested the same impressive growth pattern as the previous six years, the 1577 tithe fell dramatically. Tithe revenues in Michoacán had escalated rapidly from 1570 to 1576. In the earlier year the total income before distribution equaled 8,720 *pesos de minas*. This figure increased steadily until it reached 23,563 in 1576. Nevertheless, the 1577 total, before division, amounted to only 13,714 *pesos de minas*. This dramatic decline must have come as a tremendous surprise for the cathedral chapter of Michoacán, for in October 1577, it had predicted a tithe collection of 30,000 pesos for the year.[13] The figures for the next three years imply only a partial recovery. While the level of the tithe receipts did not decline again as precipitously as it did in 1577, neither did it demonstrate the rapid growth it exhibited before 1576. If these figures for 1577–80 are accurate, the income to the Michoacán church fluctuated dramatically, finally stabilizing near the 17,000-peso level.

The Michoacán case appears even more severe in the province of Colima since the Indian epidemic coincided with a killing frost, which completely devastated the cacao crop. In 1576 the cacao tithe from Colima reached 1,214 *pesos de minas*. In 1577 nothing remained to tithe. In fact, the total cacao tithe for the whole diocese that year barely amounted to 650 pesos.

The curve described by the tithe collections from Guadalajara closely follows that of Michoacán. The tithe grew rapidly between 1570 and 1574, with collections reaching 9,360 pesos in the earlier and 14,310 in the latter year. Nevertheless, in Guadalajara no tremendous drop in the tithe receipts occurred following 1576; rather they leveled off at the 14,000-peso level. This implies a period of economic stagnation, if not depression, for the church in that region. Their first decline, in 1574, probably resulted from routine fluctuations, while the extended flattening out of the revenues resulted from the aftereffects of the epidemic.

Comparing these trends to the situation in Mexico, the severe economic crisis suffered in 1577 had its impact some four or five years later when the cathedral chapter felt the tithe pinch. The curve of tithe collections in Mexico closely repeated the pattern established by the other two dioceses. Both Mexico and Guadalajara felt the first impact of stagnation in 1574. Unfortunately, no records remain for the crucial years following 1576 in Mexico. Nevertheless, the story told by the events of 1582 bears witness to the effects of a diminished tithe revenue. When the agricultural economy suffered its crisis in 1576, the cathedral chapter did not begin to cut back on expenditures. In fact, the chapter joined the other corporations and religious institutions in Mexico City to help lessen the suffering of the Indians during the epidemic.[14]

Even when finances became tight for the cathedral, nothing was done. The cathedral budget was being pinched, after all, not only by declining tithe revenues, but also by the absence of the king's fund. That fund had been allocated to the fabric account, from which the musical staff was paid. Thus, those employees became the first casualties of the drop in income. Only after the musicians began to file suits against the chapter for back wages did it take any action. Perhaps the administrators of the tithe, as well as the full chapter, did not recognize the magnitude of the financial crisis, or the potential crisis, at the time. Because of the slowness of the tithe collection, often at least three years would pass before all the money reached the coffers of the archdiocese.[15]

In 1583 the Mexican crisis eased. The royal grant did arrive, effective January 3, 1583.[16] One year later the chapter authorized the staff to collect their full salaries, not even discounting the ten nonexistent days between October 5 and October 15, 1583, when the colony changed over to the new Gregorian calendar. The royal accountants, however, assiduously subtracted ten days' pay from all royal pay vouchers. The severity of the Mexican experience appears even more significant when one considers that between June 1579 and December 1584 the cathedral did collect over 24,000 pesos from the royal treasury on the old royal grant and from the tithe that the monarch had to pay on tribute paid to him in kind.[17] With the normal gross annual income from the tithe amounting to over 30,000 *pesos de oro común*, the cathedral's financial straits were such that even these infusions of cash from the royal treasury could not avert the financial predicament. In late 1584 the crown began to refurbish the cathedral, thus relieving the fabric of further expenditures.[18] While the church certainly welcomed, encouraged, and pleaded for these payments from the crown's treasury, as shown by Moya's words of optimism in the depths of the crisis, these funds in no way permitted the cathedral to return to its previous level of spending.

In the late 1580s, the economic problems of the Mexican cathedral seem to have abated. The chapter did pass certain resolutions pertaining to pay cuts and tithe administration, and others enjoining employees from filing suit for back pay, but none of these showed the frenzied concern of the 1582–83 crisis. By the early 1590s, chapter revenues had increased, as had the tithe, reaching the preepidemic high. The tithe reportedly reached 42,000 *pesos de oro común* in 1594, which meant a salary of 1,293 pesos for the dean and 1,120 for the other dignitaries. These figures compare favorably to the pay scale for 1571 but are still 25 percent below the 1576 level.

Certain changes in bookkeeping in the late 1580s and early 1590s might have contributed in part to lower chapter salaries. First of all, in the 1580s the cathedral accountants began to follow the proportions stipulated in the constitutional bull. The chapter members also decided to receive part of their tithe portion in kind and not money, and this may or may not be reflected in the record of the salaries. But these two factors cannot totally account for the sharp decline in general cathedral revenues and the decline and depression of cathedral salaries between 1576 and 1582. Changes in allocation, allotment, or even bookkeeping of the tithe do not adequately explain the drop in overall church revenues suffered in three different dioceses. Thus, while malfeasance on the part of the collectors, collusion on the part of the chapter, or avoidance on the part of the producers might explain annual fluctuations in one diocese, it is unlikely that three separate dioceses would suffer the same decline in revenues from these man-made causes all at the same time.

Other church records also indicate that a financial crisis was at hand following 1576. As late as the turn of the century, the church was still resolving some of the collection contracts for 1576. In 1597 the chapter agreed to renegotiate the rental contract for the tithe on wool, cheese, milk, and butter for 1576. The original obligation had been for 4,670 *pesos de minas*, but by 1597 the renters still owed 3,318. The failure was directly attributed to the "*cocolistli* and general mortality which occurred among the Indians that year."[19] Similarly several contracts for later years were also being renegotiated. In 1600 the chapter, through the tithe administrator Canon Antonio de Salazar, agreed to extend the obligation of the renter of the tithe from Tulancingo for 1582–85.[20]

The failure rate of tithe rental contracts clearly had much to do with the health of the agricultural economy. Tithe renters based their bids on past production, plus whatever insight they might have had into the current conditions. In times of an expanding agricultural economy the error was usually on the side of the renter, thus allowing him a greater profit. In times of a contracting economy, however, the actual value of the tithe could be far below the bid price, thus ultimately leading to default. In bidding for any given year the renter wished to remain below what he believed the actual value of the tithe would be, yet still high enough to win the contract over other bidders. His margin for error was actually quite small. Since the church relied so heavily on the tithe for its day-to-day operations, especially in the cathedrals, a miscalculation by the tithe renters could be disastrous, as seen in the previous example.

Taking a further look at the tithe receipts for all of New Spain, the impact of the epidemic is clear. Only the dioceses of Oaxaca and Puebla did not suffer outright declines in their tithe revenues. As noted, they did go into a period of little or no growth. Comparing the gross tithe income for the entire *gobierno* of Mexico in 1562, 1576, and 1580, one can begin to study the overall effect of the epidemic on the agricultural economy. The gross tithe for all of New Spain in 1562 was 58,297 pesos, which means that the value of the total agricultural production was nearly 583,000 pesos. One can obtain a rough estimate of gross agricultural production by multiplying the total tithe revenue by ten, although this is far from exact. The rate on some commodities was less than 10 percent, but the practice of tithe renting also netted less revenue to the church than a full 10 percent of production. In general, the error-producing factors tend to cancel out one another. For 1576 the gross tithe for New Spain was 146,819 pesos, fully twice that of 1562, indicating a global agricultural economy of 1,468,000 pesos. In 1580, in the throes of the epidemic and depression, the aggregate tithe revenues reached only 134,108 pesos, from a calculated overall agricultural output of 1,341,000 pesos. One can conclude that the decline experienced by Michoacán, Guadalajara, and Mexico, combined with the stagnation of Oaxaca and Puebla, yielded a colony-wide depression of the agricultural economy.

This analysis merely addresses the question of total production in monetary terms. In a preindustrial society with only market forces at work, the supply and prices of goods fluctuate in a fixed ratio as long as the demand remains constant. If one assumes that the Indian population acquired its food through subsistence agriculture, rarely relying on the Spanish marketplace, then the demand for agricultural goods in the Spanish market would be generated by the Spaniards and other non-Indians.[21] The population of those groups tended to increase as the Indian population declined, perhaps doubling between 1570 and 1640.[22] Thus, during the actual epidemic, since the labor force was rapidly dying, the overall production of food should have declined. If the demand was constant, the unit price would rise. If the demand increased, the unit price would increase even faster. One can also imagine that when faced with widespread pestilence, Indians had to rely on purchased food, thus increasing the global demand. In short, prices should have increased as a result of the epidemic, and there is evidence they did.[23] A price increase means that the decline in tithe revenues actually represents an even greater decline in the total quantity of agricultural goods being produced.

At this point it is impossible to know for certain if the epidemic and subsequent depression had any immediate effect on church financial policy. Conditions for tithe renters became more stringent, and they had to post higher bonds. As seen, the cathedral chapter actively petitioned the crown for an extension of the donation of the royal ninth. At the same time, church officials sought to increase revenues out of the tithe in every possible way, including taxing the Indians and the religious orders, and attempting to increase the taxation district. But all of these actions merely demonstrated that the church remained committed to the tithe as the major source of revenue. As will be seen later in this chapter, the epidemic of 1576 had a further impact on the overall economy which directly affected the financial basis of the church. Changes in the agricultural sector leading to the formation of the great haciendas and developments in mining and commerce all created a group of wealthy individuals willing to invest in the church in the form of pious works. Thus, it is possible that *capellanias* began to play a greater role at this time. The limited cases available suggest that by century's end the number of chantries began to grow rapidly; certainly the invested capital of the chantry provided a more constant source of income than did the tithe.

The Ordenanza del Patronazgo

In the countryside the tithe had never played a particularly important role in paying clerical wages. Yet during the decade 1575–85 another important change occurred— the promulgation and implementation of the Ordenanza del Patronazgo of 1574.[24] The major thrust of this code was to increase the power of the secular clergy at the expense of the regulars. Furthermore, it placed all parish clergy, secular and regular, more firmly under the control of the monarch and the royal bureaucracy.

The Ordenanza de Patronazgo had a profound impact on the secular clergy. The Ordenanza began with a brief discussion of the concept of royal patronage and a historical justification of the Spanish kings' claims to such powers. The next part defined the royal patronage over all positions receiving a benefice and over all ecclesiastical buildings, such as churches, monasteries, votive chapels, convents, and the like. The only two items not strictly included in the royal patronage were private chapels and privately endowed *capellanias*. The latter clearly did not fall under the crown, since private funds created them. The cathedral chapter, when asked for an opinion on the subject, replied that to declare all *capellanias* under royal patronage would deny a living to the majority of priests, since there would be little incentive for private parties to create the posts.[25]

The third paragraph of the Ordenanza clarified the archbishop's right to substitution on the cathedral chapter. The resolution presented in the Ordenanza restricted the prelate's appointive power to only four substitutes and only in the event that fewer than four prebends still served their posts. In this way the archbishop could promote all four substitutes only if no royal appointees still served. The ordinance effectively eliminated the archbishop's power to appoint to the chapter, since by 1578 the chapter had its full complement of twenty-seven members. As a clarification of this paragraph, the Ordenanza further stipulated that no substitute could receive canonical possession of a prebend unless he also received a royal appointment. Thus the substitutes served only *ad interim* until a royal appointee could arrive. The Ordenanza also assured that all recipients of royal presentations, both to prebends and to simple *beneficios*, would receive the fruits of their posts quickly. The subsequent two items in the ordinances required that all persons presented to prebends hold university degrees, that they receive quick possession of their seats, and that four special canonries take the place of the first four to become vacant. This stipulation followed a decree of the Council of Trent that four titular canonries be established on each chapter. These posts became important in the seventeenth and eighteenth centuries in Mexico and fall beyond the scope of this work. The first of them appeared in 1597 in Puebla-Tlaxcala.

The middle section of the Ordenanza outlined the procedure for filling simple benefices. These, as noted, fell directly under the royal patronage because the crown assumed the ultimate responsibility for paying the wages. The ordinances declared that once such a post became vacant, for whatever reason (all were considered vacant upon creation), the archbishop had to announce the vacancy publicly and call for applicants to the post. All those who applied for the post had twenty days within which to present their credentials. All then participated in a public competition and examination for the job, an *oposición*. Upon presentation as an *opositor*, each person if unknown to the archdiocesan officials, had to file a declaration telling, first, if he was a conqueror's son and, second, how long he had spent in the administration of an Indian parish, either within the archdiocese or elsewhere. These two points entitled the applicant to special consideration. Three or four high-ranking clerics formed the board of examiners, appointed by the archbishop from among chapter members and university professors. The examination itself first dealt with the candidate's competency in an Indian language, usually Nahuatl or Otomí. A test of general knowledge over any subject taught in the schools followed, along with a quiz on the details of the latest breviary. These three tests allowed the examiners to ascertain whether or not the candidate could handle an Indian parish according to the current norms and whether or not he had any general education beyond purely ecclesiastical matters.

The board of examiners then recommended two clerics from among those tested to the viceroy, who acted as vice-patron for the king. Invariably the viceroy chose the first of the two persons recommended. Acting within the royal patronage he then gave the chosen cleric a *provisión real* for the benefice. This document, carrying the royal seal, named the parish, the salary, the source from which to collect the salary, and any conditions placed on the appointment. The provenance of the salary was important in parishes that included towns both in encomienda and under the crown.

The chosen priest then presented his *provisión* to the archbishop, or the provisor, who ordered the examiners to test the appointee once more, to ensure that he could serve the post capably. This second exam invariably occurred and constituted a major obstacle for priests arriving from Spain carrying *provisiones reales* from the king. After the second test the priest then received his canonical institution to the post, allowing him to enjoy the revenues from it perpetually. Theoretically the archbishop could withhold or withdraw the ecclesiastical recognition, *colación*, of the *beneficiado*. The *colación* granted the ecclesiastical right to administer the sacraments in the *beneficio*. The archbishop seldom withheld the *colación*, fearing a major church-state conflict. The *colación* gained real importance, once again, with priests who figured outside the *oposición* system, carrying *provisiones* from Spain. After receiving *colación*, the priest then had to present himself with all these documents in the *partido* within a given time limit and take actual possession of the benefice.

The last section of the Ordenanza defined the criteria for judging all candidates for benefices and prebends. First of all, those priests who had served in the conversion and instruction of the Indians, in the administration of the sacraments to them, or in other direct service to them were preferred over all others. Following these, the sons of the conquerors and others who had served the king ranked next in consideration. All those interested in receiving a benefice from the crown had to present a *relación de méritos* to the king and Council of the Indies and file a copy with the local ecclesiastical authorities before participating in an *oposición*.

The promulgation of the Ordenanzas had two major effects on the financial basis of the church in Mexico. On the one hand, it gave the local parish priest even further guarantees on the security of his salary. On the other, it established the principle that the regular orders would eventually leave parochial service and be placed under the jurisdiction of the local bishop. These two goals took years to come to fruition. Immediately, however, the parish priests began to feel the increased certainty of their salaries. The royal provision that granted them the benefice clearly outlined the responsibilities for payment of the clerical salaries between encomenderos and the royal treasury. This legal principle gave the parish priest the opportunity to have recourse to the royal courts for collection of his past due salary, thus further strengthening his ability to collect. In fact, in the ensuing years these suits did crop up.[26] The parish priest then enjoyed the full force of the royal government when it came to collecting his salary.

The other effect, of limiting the role of the regular clergy in the countryside, was long in being fully elaborated. It was not until the eighteenth century that the regular clergy finally left their rural parishes. In the intervening centuries there were some tremendous battles between the seculars and the regulars over questions raised by the Ordenanza. The greatest of the battles was whether or not the regulars fell under the jurisdiction of the local bishops. Claiming papal privilege, the orders declared themselves free of both episcopal and royal control. When the battle was finally joined in the seventeenth century it was precisely over the question of ecclesiastical revenues. The bishops demanded that the regular orders pay the tithe on the agricultural production of their rural estates. The Jesuits in particular refused to pay, citing the privileges outlined above. The bishop replied that until the order placed itself under his jurisdiction, especially in questions pertaining to parochial administration, the order could not be considered an ecclesiastical institution for the purposes of avoiding the tithe.[27] Other religious groups, such as the Order of San Hipólito, did pay the tithe on their rural estates, and so the question was by no means a clear-cut one.

The timing of the Ordenanza was particularly appropriate in light of the severe financial crisis felt economically by the church as a result of the Indian mortality. At the same time that the church was recovering from the effects of the epidemic, the regular orders were beginning their rapid acquisition of rural property.[28] This movement was spearheaded by the Jesuits, but other orders followed suit, with the exception of the Franciscans. Thus, the competition for sources of income created further tension between the secular and regular clergy. Interestingly enough, the decade of the 1570s marked another watershed because the regular orders by that time had reached their greatest territorial expansion. From that time on they would slowly lose parishes, while their membership increased. Thus the very nature of competition between the secular and regular clergy changed at the time of the promulgation of the Ordenanza del Patronazgo and the epidemic of 1576. As will be elaborated later, before the 1570s the competition centered on the acquisition of parishes; afterward, the competition focused on securing revenues.

Third Provincial Council

Further changes involving the secular clergy resulted from the famous Third Provincial Council of 1585.[29] This meeting of the bishops of the ecclesiastical province of Mexico had as its goal the implementation of the reforms of the Council of Trent in New Spain. The decrees of the provincial council were to govern Mexico well into the twentieth century. Four major documents came from the meeting. The most important were the decrees themselves.[30] Yet accompanying these orders were three other landmark works. One was a catechism to be used throughout the ecclesiastical province. This catechism was destined to be translated into several native tongues.[31] Also published with the decrees were the statutes of the cathedral of Mexico, collected by Don Sancho Sánchez de Muñón. The statutes were decisions of the cathedral chapter of Mexico for its own internal governance, which were made the standard for the entire province, including all suffragan dioceses. The last document, the only one to go unpublished following the council, was the *Directorio*.[32] This document was a primer and handbook for parish clergy, outlining the rudiments of the Christian doctrine and faith and providing helpful explanations of problems likely to be encountered in parochial administration.

The main purpose of the Third Provincial Council was to bring Mexican canon law in line with the reforms instituted by the Council of Trent. The Second Mexican Provincial Council (1565) had in fact adopted the Tridentine reforms as canon in Mexico, but did so without having seen a copy of the canons, since Trent had concluded shortly before the Second Council began. Thus, the Third Council more completely revised the Mexican church. The purpose of the catechism and *Directorio* was to establish common practice in parochial administration throughout the ecclesiastical province. The decrees were aimed at general moral questions facing the territory, while the statutes governed the cathedrals. A major thrust of the decrees, and to a lesser degree the *Directorio,* was to curtail abuses against the Indians. A great deal of the legislation governed the financial life of the colony and church.

Within the decrees of the council, the Third Section (Libro III) specifically dealt with the financial life of the church and of the priests. This section touched on three themes of importance to church wealth and parochial income. The decrees ordered the creation of an *arancel,* or fee schedule, for each diocese, as seen earlier. This was to be used for determining clerical fees in Spanish parishes. Moreover, the decrees prohibited parish priests from collecting anything from the Indians beyond the specified salary. In so doing, nevertheless, it clearly recognized that parish priests could and did accept some income and food from the Indians, at a level that was publically specified (*tasación*). There are no documents today to show how this specification was made. In a later section, the decrees established that fees would be the basis for parochial income, specifically including Indians, with the caveat that no fees could be involuntarily exacted from parishioners.[33] The only reference to the tithe required that all the faithful must pay as an obligation. Anyone who refused to pay or who urged others to refuse would suffer excommunication.[34]

Another major theme of this section of the council decrees was the general question of livelihood for priests. It reiterated the need for a guaranteed income before ordination, specifically mentioning the chantry or patrimony. Two paragraphs outlined the prohibitions on clerical employment outside the church. Priests were totally prohibited from exercising any base trade or office, including veterinary. They were also prevented from being servants, pages, or mayordomos for the laity. Then, in one very long part, the decrees specified the limits within which a priest might be economically active within his own parish. For instance, he could not have an estate or hacienda, even if it was inherited, within the parish he served. He was enjoined from purchasing tribute goods from the encomendero and from being a merchant. These rules clearly stipulated the norms of acceptability in the behavior of the priest within the economic and commercial world.[35]

The third topic dealing with church wealth concerned the question of patronage in the foundation of pious works, churches, and chapels. Much of this section enhanced royal law already in force after the promulgation of the Ordenanza del Patronazgo. Further, these decrees ordered that all such endowments had to be approved by the local bishop and enjoy sufficient capital for the income required. In case the founder did not indicate the endowment, the work would be established on all his estate. One interesting regulation ordered that no one within the third degree of parentage could receive the endowment of either land or capital of the work. This restriction covered relatives of the patron, chaplain, or administrator. In the case of corporate bodies, the rule applied to all their members and members' relatives. The chaplains were required to fulfill their obligations by saying all the masses stipulated, and the patrons had to see that the investment of the chantry was protected. Lastly, the bishops were called upon to investigate those pious works founded upon real estate to see if the value had diminished, and if so to moderate the obligations of the chaplain in keeping with the income.[36]

The *Directorio*, as a manual for parish priests, dealt less with general requirements and more with guidelines for the daily life of the laity. It contained extensive sections on business dealings, contracts, the difference between usury and legal income from capital, methods of extending credit, and many more. In a very general sense these precepts related to the financial dealings of the church. The work was written in a catechistical style, so it functioned not so much as a legal code or compilation, but rather as an extensive discussion of moral and ethical precepts for life. Perhaps most important is the discussion of the divine virtue of charity.

In the *Directorio*, of the divine virtues (faith, hope, and charity), charity is the most important because it caused one to approach God, and because it ordered and moved all the other virtues to their logical goal, which is God. Within the general realm of charity, the most important act was the giving of alms, both physically and spiritually. Yet the *Directorio* clearly required that if a person without charity did a good work it would not benefit him.[37] Thus the virtuous man would engage in good works to the maximum extent of which he was capable. Beyond this, charity, as the supreme virtue, meant that good works were the leading action of virtue. Clearly, this indicates that the Third Provincial Council was conforming to the general Tridentine principle that good works were to be emphasized, as a clear point of divergence from the Protestant Reformation.

In both its specific canons and in its guidelines for Christian living, the Third Provincial Council established an important context for the creation of chantries. In general, the emphasis on popular piety stressed in the Counter-Reformation also placed great stock in chantries and other visible forms of good work. Thus, by the end of the sixteenth century, there was a spiritual atmosphere that encouraged the formation of chantries, which went beyond the other social and economic reasons for the institution.

Closely related to this, the decrees of the council had established stringent rules about clerical income. The most important for the future development of the church and clergy were the income requirements placed on candidates for the clergy. The growth in *capellanias* can also be seen as tied to these demands. If earlier in the century a youth could enter the priesthood with little financial support from his family, by the last quarter of the sixteenth century they had to provide him with a living endowment, or provide him with the education necessary to win a benefice, to gain a canonically guaranteed income. Thus, the requirements for ordination tended to feed into the other forces behind the growth of the number of *capellanias*. Likewise the requirements of income complemented the royal program outlined in the Ordenanza del Patronazgo in the creation of rural benefices.

In the end, one can see that the pressures placed on the church in the last quarter of the sixteenth century brought about some important realignments, which would lead to the creation of the institution known to later centuries. If the church began the sixteenth century as a relatively poor but fervent missionary institution, by the end of the century it had become a relatively wealthy, well endowed, largely urban institution. Church finances served the twofold goal of providing adequate income to the individual priests and operating capital to the larger institution. While the tithe always formed a major source of income, the experiences of the sixteenth century encouraged the development of other secondary sources. More and more, the church was not seen as necessarily providing an income to all members of the clerical estate. The employment offered by the church was elitist and subject to the stiffest competition. Thus, while becoming wealthier as an institution, the church tended to become even more fragmented than before. The process of regulating the hierarchy belongs in a different study, but suffice it to say that parallel to the trend toward diversification of income was a trend toward centralization of power. The church grew to be by far the most powerful and important institution in Mexico.

The decade 1575–1585 saw three events of tremendous importance for the church. The epidemic of 1576 forced a serious reassessment of the church's reliance on the tithe as a source of income. The Ordenanza del Patronazgo, implemented at about the same time, placed the burden of support for the rural parishes firmly on the shoulders of the encomenderos and the crown, while establishing the principle that the secular clergy would have dominance in the parishes. Last, the Third Provincial Council, in its mammoth regulations, established both the legal and moral context within which the clergy and the church as a whole would respond to the new pressures placed on them at the century's end. The following chapter will analyze that response and the changes that occurred in the colony as a whole and investigate the long-term effects of these changes on colonial New Spain.

6. Conclusions

The epidemic of 1576 had far-reaching repercussions on the economy of colonial New Spain. The extent to which changes occurred has been the subject of much debate in recent years. The earliest hypothesis suggested that following the pestilence the economy fell into a century of depression. This vision was reinforced with known facts, which indicated that in the first few decades of the seventeenth century the colonial economy had suffered major setbacks.[1] In keeping with this theory, and inspired by similar patterns seen after the fall of the Roman empire, other scholars suggested that in the contracting economy the great estate, or hacienda, emerged as the dominant institution, providing both economic security and social stability to its inhabitants. The estate also served as a means of allocating and regulating the now severely diminished Indian work force.[2] The theory ran that when the Indian work force declined, new patterns of production were created to deal with the new conditions. The use of wage labor and debt peonage became the rule, and thus the Indians became tied to, or at least dependent on, the hacienda.

Nevertheless, in recent years many scholars have begun to question the nature and extent of economic dislocation caused by Indian mortality in general and the 1576 epidemic in specific. What has emerged from this analysis is a far more complex picture of the Mexican economy at the end of the sixteenth century. These studies have sought to determine the differential effect of the mortality and depression on the various sectors of the economy. Mining, principally in Zacatecas, suffered an immediate decline following the epidemic. Silver presented for taxation fell from a 1575 high of 171,004 marks to 165,166 for 1576 and then to 117,368 for 1577.[3] This represents a 30 percent decline over the two years. Production did not return to the preepidemic high until 1611.

In the realm of overseas commerce a similar trend occurred. The level of silver bullion remittances from Mexico to Spain reached a peak in 1577 at 1,111,202 pesos. This declined steadily until 1581 when a low of 521,883 was reached. The trade then grew again, regaining the old high volume by 1586.[4] Tonnage shipped out of Veracruz to Spain peaked at 4,800 in 1576 and fell to 1,400 for 1578. It then fluctuated between 2,200 and 3,850 for the next decade until a new high occurred in 1589 at 5,250 tons.[5]

While these data are fragmentary, they tend to reinforce trends seen elsewhere. The economy of New Spain seems to have undergone a crisis of some sort at the end of the sixteenth century. The fluctuations in mining production can partially be attributed to Indian mortality, but probably by 1585 continued stagnation was due to limited supplies of mercury.[6] In the final estimation, then, the major impact of the epidemic was to cause a depression, or stagnation, of the Mexican economy for as much as twenty years. But certainly by the last decade of the century most areas demonstrated a renewed growth. Thus, rather than a century of depression, what occurred was nearer to a decade of depression and a decade of stagnation.[7]

The two schools of thought, however, do agree that the large estate came into being at about the same time as the epidemic and ensuing repercussions. The explanation for this relationship differs between the two. The older school saw a contraction of the economy until it reached the lowest level of production, the estate, and then a consolidation around that level, leading to the great hacienda. The more recent studies have seen the large estate as proceeding from earlier institutions. The encomienda did not include a grant of land. Land was acquired through grants from the central government or by purchase. These small estates, estancias, are a ubiquitous feature of the sixteenth century. Land was an important adjunct component to the encomienda, since before the 1550s and the abolition of labor services, the institution had served as a means of labor allocation. Similarly, the *repartimiento* served to distribute limited Indian labor within the economy. Both institutions encouraged the formation of agricultural estates and other labor-requiring endeavors to maximize income, especially of the encomienda. As seen earlier, the successful encomendero diversified his holdings so as not to rely totally on the grant income for living expenses. Thus, many features of the labor allocation system encouraged the formation of agricultural estates. The hacienda then grew from two earlier institutions: in terms of landholding it resulted from the growth and consolidation of smaller estancias; in terms of its effect on the system of labor allocation within the economy, it sprang from the encomienda and *repartimiento*. It also marked a shift from governmentally supervised and regulated systems to private systems.[8]

Rather than being an institution of entrenchment, the hacienda probably evolved simply to deal better with conditions created by the labor uncertainty of the postepidemic world. As noted in an earlier chapter, the Spanish population was largely untouched by the pestilence. In fact a severe depression in Spain, caused by the 1576 bankruptcy of the crown, resulted in an increase in immigration to Mexico. This increased Spanish population placed greater demands on the agricultural markets of the cities, as evidenced by the creation of regulating institutions. In Mexico City between 1576 and 1580 the city council mandated the creation of both grain and meat regulatory institutions.[9]

The increased demand for food caused by added Spanish population occurred at a time when the agricultural sector could least respond. The labor force had become unstable, and the little production that had entered the market from

Indian producers was now disappearing. Added to this, Indians unable to acquire food in traditional markets were forced to enter the Spanish market for supply, just as that sector also felt added demand. This demand unleashed a period of inflation caused by scarcity of food. The response on the part of the elite was to increase investments in land, for several reasons. Clearly if labor could be obtained, agriculture was open for new investors to begin to meet the increasing demand. Land, in times of inflation, and especially when it can signify the production of a valued commodity, has always served as a hedge.[10]

Miners similarly confronted by unstable labor supply and inflation realized the waning productivity of their efforts. Each unit of production purchased less. When their situation was compounded by problems of supply in mercury, the logical response was to take whatever capital they could and also invest it in land. In general, the economy of scale dictated that production of foodstuffs could be maximized by creating larger, rather than smaller, estates. In areas with a suitable climate, a medium-sized labor force could be occupied throughout the year on a large estate, with only small increases of seasonal labor at critical times. But regardless of size, the estate was becoming an increasingly commercial institution. Thus, rather than falling back in isolation on the rural estates, entrepreneurs invested in land and agriculture for commercial reasons; food was scarce and land relatively plentiful. The response carried the economy forward into a new era of commercial agriculture rather than back into a quasi-feudal one.

The economic instability in Spain caused further effects in Mexico. Certainly in the realm of public finance, the monarch was desirous of increasing royal revenues prior to the bankruptcy. His unwillingness to extend the redonation of the ninth of the tithe demonstrates that. Yet in the larger economy, as certain finished goods became difficult to obtain from Spain, entrepreneurs sought to produce them locally. This stimulated the creation of the *obraje* complex for textiles, especially in the Puebla region, for example. The protoindustrial complex, in turn, placed further demands on agriculture to produce raw materials, such as wool, and to feed the now nonagriculturally productive labor force. It too was dependent on acquiring part of the diminished labor force.

The economic response to the epidemic further unified the three main sectors of the economy. More and more the commercial and mining sectors became reliant on agriculture. Individuals with land, labor, or the capital with which to acquire them could ride out the storm fairly well. In the absence of these resources, the Spaniard in the lower levels of the elite would be pressed further down on the socioeconomic scale. The process probably resulted in the creation of splits within the elite, splits that could feed into long-term grudges on the part of those conqueror and encomendero families who had been slowly pushed out by latecomer entrepreneurs.

In the countryside, several distinctive changes came with the evolution of the new economic system. Clearly, more and more land had become vacant, owing to Indian mortality. This was a positive benefit for those seeking to capitalize on the trends of the day. The pestilence also created a less dense rural population. The lack of population density eventually was seen as an undesirable result. At the century's end the civil authorities undertook an ambitious program of bringing the remaining Indian population into centrally located villages.[11] This *congregación* program further disrupted traditional Indian social and political institutions and freed up still more land in the zones from which Indian population was taken. The now more mobile Indian population would also be more attracted to the large estate as an institution of stability in a world of flux.

Proponents of the hacienda-as-retrenchment theory held that the responses seen here continued relatively unchanged for approximately a century, the duration of the depression. The critics of the argument hold that the downturn of the economy, if there was one at all, lasted only briefly, perhaps for two decades. Following the period of consolidation, capital, which had been created by the skillful entrepreneurs during the time of trouble, could then be reinvested in the economy, especially in mining and commerce. The reinvestments further stimulated the overall growth of the economy and fostered capital formation in the other two sectors, as their recovery began.

All of these changes had a critical effect on the financial life of the church. As seen, the instability of the agricultural market following the epidemic of 1576 caused tremendous uncertainty in the church. The traditional reliance on the tithe was questioned, and other sources of income, such as pious works and the collection of fees, took on an added importance, especially for the lower clergy, where it was realized that the tithe would never be able to provide adequate support. Nevertheless, once the two decades of crisis were passed, the church emerged in a far stronger position. The growth of the hacienda and the increase of commercial agriculture inherent in that growth provided the church with previously unknown levels of income. Almost by definition, commercial agriculture was subject to tithe. Even the Indian production benefited the church, since part of it, that destined to the Spanish commercial market, consisted of the traditional Spanish foodstuffs, wheat, and cattle.[12] Beyond the production of foodstuffs, sheep also provided the church with tithe income from the demand for wool from the newly stimulated protoindustrial complex. Silk also was being produced for the textile industry, until imported Philippine goods undercut the market. Thus, the shift toward commercial agriculture represented a positive trend for the church. Data on tithe income for the last decade bear out this view.

While not linked to the decline in Indian population, the increase in Spanish population also represented an additional benefit for the church. With more Spaniards, and more of them engaged in agriculture, more tithes could be expected. Furthermore, as the Spanish population grew, more parishes had sizeable Spanish populations from which the curates could rightly expect fees for services. At the same time, the somewhat unclear rulings of the Third Provincial Council had begun a trend toward the collection of fees from Indians, which served to improve income in all parishes.[13] The concentration of population on the haciendas also opened up some jobs for priests as chaplains on the estates.

The formation of the haciendas also affected the church through the creation of pious works. For the marginal Spanish family, a time of inflation could cause serious damage to family wealth. The pious work offered them the ability to invest capital to provide an on-going income for a son. Although the value of the income in terms of purchasing power would decline with inflation, at least it was secure. Further, the offering of the endowment's capital for investment on land must have provided many estate owners with the opportunity to increase their holdings. Since more land came available just as the demand increased, there was no noticeable increase in property values. At this point the estate owner could afford to take on a mortgage without fearing a later decline in property values. As far as could be seen, the value of the property would remain constant, if not increase. Once the economy slowed down, later in the seventeenth century, no doubt many landowners found themselves overextended. For miners who might have capital available to invest in land, the period was full of potential. Once they had acquired land, it could be then used as security for additional loans, either to develop the estate or to reinvest in mining. Thus, when the economy improved in the 1590s, many entrepreneurs would be ready to expand their investments.

The period did hold one major disadvantage for the secular clergy with respect to land. It saw the meteoric rise of the Jesuits as landowners, followed closely by all the other orders, except perhaps the Franciscans.[14] The lands thus acquired by the regulars were lost to the seculars in terms of tithe income. Furthermore, with a general concern over clerical income, the traditional battle between the regulars and the seculars became more involved with income and revenue. The coming confrontation over the tithe clearly had its financial aspect.

Beyond this, the Ordenanza del Patronazgo mandated the removal of the regulars from the parishes. After 1574, each parish occupied by the regulars constituted one less parish available to a secular priest. Given the income requirement for ordination, the presence of the regulars in the parishes was an economic threat to the seculars. Moreover, in a period in which the Indian population was declining, there ultimately would be fewer parishes, or so the crown ordered. Moves to limit the number of parishes tended to increase the tension between the seculars and regulars. At the same time that the regular clergy was expanding and acquiring agricultural property, engaging like the lay population in commercial agriculture but refusing to pay the tithe, the regulars also refused to give up parishes which would provide income to secular priests. In both instances the crown sided with the seculars. It is clear that the confrontation between the seculars and regulars ultimately became one of a conflict over the control of wealth.

The regular clergy came under attack from within the church as well as from the crown. Part of the Counter-Reformation consisted of the elimination of laxity and corruption among the regular clergy. In general, the orders were required to return to their monasteries and eschew secular things. Some of the movement for secularization can be seen in the decrees of the Third Provincial Council. Even more important than returning to the monasteries, the regulars were increasingly made to recognize the local authority of the bishop, especially as a supervisor, to avoid their previous excesses of the orders. Thus, the period after 1571 does see the regular orders in retrenchment, after the very rapid expansion following the conquest. Oddly enough, the Jesuits were initially greeted as allies by the seculars. Not until the 1640s did the two come into conflict, by which time the Jesuits had become the leaders of the regular clergy, at least in terms of wealth.

In the last decade of the sixteenth century, the secular clergy began to benefit additionally from the improvement of the economy. As the mining and commercial sectors expanded again, they created excess capital. Given the advantages of the pious work as a means of administering capital within a family, the wealthy miners and merchants began to endow heavily not only chantries but other pious works as well. These endowments then provided additional sources of income for the increasing number of young men entering the priesthood.

The foundation of the University of Mexico in 1553 had been the cornerstone of the creation of a local educational establishment for the training of priests. The Third Provincial Council, in both the decrees and the *Directorio*, addressed the requisites for clerical training, and the university figured prominently among them. The Jesuits also provided an essential component for the overall system through the foundation of their colleges, which functioned at times parallel to the university, at times in conflict. The growth in the number of educational facilities at the end of the sixteenth century is impressive. Some can be seen as further examples of pious works, along with the foundation of hospitals and other institutions.

By the end of the sixteenth century the church found itself in a period of impressive growth on almost all fronts. The system of tithe collection and division had grown from meagre beginnings to a complex and lucrative venture. With the increasing complexity came additional problems. Many of the problems became obvious after 1576, and it was the response to that crisis that ensured the later growth in the level of tithe income.

The evolution of the tithe can be divided into four periods. The first began with the conquest and continued until about 1550. By that date all of the dioceses had been erected and their tithe collection procedures implemented. Furthermore, legislation concerning the encomienda had established the norms for that institution. In general all of the mechanisms involved in the collection and distribution of the tithe were in place. The period from 1550 to 1576 witnessed a rapid increase in tithe remittances as Spanish agriculture began its middle-age expansion. The agricultural sector had followed a similar pattern, emerging after 1550 having suffered the effects of an earlier major epidemic (1545) and the restructuring of the encomienda. The growth of agriculture and the tithe ended in 1576 with the epidemic of that year. Both went through an unstable period, 1576–1590. For the tithe, serious problems emerged by the 1580s, but eventually conditions stabilized by the 1590s. For agriculture, demand was high and supply variable, thus increasing the attractiveness of investments in agriculture. The final period of the evolution of the tithe began in about 1590, lasting into the seventeenth century, as the church grew prosperous with the expansion of commercial agriculture and the hacienda.

The distribution of the tithe also went through four periods. The first saw a reliance on distribution in kind and specie. The market patterns were poorly defined enough to make retention of some goods desirable. The second period, marked by the growth of agriculture, was characterized by the distribution of cash, since there was a fairly stable pattern of supply for foodstuffs. The 1576–90 period created added pressures on the distribution system. The inflation, price fluctuations, and increasing value of agricultural goods meant that distributions in kind would again gain favor, allowing the church and its officials and constituent institutions to prefer holding some goods for use and others for speculation. By the final period a hybrid system had developed in which cash distribution became the norm, but some key goods were held for speculation.

In this period the church began to resell the tithe grain as seed grain.

In terms of parish salaries and income, the sixteenth century saw a great improvement in the security of income. Although the early period is unclear, the wages of the parish priest must have been uncertain until the proper mechanisms were in place to handle the administrative problems. In the earliest period, the salary was a contractual arrangement between the encomendero and the priest. As the episcopal hierarchy fell in place, it began to take over the assignment of priests to parishes, thus replacing the encomenderos, who now became obligated to pay whomever was appointed. In the early period the parish priest also had greater opportunity to extract additional sums from his parishioners. As the entire administrative hierarchy was developed and the local bishops exercised more oversight, many of these excesses were eliminated, but many remained. The Ordenanza del Patronazgo, the Third Provincial Council, and the *congregación* program following the epidemic of 1576 all helped to create job security for the parish priest, guarantee him a base wage, and offer the potential for augmenting that wage through the collection of fees. The development of the *arancel*, as a method of reducing coercion, ultimately served to legalize the payment of fees to the parish priest. Furthermore, the granting of *repartimiento* labor to the parish priest, as household servants, also improved conditions. Nevertheless, the growth of the number of secular clerics was not matched by a similar growth in the number of parishes, and many priests had to look elsewhere for employment. This situation created additional animosity against the regular clergy by the end of the century.

Pious works, and specifically chantries, provided the needed source of income for the growing number of secular clerics. In the first part of the sixteenth century the chantry was popular because it not only provided a son with an income, allowing him to enter the clergy, but it provided an additional means to pass on family wealth in avoidance of inheritance laws. In this it served a similar function as the *mayorazgo*. In another manner, the chantries, and pious works in general, skimmed the excess capital off of the economy and invested it in real estate. With the Ordenanza del Patronazgo, the Third Provincial Council, and 1576 epidemic, the chantry underwent a change. It still fulfilled the primary functions, but as a result of these events it took on an importance it had not had before. Pious works became favored methods of opposing the Protestant Reformation, as well as being excellent methods of passing on family wealth, providing for children, and putting capital back into the economy. In the trying times following the epidemic, pious works must have been especially important in their capital redistribution role. With the growth of the economy at the end of the century, pious works, and specifically the chantry, became central institutions in the economic and religious life of the colony.

The patterns of growth and development of church finances established at the end of the sixteenth century continued through the rest of the colonial period. Many of the disputes begun in the earlier period continued until the later. Controversies remained between the secular and regular clergy. The issue of secularization of the parishes was not resolved until the eighteenth century.[15] Religious orders were defiant with regard to the payment of the tithe, although all, including the Jesuits, finally acquiesced.[16] The volume of capital and land handled by the chantry court continued to grow, as pious works continued to be popular. Parish priests exacted fees from all their parishioners, Indian and Spanish, and the *arancel* became ubiquitous. Yet the church ultimately fell to the growing power of a strong centralized monarchy, as the Bourbon rulers of Spain sought to broaden their hold on the church under the provisions of the Patronato Real.

Tithe collections in the Archbishopric of Mexico reach almost unimaginable heights by the end of the eighteenth century. Alexander von Humboldt calculated that in the decade 1771–80 tithe collections in the archdiocese exceeded four million pesos and climbed to seven million in the next decade.[17] Tithe collections in Puebla were two million and two and a half million pesos for the same two decades.[18] Fragmentary data for Oaxaca indicate a similar relative level, with annual collections falling just short of 100,000 pesos.[19]

Yet these impressive sums fall short of the levels of capital represented by the endowments for pious works. As noted earlier, figures on total endowment are difficult to assess, since by the eighteenth century so many pious works were founded not on cash endowments but on voluntary impositions. Even keeping this in mind, the figure of 44.5 million pesos in total endowment is truly impressive. Of that, 9 million was administered by the chantry court of the Archdiocese of Mexico, while 18.8 million was administered by the religious orders and other church institutions.[20]

In the parishes a similar growth in income had occurred. Widespread use and misuse of the *arancel* had helped to increase parish revenues. Like their lay counterparts, the corregidores, parish priests engaged in the *derrama* or *repartimiento de bienes* (the forced sale of goods to Indians). The differential of income between a rural parish and an urban one, however, continued to be great, adding a continuing dissatisfaction among the ranks of the parish clergy.[21]

In spite of the general fiscal well-being of the church at the end of the colonial period, there were some drawbacks. With the secularization of the parishes, the clergy ultimately became more closely governed by the royal bureaucracy. The Bourbon monarchs were insistent on the enforcement and extension of their powers of patronage, further centralizing the church under their control. In 1776, the Fourth Provincial Council was held. Its decrees were so totally regalistic that even the monarch could not approve them in all conscience. The tremendous wealth of the church also attracted envy from a continually poverty-stricken monarch. Thus, in 1804, the capital was called in by the crown, in return for interest-bearing bonds. The king further restricted the clergy's role in making wills for the laity, serving as executors and heirs, and limiting bequests to the church. These and other reforms would create a great sense of dissatisfaction among the clergy on the eve of the wars for independence.

Church finances and ecclesiastical revenues grew from very modest beginnings after the conquest to rank as one of the largest economic institutions in the colony. Just as the ecclesiastical bureaucracy rivaled the royal bureaucracy in size, so only the Royal Treasury rivaled the wealth of the church. Through its various sources of revenue and economic activity, the church entered every social stratum and way of life. Having passed through a time of troubles and having been reformed and reorganized from within and without, by the end of the sixteenth century the Catholic church was well on its way to becoming the single most important institution in all of New Spain.

Notes

Abbreviations

ACEM–Archivo del Cabildo Eclesiástico de México, Cathedral of Mexico, Mexico City.
ACTAS–Minutes of the Cathedral Chapter of Mexico, held in ACEM.
AGI–Archivo General de las Indias, Seville, Spain.
AGN–Archivo General de la Nación, Mexico City.
ANDDF–Archivo de Notarias del Departamento del Distrito Federal, Mexico City.

Introduction

1. Nancy Farriss, *Crown and Clergy in Colonial Mexico* (London, 1968); Michael Costeloe, *Church Wealth in Mexico* (Cambridge, 1967).
2. For a fuller discussion of the tithe, see Chapters 1 and 2.
3. W. Eugene Shiels, *King and Church* (Chicago, 1961).
4. Woodrow W. Borah, *Price Trends of Some Basic Commodities in Central Mexico, 1531–1570* (Berkeley, 1958), 9–10; Earl J. Hamilton, *American Treasure and the Price Revolution in Spain, 1501–1600* (Cambridge, 1934), 46–72; Wilbur T. Meek, *The Exchange Media of Colonial Mexico* (New York, 1948).
5. Nicolas P. Cushner, *Lords of the Land: Sugar, Wine, and Jesuit Estates of Coastal Peru, 1600–1767* (Albany, 1980); Herman W. Konrad, *A Jesuit Hacienda in Colonial Mexico: Santa Lucia, 1576–1767* (Stanford, 1980).
6. Leslie B. Simpson, *The Encomienda in New Spain* (Berkeley, 1966), 32–33, 131; Silvio Zavala, *La encomienda indiana* (Mexico, 1973), 72–91.

7. *Cartas de Indias* (Madrid, 1877), 196–218.

8. A.G.I., Patronato, 183, Num. 1, Ramo 3, "Relacion de los clerigos que al presente ay y residen en el obispado de Tlaxcala."

9. The estimate was made as follows: Mexico 165, Oaxaca 100, Michoacán 75, Puebla 115, Guadalajara 75. Cuevas cites 470 parishes to which one must add to account for multiple clergy in some parishes, cathedral clergy, administrative staff, and others. Mariano Cuevas, *Historia de la iglesia mexicana*, 5 vols. (Mexico, 1921–28), vol. I, 151.

10. Ibid., II, 297–98.

11. Ibid., II, 299.

12. Clarence H. Haring, *The Spanish Empire in America* (New York, 1947), 117.

13. John L. Phelan, *The Kingdom of Quito* (Madison, 1967), 148.

14. Parish priests eventually received a guaranteed 150 *pesos de minas* salary ($248^{3}/_{8}$ *pesos de oro común*). The guarantee was considered sufficient to allow ordination. See Chapter 3.

15. For general discussions of colonial Spanish-American society, see James Lockhart, *Spanish Peru* (Madison, 1968); Colin MacLachlan and Jaime Rodriguez, *The Forging of the Cosmic Race* (Berkeley, 1980), 196–228; James Lockhart, "Introduction," in Ida Altman and James Lockhart, eds., *Provinces of Early Mexico* (Los Angeles, 1976), 3–28.

16. An extensive bibliography deals with the encomienda. For the basic outlines, see: Charles Gibson, *Spain in America* (New York, 1966); and his *Aztecs Under Spanish Rule* (Stanford, 1964), 58–97. See Note 6.

17. Jose Miranda, "La función económica del encomendero en los orígenes del régimen colonial en la Nueva España (1525–1531)," *Anales del Instituto Nacional de Antropología e Historia* 2 (1941–46), 421–62; and his *El tributo indígena en la Nueva España* (Mexico, 1980).

18. For the practical implications of this in the sixteenth century, see John Frederick Schwaller, "Tres familias mexicanas del siglo XVI," *Historia mexicana* 31 (October–December 1981), 171–96.

19. The recent historiography dealing with the agricultural

sector is reviewed by Eric Van Young, "Historiography of the Colonial Hacienda," *Latin American Research Review* 18 (1983), 5–61.

Chapter 1

1. Woodrow Borah, "Collection of Tithes in the Bishopric of Oaxaca During the XVI Century," *Hispanic American Historical Review* 21 (1941), 386–93.
2. Shiels, *King and Church*, 90–91, 113–15.
3. *Recopilación de las leyes de Indias*, Libro I, Título 16, Ley ii.
4. Borah, "Collection," 389.
5. *Recopilación*, I, 16, lxxi. A fine study of the relationship between the creation of the church in Granada and that of the New World is Antonio Garrido Aranda, *Organización de la iglesia en el reino de Granada y su proyección en Indias* (Seville, 1979), esp. 55–57, 177–92. See also Jesús María de la Casa Rivas, "Los diezmos como fuente de ingresos de la iglesia dominicana (1492–1577), *Casas Reales* (May–August, 1980), 43–73; and Rafaela González Díaz, "El estado financiero de la iglesia dominicana: Los diezmos (1578–1650)," *Casas Reales* (May–August, 1980), 77–93, for a discussion of American precedents before the creation of the Mexican dioceses.
6. Shiels, *King and Church*, 113–15, 123–26.
7. *Recopilación*, I, 16, i.
8. Ibid., I, 16, xvi.
9. The *peso de ley perfecta* or *castellano* had 485 *marevedises* as opposed to *pesos de oro de minas* with 450.
10. Hernán Cortés, *Cartas y documentos* (Mexico, 1963), 239.
11. AGI, Mexico, 2705, March 31, 1525; Fabián de Fonseca, *Historia de la Real Hacienda de la Nueva España*, 6 vols. (Mexico, 1845–53), III, 144.
12. Agustín Millares Carlo and Ignacio Mantecón, *Indice y extractos de los protocolos del Archivo de Notarias*, 2 vols. (Mexico, 1946), I, 37.
13. *Recopilación*, I, 16, xii.
14. Alberto María Carreño, *Un desconocido cedulario del siglo*

XVI perteneciente a la catedral metropolitana (Mexico, 1944), 165.

15. *Recopilación*, I, 16, xvii.
16. Borah, "Collection," 399–408.
17. Woodrow W. Borah, *Silk Raising in Colonial Mexico* (Berkeley, 1943).
18. Carreño, *Desconocido*, 82.
19. Ibid., 190, 291–92. For several major suits on the Indian tithe, see AGI, Justicia, 158, Num. 3 and Justicia, 160, Num. 2.
20. *Recopilación*, I, 16, xxiii.
21. AGI, Indiferente General, 2978.
22. Millares Carlo, *Indice*, II, 23.
23. ANDDF, Andres Moreno, various contracts 1592–1602.
24. Millares Carlo, *Indice*, II, 132.
25. *Recopilación*, I, 16, ii.
26. Borah, "Collection," 397–99.
27. AGI, Mexico, 375, "Cuenta de los dos novenos" Michoacán, 1594.
28. *Recopilación*, I, 16, xx.
29. *Descripción del arzobispado de México hecha en 1570* (Mexico, 1897), 298–301; AGI, Contaduría, 782.
30. Borah, "Collection", 393–94.
31. Mariano Galván Rivera (ed.), *Concilio III Provincial Mexicano* (Mexico, 1859), "Estatutos," cv.
32. ACTAS, December 11–24, 1576.
33. ACTAS, January 24, 1576.
34. AGI, Contaduría, 676, 683, 686, 687, Cargo-Tributos, "Diezmo de la provincia de Pánuco."
35. AGN, Bienes Nacionales, 1040, sin número, "Antonio Nuñez contra los indios de Tantoniga."
36. ACTAS, January 31, 1576; AGI, Mexico, 339, Dean y cabildo of Mexico to King in Council, November 5, 1576 and October 31, 1577.
37. ACTAS, May 17, 1596.
38. ACTAS, July 15, 1580; ACEM, 47, exp. 22.
39. *Recopilación*, I, 16, iii.
40. AGN, Bienes Nacionales, 325, exp. 1.
41. The process of commutation was exceedingly complex and varied across time. Some of the tribute to be paid in goods was commuted to cash or service, in the early years. Thus, the com-

muted service was subject to tithe since initially it was paid in goods. The confusion heightened when service was outlawed after 1550. Labor service was then commuted to corn and cash. Miranda, *Tributo*, 268–76.

42. ACTAS, September 4, 1590.
43. *Recopilación*, I, 16, xii.
44. AGN, Clero secular y regular, 12, exp. 1.
45. ANDDF, Pedro Sánchez, December 12, 1576.
46. AGI, Mexico, 20, doc. 126; Mexico, 21, doc. 20; Mexico, 109, ramo 4.
47. ACTAS, September 4–17, 1577.
48. ACEM, 12, exp. 10.
49. ACTAS, March 8, 1578.
50. ACTAS, June 10, 1578.
51. ACTAS, June 26, 1578.
52. ACTAS, September 30, 1578.
53. ACTAS, November 11, 1578.
54. ACTAS, April 14, 1579.
55. ACTAS, April 15, 1578, January 16, 1579.
56. ACTAS, July 15, 1580; ACEM, 47, exp. 22.
57. ACTAS, August 7, 1582.
58. AGI, Mexico, 218, doc. 14, September 18, 1585.
59. ANDDF, Andres Moreno, 1597, 297–99v.
60. *Recopilación*, I, 16, xxxi.
61. AGN, Inquisición, 140, exp. 2.
62. ACTAS, July 12, 1591.
63. ACTAS, July 12, 1594.
64. Borah, "Collection," 408–9.
65. *Recopilación*, I, 16, xi.
66. Lilly Library, Latin American Manuscripts, Mexico II, miscellaneous documents pertaining to the Mexico cathedral, Libranza, March 16, 1583.
67. Data provided by Elinor Melville from royal tribute auctions of grain from the province of Tula, AGI, Contaduría, 667–702.
68. Lilly Library, Tacubaya and Atzcapotzalco Libranzas, February 1, 1583 and December 4, 1584.
69. The nuances of storage and division of the tithe will be dealt with in Chapter 2.
70. ACTAS, February 20, 1579.

71. ACTAS, November 20, 1583.
72. ACTAS, June 8–15, 1584.
73. ACTAS, August 20, September 24, and November 8, 1585.
74. Charles Gibson, *Aztecs under Spanish Rule* (Stanford, 1964), 453.
75. ACTAS, March 4, and August 18, 1586.
76. ACTAS, November 20, 1590.
77. ACTAS, October 8, 1577.
78. ACTAS, June 20, 1586.
79. ACTAS, February 14, 1597.
80. ANDDF, Andres Moreno, 1597, 260v–61, 280–81.
81. ACTAS, July 12, 1591.
82. ANDDF, Andres Moreno, 1600, 177–78.
83. *Recopilación*, I, 16, xxiv.
84. AGN, Archivo Histórico de Hacienda, 1509, 209.
85. AGN, Archivo Histórico de Hacienda, 1291, 215.
86. AGI, Indiferente General, 77, March 1, 1608.
87. Aristides Medina Rubio, "Elementos para una economía agrícola de Puebla: 1540–1795," Ph.D. dissertation, El Colegio de Mexico, 1974, 238.
88. *Recopilación*, I, 16, xxv.
89. AGI, Mexico, 211, doc. 39; AGI, Indiferente General, 2859, vol. I, 63; *Cartas de Indias*, 200; Peter Gerhard, *A Guide to the Historical Geography of New Spain* (Cambridge, 1973), 218, 391.
90. ANDDF, Andres Moreno, years 1600–1602.
91. Biblioteca Nacional de Antropología e Historia (Mexico), Fondo de Micropelícula, Oaxaca, 100.
92. AGI, Mexico, 375.
93. AGI, Guadalajara, 64; AGI, Guadalajara, 55, exp. 8, "Relacion de beneficios . . . 1572."
94. ACTAS, June 9, 1589.
95. ANDDF, Andres Moreno, 1601, 139.
96. ANDDF, Andres Moreno, 1601, 30v.
97. ACTAS, May 26, 1587.
98. ACTAS, October 22, 1591.
99. ANDDF, Andres Moreno, 1597, 34, March 4, 1597.
100. ANDDF, Andres Moreno, 1597, 262–63, February 25, 1597; 265v–66, February 27, 1597.
101. ANDDF, Andres Moreno, 1597, 263, February 25, 1597.

102. ANDDF, Andres Moreno, 1597, 264–65, February 27, 1597.

103. Gerhard, *Guide*, 312.

104. ANDDF, Andres Moreno, 1600, 96v–97, March 8, 1600; 1601, 95v–97, March 29, 1601.

105. AGN, Archivo Histórico de Hacienda, 1219, 215; 1516, 320; AGI, Mexico, 112, R. 1, num. 1, Diego Mexia de la Cerda.

106. ANDDF, J. B. Moreno, 1592, February 26, 1593; Andres Moreno, 1600, 308v–9, October 17, 1600.

107. ANDDF, J. B. Moreno, 1592, December 19, 1592; Andres Moreno, 1600, 8–10, January 3–7, 1600; 1601, 8v–9, January 24, 1601.

Chapter 2

1. Borah, "Collection," 390–92.

2. Garrido Aranda, *Organización*, 180.

3. *Recopilación*, I, 16, xxiii.

4. AGI, Indiferente General, 2978, "Relacion de los diezmos deste obispado de Mexico," 1538.

5. AGN, Bienes Nacionales, 1044, sin número. John F. Schwaller, *Partidos y párrocos bajo la real corona en la Nueva España, siglo XVI* (Mexico, 1981); AGI, Contaduría, 683, Cargo-Tributos, Diezmo de Pánuco.

6. Joaquín García Icazbalceta, *Don Fray Juan de Zumárraga*, 4 vols. (Mexico, 1947), I, 305–12.

7. Fintan B. Warren, *Vasco de Quiroga and His Pueblo-Hospitals of Santa Fe* (Washington, D.C., 1963).

8. José Ignacio Dávila Garibi, *Apuntes para la historia de la iglesia en Guadalajara*, 6 vols. (Mexico, 1957–62), I, 656–57.

9. Luis García Pimentel (ed.), *Relación de los obispados de Tlaxcala, Michoacán, Oaxaca y otros lugares en el siglo XVI* (Mexico, 1904), 1–2.

10. The closest one can come to data on the bishop's fund is a suit between Fr. Bartolomé de Ledesma and the cathedral over his pay as administrator of the diocese for the ailing Archbishop Fr. Alonso de Montúfar: AGN, Bienes Nacionales, 1392, exp. 2; and ACEM, 12, exp. 9.

11. John F. Schwaller, "The Cathedral Chapter of Mexico in

the Sixteenth Century," *Hispanic American Historical Review* 61 (1981), 651–74.

12. Galván Rivera, *Concilio*, xxviii–xxix.
13. Carreño, *Desconocido*, 75–77.
14. Ibid., 58–68; AGI, Patronato, 180, ramo 39.
15. AGI, Indiferente General, 2978.
16. Carreño, *Desconocido*, 109, 162, and 197; ACTAS, January 5, 1545.
17. AGI, Justicia, 209, num. 1.
18. Schwaller, "Cathedral Chapter," 662–67.
19. AGI, Mexico, 339, "Testimonio de votos, 1548."
20. Archivo de la catedral de Burgo de Osma, *Directorio* del Concilio mexicano, f. 17v.
21. ACTAS, July 30, 1566.
22. John Carter Brown Library, Codex, Spanish 37, "Declaracion del quadrante . . ." [Mexico, 1700?] is an example.
23. AGI, Mexico, 343, October 17, 1582; Mexico 1090, June 24, 1573; Mexico, 290, March 2, 1575; Cuevas, *Historia*, II, 293.
24. AGI, Mexico, 339, October 17, 1597.
25. Galván Rivera, *Concilio*, xxix.
26. Ibid., cviii.
27. Ibid., cxiv.
28. ACTAS, July 30, 1566.
29. Fr. Alonso de Montúfar (ed.), *Ordenanzas para el coro de la catedral mexicana* (Madrid, 1964), 54–59.
30. Ibid., 40–43.
31. Ibid., 38–39.
32. AGI, Mexico, 339, October 17, 1597.
33. Lilly Library, Latin American Manuscripts, Mexico II, Dr. Esteban del Portillo, August 1, 1979.
34. Ibid., January 19, 1593–January 9, 1598.
35. ACEM, 12, exp. 21.
36. ACTAS, January 22, 1592, December 10, 1596.
37. AGI, Mexico, 343, Bishop of Tlaxcala to King, October 17, 1581; Mexico, 374, Bishop of Michoacán to King, March 8, 1581.
38. AGI, Justicia, 209, No. 1; Justicia, 219, No. 2; Mexico, 339, Dean y Cabildo of Mexico to King, March 30, 1578.
39. AGI, Mexico, 1064, F-2, 101v–102, March 31, 1582.
40. Galván Rivera, *Concilio*, lvii–lviii.
41. AGI, Contaduría, 782.

42. For examples see ACTAS, August 19 and November 7, 1559, discussions on the number of choirboys, and January 29, 1566 when three new ones were received.

43. ACTAS, July 6, 1582.

44. ACTAS, February 26, 1583, March 6, 1584.

45. ACEM, 69 and 70; AGN, Historia, 112.

46. "Tepotzotlán," *Artes de Mexico*, num. 62/63 (1960), 198.

47. Ibid., 169.

48. AGI, Contaduría, 782.

49. ACTAS, June 16, 1590.

50. ANDDF, Pedro Sánchez, June 22, 1583.

51. ANDDF, Andres Moreno, December 16, 1601, March 15, 1602, June 16–20, 1602.

52. AGI, Mexico, 343, Bishop of Tlaxcala to King, January 12, 1597.

Chapter 3

1. Luis García Pimentel (ed.), *Descripción del arzobispado de México hecha en 1570* (Mexico, 1897), 276.

2. AGN, Bienes Nacionales, 775, exp. 14, April 15, 1564.

3. AGN, Bienes Nacionales, 1044, exp. 10, June 28, 1583.

4. Ibid., September 30, 1589.

5. ACTAS, July 12, 1585.

6. ACEM, 12, exp. 19.

7. ACEM, 12, exp. 21, f.5.

8. Cuevas, *Historia*, III, 121–22.

9. Gerhard, *Guide*, 181.

10. AGI, Mexico, 217, doc. 34, November 17, 1583.

11. See Chapter 4.

12. AGN, Bienes Nacionales, 1124, exp. 13.

13. AGN, Bienes Nacionales, 1269, exp. 11.

14. AGN, Bienes Nacionales, 224, exp. 3, September 17, 1596.

15. García Pimentel, *Relación*, 79–81.

16. AGI, Contaduría, 671, Data–Lo Espiritual, June 30, 1567; García Pimentel, *Descripción*, 160 and 165.

17. AGI, Guadalajara, 55, exp. 8.

18. García Pimentel, *Descripción*, 181–82; AGI, Mexico, 336-A, doc. 104(5), 19v.

19. García Pimentel, *Descripción*, 211–12; AGI, Mexico, 336-A, doc. 104(7), 27v.
20. AGN, Bienes Nacionales, 78, exps. 98 and 124.
21. Galván Rivera, *Concilio*, 49.
22. For practical examples of the encomendero paying the parish priest, see ANDDF, Pedro Sánchez, June 20, 1555; Andres Moreno, June 8, 1584.
23. See Chapter 5.
24. AGN, Reales Cédulas Duplicadas, 3, exp. 204, 190.
25. AGN, General de Parte, 1, exp. 201, 40v–41.
26. Schwaller, *Partidos*.
27. Ismael Sánchez Bela, *La organización financiera de las Indias, siglo XVI* (Seville, 1968), 254.
28. Miranda, *El tributo indígena*, 126–28, 225–40. Although this relates to secular officers it applied equally to priests.
29. AGN, General de Parte, 1, exp. 136, 27.
30. *Recopilación*, I, 13, xix.
31. Schwaller, *Partidos*.
32. AGI, Contaduría, 667-A, Data–Lo Espiritual, July 26, 1561 and May 8, 1562.
33. John F. Schwaller, "Implementation of the Ordenanza del Patronazgo of 1574," *Church and Society in Latin America* (New Orleans, 1984), 38–50; AAM, Ordenes Sacras, I, March 23, 1579.
34. AGI, Contaduría, 680, Data–Lo Espiritual, January 13, 1580.
35. AGI, Contaduría, 686, Data–Lo Espiritual, June 28, 1585.
36. Gerónimo de Mendieta, *Historia eclesiástica indiana* (Mexico, 1870), 373–74; AGN, Bienes Nacionales, 325, exp. 17.
37. José A. Llaguno, *La personalidad jurídica del indio y el IIIer concilio provincial mexicano* (Mexico, 1963), 172 and 179.
38. *Recopilación*, I, 13, vii–viii.
39. Galván Rivera, *Concilio*, 49.
40. Llaguno, *Personalidad jurídica*, 172.
41. *Libro de tasaciones de los pueblos de la Nueva España–siglo XVI* (Mexico, 1952), 390, 406–8, and 522.
42. AGI, Mexico, 336-A, doc. 117.
43. AGI, Mexico, 69, ramo 4, March 26, 1574.
44. AGI, Mexico, 105, R.3, No. 33.
45. Nicolás León (ed.), *Codex Sierra* (Mexico, 1933); Barbara Dahlgran-Jordan, "Cambios socio-económicos registrados a me-

diados del siglo XVI en un pueblo de la Mixteca Alta, Oaxaca, Mexico," *International Congress of Americanists* (Paris, 1979), vol. 8, 103–19.

46. *Recopilación*, VI, 10, xii.
47. AGN, Inquisición, 115, exp. 4.
48. AGN, Inquisición, 68, exp 4.
49. AGN, General de Parte, 1, exp. 246; AGN, Indios, 2, exp. 31.
50. AGN, General de Parte, 1, exp. 610.
51. AGN, Bienes Nacionales, 546, exp. 1.
52. AAM, Ordenes Sacros, I, April 27, 1605.
53. Miranda, *Tributo*, 263–69; *Recopilación*, VI, 12, 1.
54. Mariano Cuevas, *Documentos inéditos del siglo XVI para la historia de México* (Mexico, 1914), 341.
55. *Recopilación*, VI, 12, vi–viii, x.
56. AGN, Inquisición, 155, exp. 4.
57. AGN, Bienes Nacionales, 546, exp. 1.
58. AGN, General de Parte, 5, exps, 289, 319, 459, and 646.
59. AGN, Inquisición, 155, exp 4.
60. AAM, Ordenes Sacros, I, April 27, 1605.
61. *Recopilación*, I, 13, xvii.
62. Galván Rivera, *Concilio*, 49.
63. Ibid., 183.
64. Condumex, "Instruccion para el beneficiado . . . 20 junio 1590."
65. Carreño, *Desconocido*, 75–77.
66. Galván Rivera, *Concilio*, xxvii, xxxix.
67. ACTAS, December 3, 1557, May 9, 1559, June 6, 1559.
68. ACTAS, March 18, 1578.
69. Lilly Library, Latin American Manuscripts, Mexico II, Dr. Esteban del Portillo.
70. Ecuario López, "Compendio de los libros de actas del venerable cabildo de la santa iglesia catedral de Guadalajara," *Boletín del Instituto de Investigaciones Bibliográficas*, Num. 5 (January–June 1971), 127.
71. AGN, Reales Cédulas Duplicadas, 3, exp. 224, September 14, 1588.
72. AGN, General de Parte, 2, exp. 1288.
73. Ibid., 1, 205. For the best description of the system as it

appeared in the late colonial period, see Brian R. Hamnett, *Politics and Trade in Southern Mexico* (Cambridge, 1971).

74. AGI, Mexico, 220, doc. 2.
75. AGI, Mexico, 219, doc. 18; Edmundo O'Gorman (ed.), *Catálogo de pobladores de Nueva España* (Mexico, 1945), 196.
76. AGI, Mexico, 212, doc. 19; O'Gorman, *Catálogo*, 200.

Chapter 4

1. Fr. Bartolomé de Ledesma (ed.), *Descripción del arzobispado de México* (Mexico, 1905), 3–7.
2. Costeloe, *Church Wealth.*
3. AGN, Bienes Nacionales, 1356, exp. 15; ACTAS, October 8, 1560. For an excellent discussion of the different types of loans, see Arnold J. Bauer, "The Church in the Economy of Spanish America: *Censos* and *Depósitos* in the Eighteenth and Nineteenth Centuries," *Hispanic American Historical Review* 63 (1983), 707–33.
4. Burgo de Osma, *Directorio*, 22v–23.
5. A *mayorazgo* is an entailed estate. Under Spanish law, parents could remove part (47 percent) of their overall estate and entail it so that it would be inherited wholly by one child, the eldest son. The estate so created, with royal permission and subject to royal taxation, was then inalienable and could not be broken up in any way. See Asunción Lavrin and Edith Couturier, "Dowries and Wills: A View of Women's Socioeconomic Role in Colonial Guadalajara and Puebla, 1640–1790," *Hispanic American Historical Review* 59 (1979), 282–86; and Marta Espejo Ponce Hunt, "The Processes of Development of Yucatan, 1600–1700," in Altman and Lockhart, *Provinces of Early Mexico* (Los Angeles, 1976), 36–37.
6. ACTAS, March 18, 1578.
7. Ibid.
8. AGI, Mexico, 374.
9. AGN, Bienes Nacionales, 643, exp. 5.
10. AGN, Bienes Nacionales, 133, exp. 3.
11. AGN, Bienes Nacionales, 416, exp. 1.
12. AGN, Bienes Nacionales, 816, exp. 13.
13. AGN, Bienes Nacionales, 858, exp. 1.
14. ANDDF, Pedro Sánchez, February 22, 1578.

15. AGN, Bienes Nacionales, 249, exp. 13.
16. AGN, Bienes Nacionales, 416, exp. 1.
17. AGN, Bienes Nacionales, 1517, exp. 4.
18. AGN, Bienes Nacionales, 661, exp. 7.
19. AGN, Bienes Nacionales, 661, exp. 8.
20. AGN, Bienes Nacionales, 1263, exp. 5.
21. AGN, Bienes Nacionales, 999, exp. 10.
22. AGN, Bienes Nacionales, 648, exp. 18; 1100, exp. 1.
23. AGN, Bienes Nacionales, 1044, exp. 10.
24. ANDDF, Pedro Sánchez, October 15, 1576, and October 6, [?].
25. ANDDF, Pedro Sánchez, December 12, 1576 and December 2, 1577.
26. ANDDF, Pedro Sánchez, January 30, 1578.
27. AGN, Bienes Nacionales, 648, exp. 18.
28. AGN, Reales Cédulas Duplicadas, 2, 368.
29. AGI, Mexico, 70, October 21, 1581.
30. *Guía de las actas del cabildo de la ciudad de México* (Mexico, 1971), December 3, 1540.
31. Ibid., April 22, 1560.
32. Ibid., September 9, 1566.
33. Schwaller, *Partidos*, xxvii–xxviii.
34. *Guía*, April 30, 1574.
35. Ibid., January 1, 1586.
36. Joaquín García Icazbalceta, *Bibliografía mexicana del siglo XVI* (Mexico, 1954), 447.
37. AGN, Bienes Nacionales, 945, exp. 1.
38. ACTAS, July 5, 1569.
39. ACTAS, September 6, 1575 and July 31, 1576.
40. ACTAS, September 6–25, 1576.
41. Josefina Muriel de la Torre, *Los hospitales de la Nueva España*, 2 vols. (Mexico, 1956–60), I, 147–50.
42. García Icazbalceta, *Zumárraga*, I, 307; Cuevas, *Historia*, I, 407–9; María Justina Sarabia Viejo, "Notas sobre el Hospital del Amor de Dios de México en el siglo XVI," *Anuario de Estudios Americanos* 30 (1973), 295–316.
43. García Icazbalceta, *Zumárraga*, III, 207–9.
44. Ibid., III, 209–17.
45. Ibid., III, 218–21; IV, 29–34.
46. Cuevas, *Historia*, I, 405–7; Muriel, *Hospitales*, I, 37–48.

47. Muriel, *Hospitales*, I, 233–42, 253–55.

48. Cuevas, *Historia*, I, 410–11; Carreño, *Desconocido*, 391–92; AGI, Mexico, 339, Dean y cabildo of Mexico to King, March 9, 1600.

49. Cheryl E. Martin, "San Hipolito Hospitals of Colonial Mexico," Ph.D. dissertation, Tulane University, 1976; Muriel, *Hospitales*, I, 187–97.

50. Warren, *Quiroga*.

51. Cuevas, *Historia*, I, 412; Muriel, *Hospitales*, I, 141.

52. Muriel, *Hospitales*, I, 55–111; Cuevas, *Historia*, I, 414–20.

53. Warren, *Quiroga*, 118.

54. Ibid., 107–12; Muriel, *Hospitales*, I, 59–60.

55. Muriel, *Hospitales*, I, 141–42.

56. AGI, Mexico, 2606; Francisco del Paso y Troncoso (ed.), *Epistolario de la Nueva España*, 16 vols. (Mexico, 1939–42), 14, 63.

57. Juan Bautista Arechederreta y Escalante, *Catálogo de los colegiales del insigne viejo y mayor colegio de Santa María de Todos Santos* (Mexico, 1796), 6–10.

58. AGI, Mexico, 216, doc. 52; Josefina Muriel de la Torre, *Conventos de monjas de la Nueva España* (Mexico, 1946), 85–90.

59. ANDDF, Andres Moreno, September 2, 1592, 73–75.

60. AGN, Bienes Nacionales, 816, exp. 13.

61. AGN, Bienes Nacionales, 391, exp. 15.

62. AGN, Bienes Nacionales, 1124, exp. 5.

63. AGN, Bienes Nacionales, 816, exp. 13.

64. AGI, Contaduría, 782; AGI, Mexico, 339.

65. AGN, Bienes Nacionales, 391, exp. 15.

66. Costeloe, *Church Wealth*, 8.

67. Arnold J. Bauer, "The Church and Spanish American Agrarian Structure, 1765–1865," *The Americas* 28 (1971), 92.

68. Linda Greenow, *Credit and Socioeconomic Change in Colonial Mexico* (Boulder, Colo., 1983), 72.

69. Bauer, "Church and Agrarian Structure," 95.

70. Ibid., 78–82.

71. Asunción Lavrin, "The Role of the Nunneries in the Economy of New Spain in the Eighteenth Century," *Hispanic Amer-*

ican Historical Review 46 (1966), 378, holds that they could not be repaid.

72. William B. Taylor, *Landlord and Peasant in Colonial Oaxaca* (Stanford, 1972), 141–42; Francois Chevalier, *Land and Society in Colonial Mexico* (Berkeley, 1963), 143.

73. Taylor, *Landlord*, 194.

Chapter 5

1. See the works of Woodrow Borah, Sherburne F. Cook, and Lesley B. Simpson; especially Cook and Borah, *The Indian Population of Central Mexico, 1531–1601* (Berkeley, 1960), and Borah and Cook, *Essays in Population History*, 3 vols. (Berkeley, 1971–80); William M. Denevan, *The Native Population of the Americas in 1492* (Madison, 1976); Henry Dobyns, "An Appraisal of Techniques with a New Hemispheric Estimate," *Current Anthropology* 7 (1966); Angel Rosenblat, *La población indídena de América en 1492* (Mexico, 1967); Nicolas Sánchez Albornoz, *The Population of Latin America* (Berkeley, 1974).

2. Cook and Borah, *Indian Population*, 48.

3. Woodrow Borah, *New Spain's Century of Depression* (Berkeley, 1951); for a reappraisal, see José Carlos Chiaramonte, "En torno a la recuperación demográfica y la depresión económica novohispanas durante el siglo xvii," *Historia Mexicana* 30 (1981), 561–604.

4. Peter Bakewell, *Silver Mining and Society in Colonial Zacatecas, 1546–1700* (Cambridge, 1971).

5. Carreño, *Desconocido*, 338. The existence of the letter is indicated in the reply cited here.

6. AGI, Mexico, 339, "Informacion de capellanias," March 21, 1578, "Informacion y cuentas de la fabrica," 1575–76; see Victoria Cummins, "Imperial Policy and Church Income," unpublished manuscript.

7. AGI, Mexico, 339, Dean y cabildo to King, April 20, 1581.

8. ACTAS, July 3, 1582.

9. ACTAS, July 6, 1582.

10. ACTAS, July 24 and 27, 1582.

11. ACTAS, August 22, 1582.

12. ACTAS, February 26, 1583.

13. AGI, Mexico, 374, Dean y cabildo of Michoacán to King, October 17, 1577.
14. ACTAS, September 28, 1578.
15. AGI, Mexico, 218, doc. 14.
16. Carreño, *Desconocido*, 348.
17. AGI, Contaduría, 678–80, Lo Espiritual, June 19, 1579, November 22, 1581, March 13, 1582, December 7, 1584.
18. AGN, Historia, 112.
19. ANDDF, Andres Moreno, 1597, 289–99v, August 20, 1597.
20. ANDDF, Andres Moreno, 1601, 98, March 21, 1600.
21. Richard Boyer, "Mexico in the Seventeenth Century," *Hispanic American Historical Review* 57 (1977), 461–62.
22. Borah, *Depression*, 18.
23. Gibson, *Aztecs*, 453.
24. Schwaller, "Implementation"; a copy of the Ordenanza is published in Carreño, *Desconocido*, 314–22.
25. ACTAS, March 18, 1578.
26. AGI, General de Parte, 1, passim.
27. An extensive bibliography has grown up around these conflicts, which focused on the bishop of Puebla, D. Juan de Palafox y Mendoza. See C. E. P. Simmons, "Palafox and His Critics: Reappraising a Controversy," *Hispanic American Historical Review* 46 (1966), 394–408.
28. Taylor, *Landlord*, 164–94; Chevalier, *Land and Society*, 29–62.
29. Juan Manuel Rodríguez, *La iglesia en Nueva España a la luz del III Concilio Mexicano* (Isola dei Liri, 1937); Llaguno, *La personalidad*.
30. Galván Rivera, *Concilio*. Originals are held in the Bancroft Library, University of California, Berkeley, MM 267.
31. E. J. Burrus, "The Author of the Mexican Council Catechisms," *The Americas* 15 (1958), 171–82.
32. Two copies of the *Directorio* exist. The earlier is held in Spain, Cathedral Archive of Burgo de Osma, Cod. Num. 204, "Directorio del Stº Concilio Provincial Mexicano . . . 1585." A later annotated version is still housed in the Mexico City Cathedral, ACEM, vol 120, "Directorio del Stº Concilio Provincial Mexicano, 1585." Rev. Stafford Poole and I are undertaking a critical edition of the *Directorio* using these two manuscripts.

33. Galván Rivera, *Concilio*, 183, 274; Bancroft Library, MM 267, 89v, 109v–110.
34. Galván Rivera, *Concilio*, 271–73; Bancroft Library, MM 267, 109.
35. Galván Rivera, *Concilio*, 231–34, 332–36; Bancroft Library, MM 267, 99v–100, 124v–25.
36. Galván Rivera, *Concilio*, 248–53; Bancroft Library, MM 267, 103–4v.
37. Burgo de Osma, *Directorio*, 9–10.

Chapter 6

1. Borah, *Century of Depression.*
2. Chevalier, *Land and Society.*
3. Bakewell, *Silver Mining*, 241–42.
4. Clarence Haring, *Early Trade and Navigation Between Spain and the Indies* (Cambridge, 1918), 332.
5. Pierre and Huguette Chaunu, *Seville et l'Atlantique: 1504–1650*, 8 vols. (Paris, 1955–60), vol. 6, 563.
6. Bakewell, *Silver Mining*, 188.
7. Chiaramonte, "Recuperación demográfica," 599–600. Andre Gunder Frank, *Mexican Agriculture, 1521–1600* (Cambridge, 1979), 36–50.
8. James Lockhart, "Encomienda and Hacienda: The Evolution of the Great Estate in the Spanish West Indies," *Hispanic American Historical Review* 49 (1969), 411–29.
9. Raymond L. Lee, "Grain Legislation in Colonial Mexico, 1575–85," *Hispanic American Historical Review* 27 (1947), 647–60; William H. Dusenberry, "The Regulation of Meat Supply in Sixteenth-Century Mexico," *Hispanic American Historical Review* 28 (1948), 38–52; Enrique Florescano, "El abasto y legislación de granos en el siglo xvi," *Historia Mexicana* 14 (1956), 567–630.
10. Part of this discussion can be found in Frank, *Agriculture*, 53–56, insofar as the pressures on the creation of commercial agriculture are concerned. His conclusions about the nature of the hacienda, its production, and the status of the labor force differ from those presented here. For a discussion of the labor force, see Gibson, *Aztecs*, 245–48.
11. Howard F. Cline, "Civil Congregations of the Indians in

New Spain, 1598–1606," *Hispanic American Historical Review* 29 (1949), 349–69.

12. Gibson, *Aztecs*, 32–36.

13. Ibid., 125–26.

14. Chevalier, *Land and Society*, 29–49.

15. For a discussion of the process and impact of secularization, see Francisco Canterla y Martín de Tovar, *La iglesia de Oaxaca en el siglo XVIII* (Seville, 1982); and Farriss, *Crown and Clergy*.

16. Konrad, *A Jesuit Hacienda*, 156–59.

17. Costeloe, *Church Wealth*, 17.

18. Medina Rubio, "Historia agrícola," 253.

19. Woodrow W. Borah, "Tithe Collection in the Bishopric of Oaxaca, 1600–1867," *Hispanic American Historical Review* 29 (1949), 511.

20. Brian Hamnett, "Appropriation of Church Wealth by the Spanish Bourbon Government: 'The Consolidación de Vales Reales,' 1805–1809," *Journal of Latin American Studies* 1 (1969), 88.

21. William B. Taylor, *Drinking, Homocide and Rebellion in Colonial Mexican Villages* (Stanford, 1979), 134–37, 141–42.

Bibliography

Altman, Ida, and James Lockhart, eds. *Provinces of Early Mexico.* Los Angeles: UCLA Latin American Center, 1976.

Arechederreta y Escalante, Juan Bautista. *Catálogo de los colegiales del insigne viejo y mayor colegio de Santa María de Todos Santos.* Mexico, 1796.

Artes de México, "Tepotzotlán," Num. 62–63 (1960).

Bakewell, Peter. *Silver Mining and Society in Colonial Zacatecas, 1546–1700.* Cambridge: Cambridge University Press, 1971.

Bauer, Arnold J. "The Church and Spanish American Agrarian Structure, 1765–1865," *The Americas*, 28 (1971), 78–98.

———. "The Church in the Economy of Spanish America: *Censos* and *Depósitos* in the Eighteenth and Nineteenth Centuries," *Hispanic American Historical Review*, 63 (1983), 707–33.

Borah, Woodrow W. "The Collection of Tithes in the Bishopric of Oaxaca During the Sixteenth Century," *Hispanic American Historical Review*, 21 (1941), 386–409.

———. *New Spain's Century of Depression.* Berkeley: University of California Press, 1951.

———. *Silk Raising in Colonial Mexico.* Berkeley: University of California Press, 1943.

———. "Tithe Collection in the Bishopric of Oaxaca, 1600–1867," *Hispanic American Historical Review*, 29 (1949), 498–517.

Borah, W. W., and Sherburne F. Cook. *Price Trends of Some Basic Commodities in Central Mexico, 1531–1570.* Berkeley: University of California Press, 1958.

Boxer, Charles. *The Church Militant and Iberian Expansion, 1440–1770.* Baltimore: Johns Hopkins University Press, 1978.

Boyer, Richard. "Mexico in the Seventeenth Century," *Hispanic American Historical Review*, 57 (1977), 453–78.

Burrus, Ernest J. "The Author of the Mexican Council Catechisms," *The Americas*, 15 (1958), 171–82.

Canterla y Martín de Tovar, Francisco. *La iglesia en Oaxaca en el siglo XVIII*. Seville: Escuela de Estudios Hispano-Americanos, 1982.

Carreño, José María. *Un desconocido cedulario del siglo XVI perteneciente a la catedral metropolitana*. Mexico: Ediciones Victoria, 1944.

Cartas de Indias. Madrid: Ministerio de Fomento, 1877.

Casa Rivas, Jesús María de las. "Los diezmos como fuente de ingresos de la iglesia dominicana," *Casas Reales* (Santo Domingo), May–August 1980, 43–73.

Chaunu, Pierre and Huguette. *Seville et l'Atlantique, 1504–1650*. 8 vols. Paris: Ecole Pratique des Hautes Etudes, 1955–58.

Chevalier, Francois. *Land and Society in Colonial Mexico*. Berkeley: University of California Press, 1970.

Chiaramonte, José Carlos. "En torno a la recuperación demográfica y la depresión económica novohispanas durante el siglo xvii," *Historia Mexicana*, 30 (1981), 561–604.

Cline, Howard F. "Civil Congregations of the Indians in New Spain, 1598–1606," *Hispanic American Historical Review*, 29 (1949), 349–69.

Cook, Sherburne F., and Woodrow W. Borah. *Essays in Population History*. 3 vols. Berkeley: University of California Press, 1971–79.

———. *The Indian Population of Central Mexico, 1531–1610*. Berkeley: University of California Press, 1960.

Cortés, Hernán. *Cartas y documentos*. Mexico: Editorial Porrúa, 1963.

Costeloe, Michael P. *Church Wealth in Mexico, 1800–1856*. Cambridge: Cambridge University Press, 1967.

Cuevas, Mariano, ed. *Documentos inéditos del siglo XVI para la historia de México*. Mexico: Museo Nacional, 1914.

———. *Historia de la iglesia en México*. 5 vols. El Paso: Editorial Revista Católica, 1928.

Cushner, Nicolas P. *Lords of the Land*. Albany: SUNY Press, 1980.

Dahlgran-Jordan, Barbara. "Cambios socio-económicos registrados a mediados del siglo XVI en un pueblo de la Mixteca

Alta, Oaxaca, México," *International Congress of Americanists* (Paris, 1979), 8, 103–19.

Dávila Garibi, José Ignacio. *Apuntes para la historia de la iglesia en Guadalajara*. 5 vols. Mexico: Editorial Cultura, 1957–63.

Denevan, William. *The Native Population of the Americas in 1492*. Madison: University of Wisconsin Press, 1976.

Dobyns, Henry E. "Estimating Aboriginal American Population: An Appraisal of Techniques with a New Hemispheric Estimate," *Current Anthropology*, 7 (1966), 395–416, 425–49.

Dusenberry, William H. "The Regulation of Meat Supply in Sixteenth-Century Mexico," *Hispanic American Historical Review*, 28 (1948), 38–52.

Estrada, Jesús. *Música y músicos en la época virreinal*. Mexico: Secretaría de Educación Pública, 1973.

Farriss, Nancy M. *Crown and Clergy in Colonial Mexico, 1759–1821*. London: Athlone Press, 1968.

Florescano, Enrique. "El abasto y legislación de granos en el siglo XVI," *Historia Mexicana*, 14 (1956), 567–630.

Fonseca, Fabián de, and Carlos de Urrutia. *Historia general de real hacienda*. 6 vols. Mexico: V. G. Torres, 1845–53.

Frank, Andre Gunder. *Mexican Agriculture, 1521–1630*. Cambridge: Cambridge University Press, 1979.

Ganster, Paul B. "A Social History of the Secular Clergy of Lima during the Middle Decades of the Eighteenth Century," Ph.D. diss., University of California, Los Angeles, 1974.

García Icazbalceta, Joaquín. *Bibliografía mexicana del siglo XVI*. Mexico: Fondo de Cultura Económica, 1954.

———. *Don Fray Juan de Zumárraga*. 4 vols. Mexico: Editorial Porrúa, 1947.

García Pimentel, Luis. *Descripción del arzobispado de México hecha en 1570*. Mexico: José Joaquín de Terrazas e hijas, 1897.

———. *Relación de los obispados de Tlaxcala, Michoacán, Oaxaca y otros lugares en el siglo XVI*. Mexico: Luis García Pimentel, 1904.

Galván Rivera, Mariano, ed. *Concilio III mexicano*. Mexico: Eugenio Maillefert y Compañía, 1859.

Garrido Aranda, Antonio. *Organización de la iglesia en el reino de Granada y su proyección en Indias*. Seville: Escuela de Estudios Hispano Americanos, 1979.

Gerhard, Peter. *A Guide to the Historical Geography of New Spain*. Cambridge: Cambridge University Press, 1973.

Gibson, Charles. *Aztecs Under Spanish Rule*. Stanford: Stanford University Press, 1964.

———. *Spain in America*. New York: Harper and Row, 1966.

———. *Tlaxcala in the Sixteenth Century*. Stanford: Stanford University Press, 1952.

Gómez de Cervantes, Gonzalo. *La vida económica y social de la Nueva España al finalizar el siglo XVI*. Mexico: Antigua Librería Robredo, 1944.

Góngora, Mario. *Colonial History of Spanish America*. Cambridge: Cambridge University Press, 1975.

González Díaz, Rafaela. "El estado financiero de la iglesia dominicana: Los diezmos (1578–1650)," *Casas Reales* (Santo Domingo), May–August 1980, 77–93.

Greenow, Linda. *Credit and Socioeconomic Change in Colonial Mexico*. Boulder, Colo.: Westview Press, 1983.

Guía de las actas del cabildo de la ciudad de México, siglo XVI. Mexico: Fondo de Cultura Económica, 1970.

Hamilton, Earl J. *American Treasure and the Price Revolution in Spain, 1501–1650*. Cambridge, Mass.: Harvard University Press, 1934.

Hamnett, Brian R. "The Appropriation of Mexican Church Wealth by the Spanish Bourbon Government: The 'Consolidación de Vales Reales,' 1805–1809," *Journal of Latin American Studies*, 1 (1969), 85–113.

———. *Politics and Trade in Southern Mexico, 1750–1821*. Cambridge: Cambridge University Press, 1971.

Haring, Clarence H. *Trade and Navigation Between Spain and the Indies in the Time of the Hapsburgs*. Cambridge, Mass.: Harvard University Press, 1918.

———. *The Spanish Empire in America*. New York: Harcourt, Brace, and World, 1947.

Hunt, Marta Espejo-Ponce. "Processes of the Development of Yucatan," in Ida Altman and James Lockhart, eds., *Provinces of Early Mexico*, Los Angeles: UCLA Latin American Center, 1976, 33–62.

Israel, Johnathan I. *Race, Class, and Politics in Colonial Mexico, 1610–1670*. London: Oxford University Press, 1975.

Konrad, Herman W. *A Jesuit Hacienda in Colonial Mexico: Santa Lucía, 1576–1767.* Stanford: Stanford University Press, 1980.

Kubler, George. *Mexican Architecture of the Sixteenth Century.* 2 vols. New Haven: Yale University Press, 1948.

Lavrin, Asuncion. "Role of the Nunneries in the Economy of New Spain in the Eighteenth Century," *Hispanic American Historical Review,* 46 (1966), 369–93.

Lavrin, Asuncion, and Edith Couturier. "Dowries and Wills: A View of Women's Socioeconomic Role in Colonial Guadalajara and Puebla, 1640–1790," *Hispanic American Historical Review,* 59 (1979), 280–304.

Ledesma, Bartolomé de. *Descripción del arzobispado de México.* Madrid: Sucesores de Rivadeneyra, 1905.

Lee, Raymond L. "Grain Legislation in Colonial Mexico," *Hispanic American Historical Review,* 27 (1947), 647–60.

León, Nicolás. *Codex Sierra.* Mexico: Museo Nacional, 1933.

Libro de las tasaciones de la Nueva España, siglo XVI. Mexico: Archivo General de la Nación, 1952.

Liss, Peggy K. *Mexico Under Spain, 1521–1556.* Chicago: University of Chicago Press, 1975.

Llaguno, José A. *La personalidad jurídica del indio y el IIIer concilio provincial mexicano.* Mexico: Editorial Porrúa, 1963.

López, Ecuario. "Compendio de los libros de actas del venerable cabildo de la santa iglesia catedral de Guadalajara, 1552–1900," *Boletín del Instituto de Investigaciones Bibliograficas,* 5 (1971), 119–361.

Lockhart, James. "Encomienda and Hacienda: The Evolution of the Great Estates in the Spanish West Indies," *Hispanic American Historical Review,* 49 (1969), 411–29.

———. *Spanish Peru, 1532–1600.* Madison: University of Wisconsin Press, 1968.

MacLachlan, Colin M., and Jaime E. Rodriguez. *The Forging of the Cosmic Race.* Berkeley: University of California Press, 1980.

Martin, Cheryl E. "San Hipolito Hospitals of Colonial Mexico," Ph.D. diss. Tulane University, 1976.

Meek, Wilbur T. *The Exchange Media of Colonial Mexico.* New York: King's Crown Press, 1948.

Mendieta, Gerónimo de. *Historia ecclesiástica indiana*. 4 vols. Mexico: Editorial Salvador Chávez Hayhoe, 1945.

Millares Carlo, Agustín, and José Ignacio Mantecón. *Indice y extractos de los protocolos del Archivo de Notarias*. 2 vols. Mexico: Colegio de Mexico, 1946.

Miranda, José. *La función económica del encomendero en los orígenes de régimen colonial*. Mexico: Universidad Nacional Autónoma de México, 1965.

———. *El tributo indígena en la Nueva España durante el siglo XVI*. Mexico: Colegio de Mexico, 1952.

Montúfar, Alonso de. *Ordenanzas para el coro de la catedral mexicana*. Madrid: Ediciones José Porrúa Turanzas, 1964.

Muriel de la Torre, Josefina. *Conventos de monjas en la Nueva España*. Mexico: Editorial Santiago, 1946.

———. *Los hospitales de la Nueva España*. 2 vols. Mexico: Universidad Nacional Autónoma de México, 1956–60.

O'Gorman, Edmundo, ed. *Catálogo de pobladores de la Nueva España*. Mexico: Archivo General de la Nación, 1945.

Parry, John H. *The Sale of Public Office in the Spanish Indies Under the Hapsburgs*. Berkeley: University of California Press, 1953.

———. *The Spanish Seaborne Empire*. New York: Knopf, 1966.

Paso y Troncoso, Francisco del. *Epistolario de la Nueva España*. 16 vols. Mexico: Antigua Librería Robredo, 1939–42.

Phelan, John L. *The Kingdom of Quito*. Madison: University of Wisconsin Press, 1967.

———. *The Millenial Kingdom of the Franciscans in the New World*. Berkeley: University of California Press, 1970.

Poole, Stafford. "Research Possibilities of the Third Mexican Council," *Manuscripta*, 5 (1961), 151–63.

Recopilación de las leyes de Indias. 4 vols. Madrid: Ediciones Cultura Hispánica, 1973.

Ricard, Robert. *The Spiritual Conquest of Mexico*. Berkeley: University of California Press, 1966.

Rodríguez, Juan Manuel. *La iglesia en Nueva España a la luz del III concilio mexicano*. Isola dei Liri, 1937.

Rosenblat, Angel. *La población indígena de América desde 1492 hasta la actualidad*. Buenos Aires: Institutión cultural española, 1954.

Sanchez Albornoz, Nicolas. *The Population of Latin America*. Berkeley: University of California Press, 1974.
Sánchez Bela, Ismael. *La organización financiera de las Indias*. Seville: Escuela de Estudios Hispano Americanos, 1968.
Sarabia Viejo, María Justina. "Notas sobre el Hospital del Amor de Dios de México en el siglo XVI," *Anuario de Estudios Americanos*, 30 (1973), 295–316.
Schwaller, John Frederick. "The Cathedral Chapter of Mexico in the Sixteenth Century," *Hispanic American Historical Review*, 61 (1981), 651–74.
———. "The Implementation of the Ordenanza del Patronazgo in New Spain," in Jeffery A. Cole, ed., *The Church and Society in Latin America*, New Orleans: Center for Latin American Studies, Tulane, 1983, 38–50.
———. *Partidos y párrocos bajo la real corona en la Nueva España, siglo XVI*. Mexico: Instituto Nacional de Antropología e Historia, 1981.
———. "Tres familias mexicanas del siglo XVI," *Historia Mexicana*, 31 (1981), 171–96.
Shiels, W. Eugene. *King and Church*. Chicago: Loyola University Press, 1961.
Simmons, C. E. P. "Palafox and His Critics: Reappraising a Controversy," *Hispanic American Historical Review*, 46 (1966), 394–408.
Simpson, Lesley B. *The Encomienda in New Spain*. Berkeley: University of California Press, 1966.
———. *Studies in the Administration of the Indians in New Spain*. Berkeley: University of California Press, 1934.
Stevenson, Robert. "Mexico City Cathedral: The Founding Century," *Inter-American Music Review*, 1 (1979), 131–78.
Taylor, William B. *Drinking, Homocide, and Rebellion in Colonial Mexican Villages*. Stanford: Stanford University Press, 1979.
———. *Landlord and Peasant in Colonial Oaxaca*. Stanford: Stanford University Press, 1972.
Toussaint, Manuel. *Colonial Art in Mexico*. Austin: University of Texas Press, 1967.
Van Young, Eric. "Mexican Rural History Since Chevalier: Historiography of the Colonial Hacienda," *Latin American Research Review*, 18 (1983), 5–61.

Warren, Fintan B. *Vasco de Quiroga and His Pueblo Hospitals of Santa Fe*. Washington: Academy of American Franciscan History, 1963.

Zavalo, Silvio. *La encomienda indiana*. Mexico: Editorial Porrúa, 1973.

Map Appendix

DIOCESE OF GUADALAJARA

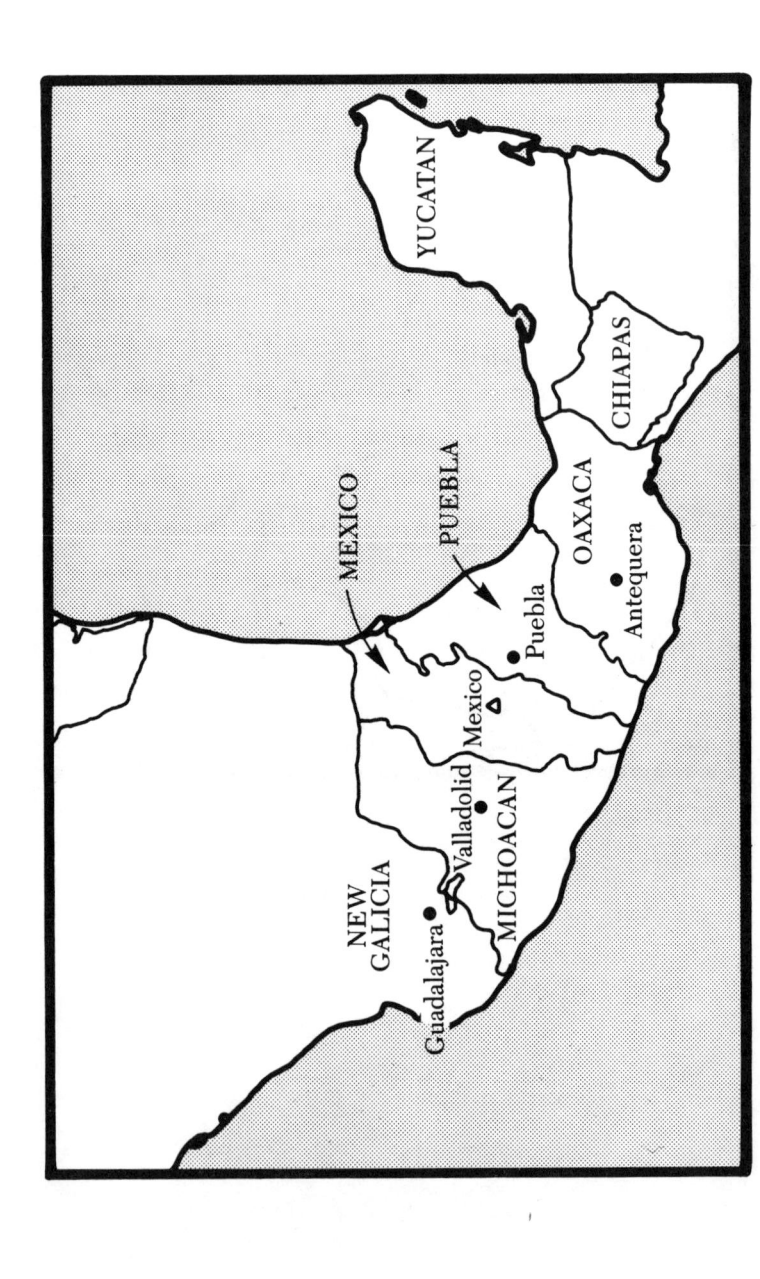

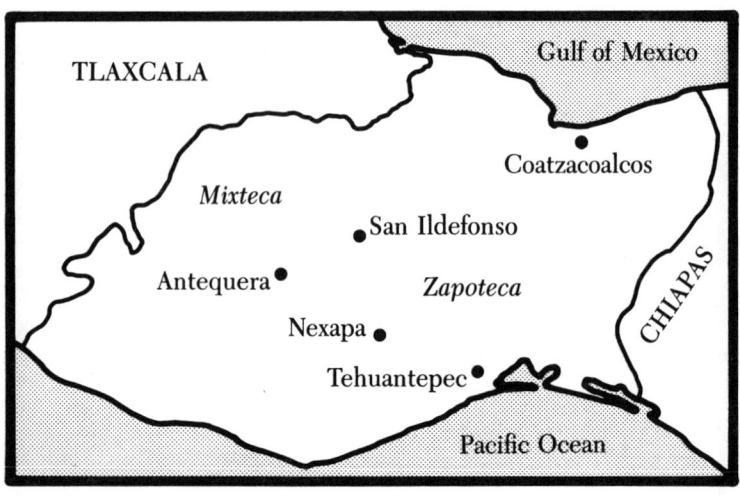

ARCHDIOCESE OF MEXICO

DIOCESE OF PUEBLA-TLAXCALA

Statistical Appendix

Obispado de Oaxaca
Tithe Collection
(oro comun)

	A	B	C	D	E	F	G	H	I
1561			297.6.4	24.6.6	165.3.6				
1562	526.3.3	702.7.0					6312	6318	
1563	525	700.4	305.7.6	31.4	138.6		6300	6300	
1564	467.2	621.6	289.5	19.7	115.5		5604	5589	
1565	492.1	656.2	297.5	19.7	91		5904	5904	
1566	463.2.6	617.5	200.3	20	90.6	28	5556	5553	
1567	397.0.1	529.3.6	281.1.3	16.4	104.1.9		4764	4761	
1568	335.7	497.6.6				34	4020	4473	
1569	376.0.3	501.0.6	229	16.4	115.4	29	4512	4509	
1570	341.3	455.3	220	16.4	154.2	25	4092	4095	
1571	412.5	551.4	220	16.4	115.4	31	4944	4959	
1572	405.3	539.4	200	12	116.1	42	4860	4851	
1573	414	550.4	286	10	88	40	4968	4950	5000
1574	541.4	722.2	400			39.2	6492	6498	6500
1575	458.2	611.4	410		165.3.6	50	5496	5499	5500
1576	500	666.5		10	250	50	6000	6000	6000
1577	500	666.5	400	13.6.3	300	55.4	6000	6000	6000
1578	500	666.5	322	13.6	300	51	6000	6000	6000
1579	500	666.5	300	10	300	51	6000	6000	6000
1580	500	666.5	330				6000	6000	6000
1581	500	666.5	325		300	70	6000	6000	6000
1582	583.2.2	777.6.2	325	25	300	70	6996	6993	7000
1583	728.4	971	340.4	30.4	300	80	8736	8739	
1584					250	75			8000
1585	636.4	847.2			250	75	7632	7623	8000
1586	666	889	345	25	250	75	7992	8001	
1587	664.2	885.6	345		250	75	7968	7965	
1588				13	242				
1589	833.3	1111.1			300		9996	9999	10000
1590					300				

A. Fabric fund
B. King's fund
C. *Excusado* Antequera
D. *Excusado* San Ildefonso
E. *Excusado* Tehuantepec
F. *Excusado* Coatzacoalcos
G. Total Tithe [Fabric fund × 12]
H. Total Tithe [King's fund × 9]
I. Total Tithe

Source: Biblioteca del Instituto Nacional de Antropologia e Historia, Mexico, Filmoteca, Oaxaca Rollo 100.

Arzobispado de Mexico
Tithe Collection
(oro de minas)
(c = oro comun)

	A	B	C	D	E	F
1523–24	5550 c					
1525	4100 c					
1528	2800.m					
1529	3700.m					
1530	6000.m (5000?)					
1535	4700.m					
1536	7000 c*					
1537	7112 c					
1538	9261.m					
1539	7000 c					
1540	5201 c**					
1541	5652.5					
1544						277.3
1545				625.7.1		278.4
1546						280.2.5
1547				766.3.3	1021.7	390.
1548				780.	1046.6.8	409.4
1549				656.6	875.4	472
1550	11103.4	2630.4	8473	691.0.8	921.3.6	645
1551	10848.6.7	2370.6	8478	690.4	921.5.4	741
1552	10649.3.9	2370.6	8278.5.9	666.3.1	901.6.10	750.6
1553	12441.1.8	2370.6	10070.3.8	825.5.7	1100.7.6	889.5.7
1554	11770.6.6	2039.1	9731.5.6	796.1	1061.3.2	929.4.6
1555	12510.2.4	2039.1	10471.1.4	776.7	1035.6.8	939.7
1556	12046.5.4	2939.1	9107.4.4	710	947.4	515.4.8
1557	13227.4.3	2939.1	10288.3	814.2.6	1085.6	848.2.8
1558	12515.5.11	2125.5	10390.0.11	811.1.6	1081.4.8	805.2.1
1559	13324.2.2	2031	11293.2.2	906	1208	732.0.5
1560	12465.0.11	2249.5	10215.3.11	923.1.3	1231.1.3	662.2.5
1561	14110.6.3	2086.7	12023.7.3	1055.3.11	1407.2.6	990
1562	16100.3.7	2086.7	14014.4.7	1040.2	1467.3.7	854.2.8
1563	18651.2.2	2146.4	16504.6.2	1255.3.11	1762.2	940
1564	16854.1.11	1134	15720.1.11	1265.6.11	1682.6.8	840.7.5
1565	18355.6.3	1025.4	17330.3.3	1378.3.8	1853.7.4	821.5.4
1566	17453.3.7	1025.5	16427.6.7	1256.1.8	1699.7.10	825
1567	16910.6.6	936.3	15947.3.6	1268.6.4	1703.2.10	736
1568	16262.7.10	963.3	15299.4.10	1154.6.4	1616.2.3	770
1569				1357.1.8	1844.3.6	930
1570	17910			1475.5.5	1990	877.6.8
1571				1699.0.4	2225.2.3	858.6
1572				1689.6.6	2267.3.6	917.4.1
1573				1895.0.1	2532.4.4	1177.2.2
1574 [oro comun]				4287.7.6	5717.2.2	2365.6.6
1575 [oro comun]				3970.1.6	5338.5.9	2202.0.2
1576 [oro comun]				3887.3.5		2331.1.6

A. Gross tithe
B. Tithe on Tribute
C. General tithe
D. Fabric fund
E. King's fund
F. *Excusado*
*Includes Michoacan
**Michoacan separated

Source: AGI, Mexico, 336-A, doc. 104(7)

Obispado de Puebla
Tithe Collection
(oro comun)

	A	B
1540	813.	586.
1541	813.	586.
1542	930.	730.
1543	1087.	860.
1544	1542.	1304.
1545	1620.	1332.
1546	1630.	1430.
1547	1701.	1498.
1548	3358.	2640.
1549	3359.	2673.
1550	3190.	2369.
1551	3651.	2532.
1552	4196.	3097.
1553	4644.	3513.
1554	5010.	3800.
1555	6205.	5068.
1556	9150.	7362.
1557	7578.	5587.
1558	16104.	14982.
1559	17639.	15452.
1560	14866.	12727.
1561	17750.	15934.
1562	18322.	16296.
1563	19995.	18064.
1564	20654.	19117.
1565	19183.	17311.
1566	16010.	13968.
1567	14905.	
1568	20528.	
1569	15231.	
1570		
1571	16247.	14151.
1572	16219.	14516.
1573	31939.	
1574	30023.	
1575	34144.	
1576	33506.	
1577	37922.	34426.
1578	41452.	38853.
1579	44286.	40734.
1580	37880.	31129.
1581	42689.	37302.
1582	59939.	53701.
1583	53451.	45043.

A. Gross tithe
B. Tithe less costs
Source: Aristides Medina Rubio, "Elementos para una economia agricola de Puebla, 1540–1795," unpublished dissertation, El Colegio de Mexico, Mexico, p. 233.

Obispado de Michoacan
Tithe Collection
(oro de minas)

	A	B	C	D	E	F
1550	3307.4	920.4	635.3.6	462.7.1		4166
1551	4000	920.4	635.3.6	466.7.5		4202.3
1552	3110	653	560.2.4	480.2.11		4323.2.4
1553	3000	727.5.6	660	487.4.2		4387.5.6
1554	2600	450	822	430.1.9		3872
1555	3135.5.3	494.0.4	730.4.2	436.0.11	4360.1.9	3925.3.6
1556	2551.1.9	573.7.6	1080.6.4	388.2.3	4205.7.9	3495.4.10
1557	2519.7.9	760.2.9	1222.7.1	484.5.10	4503.1.7	4272.2.5
1558	2732.3	795.1.7	1477.6.4	533.3	5005.2.11	
1559	3157.0.7	722.5.7	1157.1.4	515.4.1	5036.7.2	
1560	3303.5.8	989.4.7	938.4.5	550.5.11	5231.6.8	
1561	3527.6.11	683.4	861.1.11	532.4.3	5072.4.10	4792
1562	4754.4	891.3	882	682.5.1		6143.6
1563	5394.5.4	903.8	762.2.9	677.4.3		6097.7.5
1564	6475.7.9	900	789.4.6	858.2.5		7724.5.11
1565	6491.0.11	821	920	770.1.11	8232.0.11	6932.0.4
1566	6089	900	855.3	721.7.8	7875.1	6497.2.11
1567	5687.3.3	700	800	705.7.5	7187.3.3	6352.1.9
1568	6114.2	864.1.9	855.1.7	757.7	7833.5.4	6819.4.7
1569	6817.6.2	924	920	853.4.6	8661.6.2	7682.3.3
1570	8298.7.8	972	950	968.7.7	10221.2.8	8720.4.4
1571	10142	948	1084.6	1264.5.6	12174.6	11382.1.9
1572	11592.2.6	1105	1275.3	1424.2.6	13972.5.6	12819.1.6
1573	12973.6.6	1455.3	1455.2.6	1667.0.4	15884.4	15002.4
1574	16065.1.1	1155	1270	1895.4.10	18490.1.1	17060.4.6
1575	17200.5	1109	1155	2097.3.3	19464.5	18876.6.5
1576	21772.2.6	1214	1337	2618.1.1	24323.2.6	23563.2.1
1577	14224.2.11		*	1523.2.11		13714.0.4
1578	14171.4.6	1000	1200	1751.3.10	16371.4.6	15775.1.5
1579	17753.2 c 6089.7.10	483.4.11	880	1983.3.9		17860.4.1
1580	30035.5.4c	899	992	1857.0.3		16733.3.1

A. Province of Michoacan
B. Province of Colima
C. Province of Zacatula
D. King's fund
E. Gross tithe
F. Tithe after expenses
Source: AGI, Mexico, 375.

Obispado de Guadalajara
Tithe Collection
(oro de minas)

	A	B	C	D	E	F
1551	346.2.10	2287.1.6	600.	145.	85.	3117.
1552	405.3.3	2518.6	573.2.5	156.5	400.	3648.5.5
1553	339.2	1827.6	898.5.2	100.	226.7.7	3053.1.9
1554	385.3.6	2022.4	1021.4	101.	425.	3469.
1555	280.0.4	1581.2	850.	123.	89.1	2520.3
1556	331.1.6	1917.1.4	938.4	125.	315.	2980.5.4
1557	339.4.8	1900.6	897.5	135.	123.	3056.3
1558	325.5.4	1827.4	804.4	252.	49.	2931.
1559	339.1.8	1977.0.6	698.2	231.4	146.1	3052.7.6
1560	368.5.6	2283.7.6	782.6	172.	79.4	3318.
1561	451.6.5	2798.	975.	172.	121.	4066.2
1562	538.	3596.7.6	800.	196.	255.	4841.7.6
1563	517.3.11					5306.
1564	673.6.8					5833.1.3
1565	790.7.7					
1566	764.6.5					
1567	679.5.1					
1568	897.0.2					
1569	937.0.7					
1570	1040.7.6					
1571	1013.7					
1572	1122.					
1573	999.6					
1574	1589.7.9					
1575	1485.5.3					
1576	1601.7.9					
1577	1609.2.4					
1578	1478.4					
1579	1443.3.6					
1580	1490.5.8					
(oro comun)						
1586	3078.5					
1587	2992.6					
1588	3002.2					
1589	2890.6					
1590	2870.3.9					

A. King's fund
B. Guadalajara Province
C. Campostela Province
D. Purificacion Province
E. Culiacan Province
F. Gross tithe

Source: AGI, Guadalajara, 64; AGI, Indiferente General, 2978.

Tithe Collection Conditions

1578: Las condiciones que se le ponen al administrador de los diezmos

Primeramente que todo lo que se hubiere de traer en especie de los diezmos sea dando quenta primero al cabildo, y asi mismo de lo que se ubiere de vender asi en esta ciudad como fuera.

Y lo mismo de todo lo que se ubiere de repartir en especie o en dineros para que se manden hazer los repartimientos que para ello sean necesarios y sea todo lo susodicho cargo del administrador y el avisar a sus tiempos de todo lo que se ubiere entregado al mayordomo en dineros o en especies.

Ha de tener en guarda de todas las escripturas de lo que se vendiere para las entregar al mayordomo en estando cumplido el plazo de las tales escripturas el qual las tiene de comenzan a cobrar dentro de los veinte dias que en sus condiciones se pone.

Ha de tener un libro donde tenga quenta y razon con todo lo que se entregare al mayordomo asi en especie como en dineros o en otra qualquier manera con dia, mes, y año y firmado del dicho mayordomo y lo que asi se le entregare ha de yr declarado de que estancias o sementeras y la cantidad de cada una de las estancias o sementeras.

Ha de procurar de tener cedulas o cartas de todos los diezmeros por donde se declare la cantidad de sus diezmos de qualquier cosa que se an firmados de sus nombres con dia, mes, y año.

Con esta misma obligacion se han de señalar y embiar los cobradores de todos los dichos diezmos o qualquier parte dellos llevando cada uno su libro donde pongan la razon de lo que cobrare y lo firmen los que lo pagaren o otro por ellos con testigos si pudiere ser para que a su tiempo se pueda mejor averiguar la verdad cotejando unos libros con otros.

Tithe Collection Conditions

Ha de ser a su cargo el procurar las personas que sean necesarias para yr a cobrar y recoger los dichos diezmos o parte de ellos y en concertase con ellos en la parte o salario que ubieren de aver los quales han de dar finazas legas, llanas, y abonadas de que haran bien y fielmente su officio salvo si al cabildo le pareciere otra cosa.

Ha de ser a su cargo procurar quien traiga los dichos diezmos que se ubieren de traer en especie a esta ciudad y concertar los salarios que se les ubieren de dar lo qual ha de pagar el mayordomo por sus cedulas del dicho administrador salvo quando le pareciere que convendra que el cobrador que embia las tales cosas y diezmos haga el tal concierto con el arriero o personas que lo truxeren a la ciudad.

Ha de poner por condicion a los que truxeren los dichos diezmos que quando truxeren algun trigo o mayz mal acondicionado conviene a saber elado, mojado, o que tenga algun otro daño que lo traigan aparte y dello den aviso al dicho administrador o al mayordomo para que se ponga a donde no dañe lo bueno y para que del tal genero se haga repartimiento particular.

Y por evitar que ninguno de los señores prebendados se pueda quexar del dicho administrador si da a uno mejor trigo que a otro, es condicion que no pueda particularmente dar a ninguno de los dichos señores prebendados ningun trigo ni maiz sin que para ello precede repartimiento de tantos o tantas hanegas de maiz o trigo o cebada o otras qualesquier cosas que estan en tal o tal pieza o aposento.

Que da libertad al Cabildo para alterar o disminuir o añadir en estas condiciones lo que quisieren conforme a lo que mostraren los tiempos que sucedieren.

Da se le salario al dicho administrador por su trabajao docientos pesos de oro comun.

Source: ACTAS, June 26, 1578, III, f. 56–56v.

1582: Condiciones para el administrador

Primeramente que a de ser obligado el dicho administrador a hazer una descreption de todos los pueblos y estancias y tierras de pan llevar y otras qualesquiera partes donde aya ganados o senenters o otras qualesquiera cosas de que se deba diezmos en todo este arzobispado en poca o en mucha cantidad y informarse y tomar cuenta en al mejor forma que aya lugar de los señores de las dichas posessiones o tierras o estancias o pueblos y otras partes donde se coge o crie o aya cogido o criado alguna cosa de que se deba y aya debido diezmo o a las personas que lo uvieren tenido o tuvieren a cargo que se hallaron presentes o despues quando uviere con ellos y que tanto ayan pagado de diezmo de los años pasados a poco mas o menos si al justo no se pudieren saver o a lo menos en el año proximo pasado y si debieren o restaren debiendo alguna cosa o parte de ello y cobrarlo en especie o en dinero o si le pareciere venderlo, lo qual se dexe a su buena rectitud y conciencia en lo tocante a lo que esta dicho, y a de ser obligado a hazer description susodicha por tan buena orden que se pueda entender en terminos de que pueblos caen y estan las tierras o estancias o partes donde se cogen o crian aquellas cosas de que se deben y ayan de pagar y cobrar los dichos diezmos, todo lo qual a de hazer dentro del diho año so pena de que si alguna cosa dexare de hazer en este dicho tiempo sea obligado a hazer la sin salario o que se probea persona que la haga por los dichos señores dean y cabildo a su costa y de lo que bendiere si fuere al fiado enbie dentro de diez dias los recaudos de ello a los dichos señores dean y cabildo para que se haga cargo de la cobranza de ello al mayordomo y si fuere al contado embielo procedido de ello dentro del dicho termino hallando persona de recaudo con quien seguramente se pueda embiar, con declaracion que en lo tocante a la provincia de Acapulco por ser tierra tan calida cumpla con encomenderlo a los beneficiados que residen en ella con obligacion de dar entera noticia y relacion de todas las huertas de cacao y maiz de los pueblos y estancias de ganados y pesquerias y simenteras de algodon y de todo lo demas que en la dicha provincia aya de que se deba diezmo y de cuyo es y lo que podran valer del diezmo de ello y si se deba algo de los años de atras.

Yten que se le da facultad y poder cumplido para poder nombrar cobradores de todos los diezmos de este arzobispado y remoberlos cada y quando que bien visto le fuere dando de ello noticias a los dichos señores de los que uviere de remober con tal que a los tales cobradores en la facultad que les diere para cobrar los dichos diezmos les señale las partes y terminos de donde an de cobrar y la parte o salario que por ello an de llebar

Tithe Collection Conditions

Tithe Collection Conditions

haziendolos obligar y que se obligue a que recogeran y cobraran todo lo que uviere de diezmos de aquel genero o generos de diezmos que se les encomendare en todo aquel territorio y partes que les fuere señalado sin dexar de cobrar cosa alguna de todo ello salbo quando los deudores no se lo quisieren pagar en tal caso con dar parte de ello a los dichos señores dean y cabildo ayan cumplido so pena de que lo que dexaren de cobrar se cobrara de ellos de sus bienes o se embiara a su costa persona que lo cobre dentro del termino que por el dicho señor racionero se les señalare o como mejor pareciere a los dichos señores dean y cabildo y que para la buena razon de ello se les da a cada uno de los tales cobradores un libro de a quarto de pliego como los que se suelen dar numerados las ojas y rubricado del dicho señor racionero Muñoz con cargo que el tal cobrador asiente en el todo lo que cobrare especificando la calidad y cantidad de lo que cobrare y que tanto es de lo bueno y de lo no tal y si fuere trigo maiz o cebada que tanto es de lo bueno y que tanto es de lo mojado o podrido o comido de gorgojo o elado que todo se firme de las personas de quien lo cobrare o de otros con testigos si los uviere si ellos no supieren firmar cada vez que alguna cosa recibiere y con dia y mes y año jurando si lo quisieren jurar y con declaracion si acaban de pagar con aquello que entregan lo que bende aquel año o de aquel genero o especie que entregan o si les queda mas si entra en ello parte o todo de alguno de los años de atras, para que por las partidas y razon de los tales libros sean obligados s dar sus quentas con pago cada quando que se les pidiere dentro de viente dias despues para ello fueren llamados o embiados a llamar en que a de ser creido por solo su juramento el que los llamare o fuere a llamar por parte de los dichos señores dean y cabildo so pena que no viniendo se pueda enbiar por ellos con cartas o otros recaudos de justicia y la persona que fuere aya a su costa con dos pesos y medio de salario por cada dia de lo que en ello se detuviere y lo a de pagar juntamente con todo lo que costaren las cartas de justicia y los demas recaudos que para ello se uvieren de sacar y las demas cosas que para ello se hizieren, y desta manera y no de otra se den los poderes a los dichos cobradores so pena de que dar el dicho señor racionero Muñoz obligado y que desde luego se obligue al cumplimiento y paga de todo ello renunciando su propio domicilio y jurisdicion y sometiendose a todas las justicias de Su Magestad y especialmente a los desta ciudad de Mexico y a la de los señores alcaldes de corte que en ela residen y que cumpla con los tales fiadores siendo abonados y tenidos por tales.

Yten a de tener un libro por si a donde asiente por su orden todo lo tocante a la description del arzobispado con declaracion de donde caen y en terminos de que pueblo todas las estancias y simenteras que uviere en los terminos del tal pueblo y sus sujetos y que es lo que se siembrare en cada una de ellas si es trigo o maiz o otras semillas y que ganados se crian en ellas asi mayores como menores y la cantidad de lo que pudiere averiguar que se suele dezmar en los años de atras y en alguno de ellos y lo deste dicho año de su administracion distinto lo uno de lo otro y todo por tal orden y tambien declarado que despues a su tiempo se pueda poner todo por buena orden en la contaduria deste santa iglesia en un libro de pliegos oradados a lo qual el se a de jallar para lo poner y declarar juntamente con el contador que lo uviere de hazer.

Yten que cada y quando sea necesario escriba dando aviso a lo menos de quinze en quinze dias o de veinte en veinte dias a los dichos señores dean y cabildo de lo que fuere administrando para que por sus cartas se haga cargo al mayordomo de lo que convenga que se haga y se le mande lo en ello aya y deba hazer assi mesmo lo que uviere de embiar en dinero de lo que uviere bendido de los dichos diezmos y para que aya razon y quenta de todo ello y a else le avise de lo que convenga quando se ofreciere de que deba ser avisado o a el se le ofreciere de que lo quiera ser.

Yten en quanto a lo que toca a la Teutalpa Temazcaltepec y Zultepec lo que encomendare a los beneficiados que en estas partes residen cumpla con que ellos solos se obliguen en la forma que esta dicha sin que den fiadores si buenamente no los quisieren dar.

Yten a de llebar cartas generales de las que suelen dar contra las personas que no an pagado asta agora enteramente sus diezmos y deben alguna cosa de ellos o que no los ayan pagado como son obligados y por derecho esta determinado haziendo fraude o represa en algo de ello.

Yten que el dicho señor racionero a de ser obligado a hazer todo los suso dicho en el tiempo y como por los capitulos y condiciones de suso antes deste esta referido y se declara y para ello se le da y señala por su travajo y solicitud que gane la gruesa

Tithe Collection Conditions

de su prebenda como absente y assi ponga en el quadrante todo lo que deste dicho tiempo de su año lo estuviere y se necesario estarlo y demas de ello se le den ocho cientos pesos de oro comun por todo este dicho año de la gruesa de todos los diezmos pagados por sus tercios.

Source: ACTAS, November 23, 1582, III, f. 160–61.

Tithe Conditions for Queretaro and San Juan del Rio

Ynstruccion de lo que a de hazer el Sr. Dr. don Alonso Larios de Bonilla chantre de la catedral de Mexico con el poder desta santa yglesia al valle de S. Juan del Rio y termino de Queretaro y Suchi.

Lo primero por virtud del poder tomar quenta a los que an tenido poder de esta santa yglesia son los albaceas o erederos del P. Cipriano, difunto, al beneficiado Miguel Izquierdo, al P. Bartolome Rodrigues, a Alonso Perez de Bocanegra y ver si conforman al asiento que con ellos se hizo si an cumplido.

Yten a de llevar consigo la executoria de la Real Audiencia que se saco en el pleyto de Queretaro donde estan nombradas todas las haziendas, estancias, del termino de Queretaro de que se tomo posesion para que paguen diezmo a este arzobispado de ganado mayor y menor y de lo demas que en las dichas haziendas se sembra y coge y saber si alguna de las dichas estancias sea substraido de pagar del dicho diezmo y que para adelante reconozcan que la paga que estan obligados a hazer del dicho diezmo a de ser a esta santa yglesia.

Yten a de llevar un libro o quaderno donde se asienten todas las estancias y las personas que las poseen y que cantidad de cada cosa orian y cogen de que son obligados a pagar diezmo y juntamente asentar en el dicho libro las haziendas que ay en el termino de Queretaro de trigo y maiz y de las demas semillas y huertas y que cantidad se suele coger un año con otro asentandose cada partida de cada hazienda aparte con el nombre de la persona que lo posee para que esta yglesia aya la claridad que convenga.

Yten a de hazer diligencia y saber muy en particular lo que toca al ganado menor que tanto tiempo del año anda repastando en el obispado de Mechuacan y que cantidad es de ganado la que alla se tresquila por quanto an sacado provision real para que en el dicho obispado de Mechuacan se pague la mitad del diezmo de la lana y borregas y si para esta averiguacion convieniese hazer alguna diligencia ante la justicia de Queretaro se hara.

Yten de todo lo que cobrare del ganado mayor se a de entender que si aventasare y sobrepasare mas del arendamiento en que lo a tenido los años pasados Alonso Perez de Bocanegra, que de aquello que sobrepasare y acresciere mas del dicho arendamiento a de llevar la decima parte dello libre y sin costas y esto se a de entender de lo que bendiere al contado o fiado segun como se hiziere la diligencia de la misma suerte a de llevar la parte que le cupiere y en el dicho quaderno a de asentar todas las manifestaciones que se hiziere del ganado mayor como arriba esta referido para que aya claridad de cada cosa.

Yten que de las otras cosas que cobrase de maiz, trigo, lana, quesos, ganado menor, fruta, uvas, nuezes, pollos, gallinas, de qualquier cosa destas o de otras que pareciere deverse diezmo a de llevar cinco por ciento en el contado o fiado que hiziese en cada cosa su parte.

Yten que de los naturales pueda cobrar de todas las cosas que cogen y crian que son de Castilla, frutas, uvas, nuezes, y ganado menor y desto a de llevar cinco por ciento y asentar en el mismo quaderno todas las haziendas de los naturales y que cantidad cogen cada una dellas.

Yten de todos los rezagos que an dejado de cobrar los que an tenido poder los años pasados se a de entender lo que cobrare desto a de llevar la decima parte dello.

Yten las escripturas que hiziere de ganado mayor de trigo o maiz o otra qualquier cosa que sea, se an de obligar ante scribano real y a la jurisdiccion desta Real Audiencia y Justicia Ordinaria y al fuero della com pena que cumplido el plazo si no pagaren puedan ir a cobrar dellos con dos pesos de salarios y esta es la instruccion que se manda dar al doctor don Alonso Larios de Bonilla.

Source: ACTAS, July 12, 1591, IV, ff. 52v–53.

Index

Acapulco, 3, 4, 35
Acolman, 47
Acolman-Teotihuacan, 35
agriculture: economic sector of, 11–12, 15–16; encumbrances and, 146; epidemic and decline of, 150, 159, 160; estate growth and, 175–77, 179; fertile areas for, 3–4; grain tithe resold, 80–81; investments in, 51; regular clergy holdings in, 31, 165, 179–81; tithe on, 48–49, 80–81, 158, 178
Alamo, Lázaro del, 74
Alavés, Esteban de, 108
Alexander VI, 19
alms, 5, 10, 140–43, 169
Alonso, Antonio, 125–26
Altamirano, Juan, 48
Álvarez, Bernardino, 136, 138
Alzórriz, Sancho de, 39
Amecameca, 35, 47
Amor de Dios, 59, 135
anniversaries, 106
Antequera, 3, 47
aranceles, 86, 88, 97, 104, 167
Atlixco Valley, 3, 15, 23

Avila, Alonso de, 45
Ayllón, Juan de, 123

Badillo, Juan de, 34
Baena, Diego, 127
Bajío, 4, 47
Bauer, Arnold, 145
Becerra, Bertolomé, 91
benefice (*beneficio*), 9, 162–66
Benítez, Miguel, 127
Bourbons, 184, 185
Bravo, Diego, 108
Breviary, 64
Bustamante, Blas de, 86–87, 128, 130

Caballero Bazán, Diego, 33–34, 35
cacao, 155
Campostela, 4, 48
Canonical Hours, 64
capellanias, 106, 112, 117, 126–27, 161. *See also* chantries
Cárdenas, Cespedes de, 131
Carolense, the, 3
catechism, 166
cathedral chapter: allocation of salaries, 60–73; attendance and salaries,

64–70, 72; burial fees, 86, 105–6; cathedral *capellanias*, 113, 117–18; cathedral chaplains, 129; cathedral maintenance, 26, 28, 74–78. *See also* fabric account; cathedral parishes, 85–86; cathedral staff, 59–63, 74–76, 153–56; dividing the funds, 63–65, 72–73; financial evaluation, 152, 156; hierarchy, 60, 68; incomes not salaries, 106, 118; opinion on royal patronage, 161; power of appointment, 161–62; statutes, 166; suits with priests, 86–88, 128; tithe collection and administration, 27–28, 55
cattle, 4, 24–25, 30
Cazano, Nicolás, 124
cédulas: defining the tithe, 19, 25, 26; on Indian fees, 97; on salaries, 23, 58, 62, 73; on the tithe, 20, 23, 58
censo perpetuo, 114
censo redimible, 114
Cervantes, Miguel, 108
Chalco, 35, 37, 47, 51
chantries, 9; *capellanias*, 106, 112, 126–27, 161; corporate, 130–33; features of, 118, 120–21; income from, 117–18; loss of capital for, 125; private, 112–27; títular, 128–30. *See also* patronage
charity, 169
Charles I, 20, 21, 23

Chiapas, 4
Chimalhuacan Atengo, 47
choirboys, 75
church, the: administrative divisions of, 1–2; general finances of, 6–7, 28, 139–40; general wealth of, 144–47, 178; individual and institutional considerations for, 6; respect for, 9–10; rules for minimum income in, 8; "treasure" of, 77, 78. *See also* cathedral chapter; clergy; parishes
clergy: controversies in the, 31, 86–88; general incomes for, 10, 86, 89, 90–92; power of attorney by, 129; remunerative activities for, 86, 87, 88; review of development of, 183–84; royal authority and, 83–84; sickleave for, 67, 72. *See also* regular clergy; secular clergy
Coatzacoalcos, 3, 23, 47, 58, 91
Codex Sierra, 98
colación, 163–64
Colegio de Donceles, 124
Colegio de Omnium Sanctorum (Todos Santos), 137, 138
Colegio de San Nicolás, 137
Colima, 47, 85, 90, 155
commerce: church capital and, 147; church tithe and, 49–50, 81–82; economic sector of, 12, 17–18; forced sale of goods, 107;

postepidemic, 174; and the rise of *obrajes*, 176–77
commodities tithed:
auctioning of, 32; categories of, 25; collection specialization in, 37; commutation of, 32–33; division of, 79–82; renters of, 51; *tres cosas*, 22–23, 25, 37, 43
commutation, 32–33
Concordat of Burgos, 20, 21
congregación, 177
Cornejo, Alonso, 126
Cortés, Hernán, 3, 21, 128, 135; Marquesado del Valle, 9, 32–33, 35
Cortés Conspiracy, 66
Council of the Indies, 66, 70
Council of Trent, 67, 162, 166
Counter-Reformation, 112, 117, 169, 180
Coyoacan, 35, 47
Crespo, Pasqual, 37
Cruz, Juan de la, 107
Cuautitlan, 35
Cuernavaca Valley, 32, 35
Cueva, Beltrán de la, 125–26
Cuevas, Fernando de, 129
Culiacán, 48
currency, overview of colonial, 4–5

daily offices, 68
derrama, 107
Díaz, Agustín, 76
diezmo, 20
diocesan clergy, 2
Directorio, 166, 167, 168–69
Divine Office, 64

Duarte, Juan Bautista, 127
ducado, 5

Ecatepec, 47
ecclesiastical hierarchy, 2, 60, 68, 84, 123, 161–64
economics: capital distribution, 12–14; currency, 4–5; effects of crown bankruptcy, 175–76; inflation, 176; investments, 13–14, 25, 51–52, 143–44, 178; loans, 115; sectors discussed, 11–13, 15–18. *See also* agriculture; commerce; mining
education, 181
encomenderos, 5, 13, 15, 16, 22, 33, 94
encomiendas, 12–13, 95, 101, 174
encumbrance, 114–15, 145, 146
endowment, 114, 122, 145
entailed estate, 14
Epazoyucan, 47
epidemic period, 29, 149–61, 173
Espinosa, Bartolomé de, 37
Espinosa, Luis de, 121–22
Estrada, Cristóbal de, 37
excommunication, 38

fabric account, 74–79; bequests accredited to, 142–43; crown support of, 60, 156–57; gross revenue divisions and, 56, 59, 60
families, growth and

235

Index

maintenance of, 13–14, 116–17, 122, 126
Ferdinand, 20
fiadores, 24, 50
fianzas, 31
First Provincial Council, 97
fondo excusado, 26, 47, 48, 59
foundling home, 136
Fourth Provincial Council, 185
Franco, Fernando, 76
Freire, Antonio, 141, 143

Galarza, Juan de, 51
Garcés, Julián, 137, 138
García, Bartolomé, 80
García, Cosme, 123, 141, 142
Garzón, Francisco, 21
Gómez Páez, Antonio, 39
Gómez Ronquillo, Francisco, 141
González, Francisco, 29
granos, 5
Gregorian calendar, 157
Guadalajara, 3, 4, 59, 92, 106, 144; the tithe in, 47–48, 150–52, 155
Guatemala, 4
Guerrero, Lobo, 67
Gutiérrez, Antonio, 50
Gutiérrez, Hernán, 48

haciendas, 15, 173, 174–77, 179
Hermanos de la Caridad, 136, 138
hermitage, 143
Hernández, Gerónimo, 77
Hernández, Juan, 35

Hidalgo de Montemayor, Luis, 98, 102, 103–4
Hidalgo, Francisco, 50
hospitals, 56, 59, 86, 128; chaplains for, 130; endowments for, 134–40
households for tithe, 26, 48
Huasteca, 96
Huehuetoca, 47
Huehuetoca-Tepotzotlán, 35
Hueyacocotla, 101
Huitzilopochco, 47, 88
Humboldt, Alexander von, 185

Indians: encomienda and, 12–13, 15–16; fee collection from, 88, 97, 179; forced sale of goods to, 107; parishes and clergy for, 5, 9, 85, 93–105, 163; protections for, 167; relocation of, 177; social place of, 11, 88; suits by, 98, 99, 101, 102, 103; tithe and, 22–23, 41, 42–43
inheritance, 13–14, 116–17, 122, 126
Inquisition, the office of, 67, 132
investments: inheritance and, 13–14; pious works and alms as, 143–44; postepidemic reinvestment, 178; tithe rentals as, 25, 51–52
Irapuato, 47
Isthmus of Tehuantepec, 3
Izmiquilpa, 47
Iztapa, 99

Iztapalapa, 88, 131, 132

Jáuregui, Lucas, 39
Jesuits, 2, 5. *See also* regular clergy
Jiménez, Antón, 141
Jiménez de Narváez, Cristóbal, 50
Jiménez, Juan, 118
Jiménez, Mari, 76
Jujupango, 45
Julius II, 19
juzgado de capellanias, 113, 123, 124, 125, 126

labor (labor service), 12–13, 15–16, 101–3, 175
La Concepción de Nuestra Señora, 135
Lamarilla, Gerónimo de, 81
land. *See* real estate
Landeras y Velasco, Diego de, 44–45
languages, competency in, 9, 163
Larios de Bonilla, Alonso, 40
Laws of Toro, 13
Ledesma, Bartolomé de, 39
León, Francisco de, 59, 125
lepers, 136
loans, legal and illegal, 115
López, Beatriz, 125
López, Bernabé, 104
López de Cárdenas, Alonso, 131
López de Proano, Pedro, 142
López, Pedro, 124, 136, 142
Loya, Francisco de, 132
Luther, 111

mandas forzososas, 142
marevedí, 51
Marqués del Valle, 9. *See also* Cortés, Hernán
Marqués de Villamanrique, 34
Martínez, Benito, 21
Martínez de Zayas, Alonso, 90, 93
Matlactonatico, 45
mayorazgo, 14, 116
mayordomos, 27, 28
Medellín, 21
memorial mass celebration, 140–42
mendicants, 2, 5
Mendieta, Gerónimo de, 96
Mendiola, Arteaga de, 98
Mendoza, Diego de, 99
Menéndez, Gonzalo, 125
mercury, 174
Merino de Meneses, Andrés, 126
Mesa, Juan de, 95–96
mesa capitular, 56
mesa episcopal, 56
Mexía, Bartolomé, 30
Mexía de la Cerda, Diego, 44, 51
Mexico, 3, 4, 6, 59, 92, 98–99; the tithe in, 21, 24, 26, 27, 28, 35, 39, 46–47, 150–53, 156, 184–85
Mexico, *gobierno* of, 3; gross tithe for, 159
Mexico City, 17, 84, 175; chaplains in, 86–87, 128; cost of living in, 7–8; hospitals in, 134–37; parishes in, 88, 89
Michoacán, 3, 4, 59, 73, 98–

99, 118, 135, 154; the tithe in, 27, 40, 47, 150–52, 155
Miguel, Cristóbal, 122–23, 125
mining: church capital and, 147; districts for, 4, 16; economic sector of, 12, 16–17; parishes for, 85, 91–93; postepidemic, 173–74, 176, 179
missionary activity, 2, 10
Mizquiahuala, 94
monasteries, 2, 84
Montúfar, Archbishop, 105
Morán, Rodrigo, 49–50
Moreno, Pedro, 125
mortmain, 144, 147
Moya de Contreras, Pedro, 66, 78, 96, 97, 154
municipal council, chaplain for, 131–32
Muñoz, Rodrigo, 35
musical staff, 74–76, 153, 154, 156

Nava, Pedro de, 77
New Galicia, 3, 23, 59, 106
New Viscaya, 4
Nexapa, 3
Nexapa-Tehuantepec, 47
nobility, 17, 22, 50–51
Nuestra Señora de los Remedios, 132
Núñez Caldera, Antonio, 30, 49
Núñez, Domingo, 51

Oaxaca, 3, 91, 98, 107; the tithe in, 26, 27, 38, 44, 47, 150–52, 159, 185

Oaxaca Valley, 3
Ocuituco, 135
oposición, 162–64
Ordenanza del Patronazgo, 94, 161–66, 180
Order of San Hipólito, 165
ordination: *capellanías* for, 113, 116–17, 121–22, 124, 127; income requirements for, 8, 169–70; sustenance (*títulos*) for, 8–9, 129
Ortega, Juan de, 71
Ortiz de Hinojosa, Hernando, 107
Our Lady of Guadalupe, hermitage, 143

Pacheco de Alarcón, Alonso, 125
Pacheco, Fernando, 125
Pachuca, 35, 47, 92, 93, 103
Palomo, Bartolomé, 50
Pánuco, 23, 30, 35, 58, 92, 95–96
parishes: base income for, 95; benefices for rural, 162–66; fees, 103–6; food from Indians to, 97–99, 101; illegal income for, 107; income evaluation for, 108; Indian villages and, 93–105; mixed populations and, 91–93; personal income for, 107–9; postepidemic growth of, 178–79; secularization of, 184; Spanish, 85–91; three secular, 84–85
patrimony (*patrimonio*), 9
patronage: administrative power of, 124–26;

archbishop and, 122–23; chaplains and, 127; cofradías and, 124–25; corporate, 117; decrees concerning, 168; inheritance and, 125, 126; private, 121; pueblo hospitals and, 138; royal, 9, 161
Patronato Real, 19, 83
Pátzcuaro, 3, 4, 103
Paz, Francisco de, 38
Pérez, Alonso, 33
Pérez, Juan, 124
Pérez Simal, Melchor, 127
peso, three types of, 4–5
Philip II, 23
Philippines, 4
pieces of eight, 5
Pinillos, Juan, 37
pious works, 10, 111–15, 133, 185; chantries, 112–33. *See also* chantries: colegio endowment, 137; convent endowment, 139; dowries, 133–34; endowment/ encumbrance contrast, 145; inflation and, 179; inheritance and, 14. *See also* hospitals
population, 11, 149, 175, 177, 178–79
Porcallo, Lorenzo, 94
Portillo, Esteban del, 69–70
Provincial Council: First, 97; Second, 77, 166; Third, 97, 104, 166–71; Fourth, 185
Puebla, 59, 94, 98, 177; the tithe in, 27, 150–52, 159, 185

Puebla-Tlaxcala, 3, 6, 73, 98, 162; the tithe in, 44, 45, 49, 81
Purificación, 48

Querétaro, 4, 25, 35, 39–40
Quiroga, Vasco de, 59, 137, 138

racionero, 35
Ramírez Becerra, Pedro, 80
Ramírez Bravo, Francisco, 123–24
reales, 5
real estate: bought/sold by church, 147; church encumbered, 146; land acquisition, 175–76, 179; land tenure patterns, 46; ownership records, 115; regular clergy holdings in, 165, 179–81; review of value decreed for, 168
Rebolledo, Hernando, 124
Rebolledo, Juan de, 122
Recogidas de la Encarnación, 139
regular clergy, 2, 10, 83–84, 164, 165, 180; income for, 5, 6, 9; land ownership by, 31, 165, 179–81; parishes and, 88–89
relaciones, 108
religious orders, 2, 22, 30–31. *See also* regular clergy
repartimiento, 13
repartimiento de bienes, 107
Ribas, Diego de, 91
Ribera, Juan de, 126
Rivero, Servan, 37

Robles Porras, Rodrigo de, 99, 103, 107
Rodríguiz de Bonilla, Alonso, 34
Rodríguiz de Paz, Gerónimo, 90
Rodríguez Santos, Francisco, 77, 137, 138
Rodríguez Tejada, Francisco, 101, 104
Rosales, Antonio, 37
royal audiencia, chaplain for, 131
royal authority, 2, 3, 14, 161; clergy and, 83–84; petitions to, 89; salary comparisons with, 8; tithe owed by, 20, 21, 22
royal treasury: defrauding the, 81; parochial salaries from, 92, 94–95; tithe collection by, 30, 43–44
Ruiz de Rozas, Andrés, 44

sacraments, 104
salaries: allocation of cathedral, 60–73, 157–58; attendance and, 64, 66–70, 72; benefices, 9, 162–66; comparisons of, 8; corporate chaplains', 131, 132; curates', 23, 56, 58, 70–72; from the fabric account, 74; institutional chaplains', 129; musical staff, 74–76, 153–56; royal officers', 5; suits for, 153, 164
Salazar, Antonio de, 35, 45–46, 80–81, 158

San Antonio Abad, hermita, 123
Sánchez de Muñón, Sancho, 7, 8, 66–70 passim, 79, 139, 166
San Hipólito, 132
San Ildefonso–Villa Alsa, 47
San Juan del Río, 25, 39–40
San Luis Potosí, 4
San Miguel el Grande, 47
Second Provincial Council, 77, 166
secular clergy, 2, 3, 6–7, 83–84; income for, 5–9, 167–68
secularization, 184
Silao, 47
silk, 22
social structure, 11, 14–15, 88
Society of Jesus, 2, 5
Solís Bristos, Francisco de, 50
Sotomayor, Agustín de, 77
sugar, 32
superavit, 59, 64, 73

Tacuba, 35, 47, 80
Tacubaya, 35, 47
tamemes, 102–3
Tampico, 92, 97
Taxco, 35, 92, 103, 123–24
Tempoal, 91, 96, 97
Tenancingo, 48
Tenochtitlán, 20
Tepeucila, 97, 99
Tepotzotlán, 47, 80
Texadillo, Jusepe de, 127
Texcoco, 35, 47, 80–81
Texupa, 98
Third Provincial Council, 97, 104, 166–71
tithe, the: administration of,

27–28, 55; allocation funds of, 56–60. *See also* fabric account: allocation salaries from, 60–73. *See also* salaries: commutation of, 32–33; delayed payment of, 38; distribution of, 36, 42, 62; in kind, 81, 153, 158. *See also* commodities tithed: fluctuation of, 150–52, 157–58; *fondo excusado*, 26, 47, 48, 59; functionaries collecting, 27–28, 34–36, 40, 46; gross revenue from (*grueso*), 56–57, 60; king's portion, 43–45; policy for, 21–26, 36, 39, 58; precedents for, 19–21; pressures on division of, 79–82; regular clergy and, 165; rent of, 23–38, 43, 46, 49–52; renegotiated, 29, 34, 37, 158; review of evolution of, 181–82; royal redonation of, 2, 20, 43–45, 152, 154–57, 176; shipping and storage of, 41–42, 80; speculation with, 42; suits for, 9, 29, 34, 38, 49, 154
títulos, 8–9
Tlacozautitlán, 94
Tlalchichilco, 101
Tlalmanalco, 80–81
Tlalnepantla, 35
Tlatlanquitepec, 97
Tlaxcala, 3, 21
Toluca, 85
Toluca Valley, 4, 15, 35, 47
tomines, 5, 41
Tonatico, 99

Torres de Loranza, Juan de, 50
Torres Ronquillo, Juan de, 126
tres cosas, 22–23, 25, 37, 43
tribute, 12, 23, 32–33, 59, 93–94, 102
Tulancingo, 51, 158
Tula Valley, 35, 47
Turicato, 99

university, chaplain at the, 107
University of Mexico, 139, 181

Valley of Mexico, 4, 15, 21, 35, 37
Vargas, Hernando de, 126
Vargas, Rodrigo de, 90
Vargas Sotomayor, Alonso de, 130
Vargas-Valadés, Cristóbal de, 126
Vega, Álvaro de, 129, 134
Vega, García de, 133–34
Veracruz, 21, 23, 137, 174
Villa Alta, 3
Villalobos, Gonzalo de, 126
Vivero, Diego de, 72

Yucatán, 4

Zacatecas, 48, 174
Zacatula, 47
Zaqualpa, 90, 93
Zumárraga, Juan de, 22, 59, 78, 135
Zumpango de la Laguna, 35
Zurnero, Juan de, 80